wadsworth.com is the World Wide Web site for Wadsworth Publishing Company and is your direct source to dozens of online resources.

At *wadsworth.com* you can find out about supplements, demonstration software, and student resources. You can also send e-mail to many of our authors and preview new publications and exciting new technologies.

wadsworth.com
Changing the way the world learns®

Right from the Start

Taking Charge of Your College Success

Third Edition

Robert Holkeboer
Eastern Michigan University

Laurie Walker
Eastern Michigan University

Wadsworth Publishing Company
I(T)P® ITP An International Thomson Publishing Company

Belmont, CA • Albany, NY • Boston • Cincinnati • Johannesburg • London • Madrid • Melbourne
Mexico City • New York • Pacific Grove, CA • Scottsdale, AZ • Singapore • Tokyo • Toronto

College Success Editor: Karen Allanson
Development Editor: Kim Johnson
Editorial Assistant: Godwin Chu
Marketing Manager: Jennie Burger
Project Editor: Tanya Nigh
Print Buyer: Barbara Britton
Permisions Editor: Bob Kauser
Production: Tom Dorsaneo
Designer: Rosa + Wesley
Copy Editor: Carol Lombardi
Cover Design: Hespenheide Design
Compositor: Fog Press
Printer: Courier Companies, Westford

Printed in the United States of America
2 3 4 5 6 7 8 9 10

For more information, contact Wadsworth Publishing Company, 10 Davis Drive, Belmont, CA 94002, or electronically at http://www.wadsworth.com

International Thomson Publishing Europe
Berkshire House
168-173 High Holborn
London, WCIV 7AA, United Kingdom

Nelson ITP, Australia
102 Dodds Street
South Melbourne
Victoria 3205 Australia

Nelson Canada
1120 Birchmount Road
Scarborough, Ontario
Canada M1K 5G4

International Thomson Publishing Southern Africa
Building 18, Constantia Square
138 Sixteenth Road, P.O. Box 2459
Halfway House, 1685 South Africa

International Thomson Editores
Seneca, 53
Colonia Polanco
11560 México D.F. México

International Thomson Publishing Asia
60 Albert Street
#15-01 Albert Complex
Singapore 189969

International Thomson Publishing Japan
Hirakawa-cho Kyowa Building, 3F
2-2-1 Hirakawa-cho Chiyoda-ku
Tokyo 102, Japan

Library of Congress Cataloging-in-Publication Data
Holkeboer, Robert.
Right from the start : taking charge of your college success / Robert Holkeboer and Laurie Walker. — 3rd ed.
p. cm.
Includes bibliographical references and index.
ISBN 0-534-56412-7 (alk. paper)
1. College student orientation—United States. I. Title.
LB2343.32.H65 1999
378.1'98—dc21 98-34985
CIP

This book is printed on acid-free recycled paper.

Brief Contents

Contents

Preface to the Instructor

About half of all first-year college students never receive a degree. About a third never make it to their sophomore year. Even highly selective colleges lose 10 percent of their first-year students within the very first semester of college.

For America's colleges, this astounding attrition rate adds up to a loss of billions of dollars in tuition revenue and thousands of faculty jobs. The loss to the nation—in tax revenue, productivity, social problems, and entitlements—is incalculable.

There are many reasons for the high dropout rate: inadequate preparation for college; poor study skills; family pressures and financial problems; and inappropriate choices about time management, friends, alcohol, and sex.

As instructors and mentors, we can help to reverse this national calamity by teaching our first-year students—whether they are eighteen-year-olds struggling to find themselves or older adults trying to balance school with a family and a job—to take control of their lives.

THE SELF-MASTERY THEME

Self-mastery is the theme of *Right from the Start: Taking Charge of Your College Success.* The theme is expressed succinctly in the title of the opening chapter: "You're in Charge!" Here students are taught the basic principles of critical thinking and strategic planning: identify the problem, consider possible solutions, select the best one, and then take action. Every chapter shows how to do it—step by step.

Some orientation texts offer motivational pep talks and soft soap. Others offer the avuncular wisdom of academic theorists and college administrators. *Right from the Start: Taking Charge of Your College Success* offers straight talk, common sense, and a time-tested strategy that works as well in the classroom as it does in everyday life.

Right from the Start: Taking Charge of Your College Success treats all first-year students as adults who are responsible for their own happiness and success. Students are taught how to manage change—how to control life's unpredictability and plan for success. *Right from the Start: Taking Charge of Your College Success* places the burden of responsibility for success in college squarely on the shoulders of the student. Each chapter reinforces the idea that success is neither an accident nor the necessary by-product of exceptional brain power. Rather, it is the result of conscious, deliberate goal setting, strategic planning, and plain hard work.

Every chapter has a common, recognizable, and useful format, beginning with a Self-Assessment and ending with a Strategic Plan, which walks students step by step through an action plan designed to bring about significant behavioral change. These recurring elements prompt students to assess their situation, define their learning objectives, and take responsibility for the results. The emphasis is on small gains and building a gradual history of success.

Each chapter also contains a Preview, a prewriting exercise called "Write Before You Read," and a Summary—elements that reinforce the SQ3R study approach outlined in Chapter 6, "How to Study (and Still Have a Life)." Here and elsewhere students are trained to survey and anticipate the content of a text and to review and recite after each reading session.

Finally, students acquire management and communication skills by spending a portion of every class period working in small groups. By taking turns as group leaders and reporters, they learn to assume responsibility for the quality and quantity of the learning that occurs in their group and to evaluate the contributions of other team members. In the process, they discover that true learning is the product of cooperation in the pursuit of a common goal, not competition for grades.

NEW IN THE THIRD EDITION

Thanks to the constructive criticism of faculty and student users from coast to coast, this Third Edition of *Right from the Start: Taking Charge of Your College Success* has been significantly improved.

- Internet exercises ("Web Search") are provided at the end of each chapter. The exercises, some of which use InfoTrac College Edition, help students become proficient in conducting information searches on the World Wide Web, now an essential competency in college and beyond.
- The collaborative, team-based focus of the text has been strengthened with many new Group Activities (now called "Collaborate") written specifically for the Third Edition.
- The chapters have been reorganized into three parts for better accessibility and comprehension of the information:

  Part I — Starting Out (discusses challenges students face during their first three weeks of college)
  Part II — Staying the Course (emphasizes academic and study skills)
  Part III — Soaring On (focuses on cocurricular, personal, and interpersonal issues)

- Chapter 12 ("Labeling is Disabling") has been incorporated into Chapter 10, now called "Values, Culture, and Relationships."
- Although colleges resemble businesses in some ways, they are very different in others. Therefore in this edition, we have reduced talk of CEOs, management techniques, board meetings, and wise investments. Instead, we have emphasized the skills needed to succeed in

any environment, such as the ability to think critically, plan strategically, collaborate, and communicate.

Other significant changes in the Third Edition include:

- Many new individual exercises ("On Your Own")
- New sidebars throughout featuring current research on learning styles, diversity, time-saving strategies, and many others
- "Self-Assessments" have been completely recast as positive statements with which a student is asked to agree or disagree
- Revised and updated section in Chapter 7 on using computers, e-mail, computer conferencing, and the Internet
- New and improved journal ideas
- New quotes
- Updated references and statistics
- Updated library information to describe online catalogs and reference tools
- Updated financial aid information
- Additional emphasis in the study skills chapters on reading and writing competencies
- Completely updated and revised Instructor's Manual
- Finally, the text has been redesigned to improve its visual appeal, sophistication, and readability.

COLLABORATIVE ACTIVITIES

Because the orientation course is ideally served by interactive learning, *Right from the Start: Taking Charge of Your College Success* contains plenty of classroom-tested group activities and hands-on exercises ("Collaborate") that require active participation and teamwork. Most are designed for small (4–5 student) groups, and a few for pairs. Learning partners and groups promote a sense of safety, candor, and cooperation. Students come to understand that many of their emotions and experiences are shared—even universal—and that learning at its best is a collaborative rather than a competitive activity.

CASE LEARNING

Right from the Start extends its focus on collaboration and team-building with case learning, a popular mode of instruction provided and explained in the Instructor's Resource Manual (IRM). Case learning promotes critical thinking, values clarification, and communication proficiency. For a fuller discussion and a selection of case studies for class use, see the IRM that accompanies this text.

WRITING EXERCISES

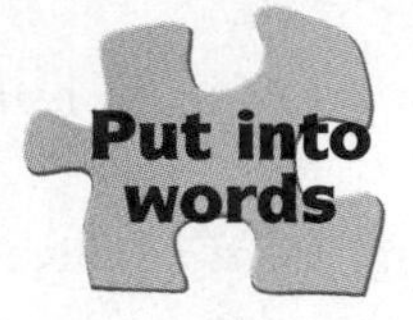

A major complaint of instructors and employers is that today's college student doesn't know how to write. *Right from the Start: Taking Charge of Your College Success* offers many opportunities for students to develop this indispensable skill.

A prewriting exercise ("Write Before You Read") at the beginning of each chapter prompts students to scan the chapter and begin thinking about how its topics intersect with their lives. Suggested topics ("Journal Ideas") for a required weekly journal entry are included at the end of each chapter. Instructions for written activity reports can be found in the Appendix (pp. 261–262). These serve the additional purpose of getting students to explore their college's "other curriculum"—lectures, sports and entertainment, meetings, and special events. Finally, each chapter contains at least one exercise that requires some writing, from a "Distinguished Alumni Acceptance Speech" (p. 38) to briefer fill-in and listing exercises. All these elements have a single purpose—to prompt students to think about and express what they have learned.

OTHER SPECIAL FEATURES

- Quotations, Tips, and Sidebars break up long sections of text and offer parenthetical information, suggestions for special populations, and inside knowledge of a practical nature.
- A Glossary at the end of the text demystifies the campus jargon that puzzles many new students—such Latinate terms as *curriculum, adjunct, baccalaureate, tenure*, and *sabbatical*, for instance. The Glossary is intended to be entertaining and instructive, not necessarily complete, and can be read with pleasure from beginning to end.

CHAPTER-BY-CHAPTER SUMMARY

Parts and chapters are arranged on a "need to know" basis. But, because each chapter is a self-contained topical unit, you can teach them in any order you wish. Here is a brief survey of the contents—chapter by chapter.

Part I Starting Out

Chapter 1
You're in Charge!

Introduction to self-management skills. Conducting a self-analysis and environmental scan. Getting to know yourself, your instructor, your classmates, and your textbook. Instructions on creating a journal (with sample journal entry). The Five Principles of Learning.

- *On Your Own*: Who Am I?; Need to Know; How I Learn

- *Collaborate*: Interview Your Instructor; Getting Acquainted; Speaking, Listening, Writing.
- *Sidebars*: Facts About First-Year Students; Generation 2001; Creating a Journal (with sample journal entry)

Chapter 2
A New Chapter
Transition issues and change management for both traditional students (culture shock, homesickness, homelessness, competition, making friends, changing values) and returning adults (self-confidence, learning skills, work and family pressures, conflicting demands). Motivation and goal-setting strategies. Critical thinking. Strategic planning for life.

- *On Your Own*: Distinguished Alumni Acceptance Speech; Challenging Assumptions; It Helps to Have a Plan
- *Collaborate*: Adjusting; Ask the Class; What Am I Doing Here?; Problem Solving
- *Sidebars*: What Critical Thinkers Do; Strategic Planning

Chapter 3
Taking Stock
Understanding the college culture. Freedom and responsibility. Understanding college instructors and their expectations of students. Behaviors of successful students. General education requirements. Academic expectations: workload, self-direction, class attendance, grades. Student rights and responsibilities. Importance of the syllabus (with sample syllabus). Grade grievance procedure.

- *On Your Own*: Design Your Own Degree; Computing Your GPA
- *Collaborate*: What Is a Successful Student?; Probation Appeal Review Panel
- *Tips*: Professorial Protocol; Digging Yourself Out
- *Sidebars*: What Instructors Look For; What Employers Expect of College Graduates; The Privacy Act; A Student's Bill of Rights

Chapter 4
Time and Money
Time management (time wasters, procrastination, prioritizing, discretionary time, balancing academic and job commitments) and money management (making a budget, debit cards, credit cards, check writing, financial aid).

- *On Your Own*: Twenty Time Wasters; How Are You Spending Your Time?; Prioritizing with a Scatterplot; Looking Forward, Looking Back; Looking Forward, Once Again
- *Collaborate*: Strategies for Avoiding Work; Money Savers; Solicitation Simulation
- *Tips*: Getting Organized; A Time-Saving Strategy Sampler; ATMs, Credit Cards, and Checks
- *Sidebar*: How Much Is Too Much?

Part II Staying the Course

Chapter 5
Going to Class

Importance of class attendance. Active listening and remembering. Active note taking (Cornell method, shorthand techniques) and after-class review. Building a powerful vocabulary. Active participation in large classes and small group discussions. Group projects. Giving a speech and managing stage fright.

- *On Your Own*: Instant Recall; Practicing the Cornell Method; Practicing Shorthand; Start a Vocabulary Notebook
- *Collaborate*: Listening and Remembering; Swap Notes; Practice Paraphrasing; Word Games; Design Your Own Class Session
- *Tips*: If You Have to Miss Class; Design Your Own Shorthand; Small Group Discussions
- *Sidebars*: When Instructors Talk Fast; Build a Powerful Vocabulary; Controlling Stage Fright

Chapter 6
How to Study (and Still Have a Life)

How much, where, and when to study. Getting motivated to study. Maintaining concentration. Active studying using SQ3R: Survey, Question, Read, Recite, Review. How to mark up a text. Remembering and forgetting. Memory tricks and techniques.

- *On Your Own*: Motivation and Goals; Mark Up Your Text; Underlining; Applying SQ3R; Your Learning Style; Making Memories
- *Collaborate*: Exercise Swap; Share What You Read; Comparing Memories
- *Tips*: Studying
- *Sidebars*: Owning Your Own Computer; On Reading Well; Lots of Learning Styles; Mnemonics for Majors

Chapter 7
The Library and Beyond: Tapping Resources

Library orientation and online information sources. Managing information by using the Internet. Using online catalogs, periodical indexes, and microfilm. Using the Internet and e-mail. Tour of all available campus resources for academic and personal support.

- *On Your Own*: Getting Acquainted with the Library; Using Microfilm; Campus Tour
- *Collaborate*: Getting to Know the Campus; Getting to Know the Campus Even Better

- *Tips*: Using the Library; Password Security; E-Mail Etiquette; E-Mail Emoticons and Acronyms; Computer Conferencing; Chronic Health Problems
- *Sidebars*: Distance Education: The Virtual Classroom; If College Were a Business

Chapter 8
Test Management

Studying for tests. Dealing with math and science aversion. Crib sheets and cramming. Effective study groups. Preparing for tests. Taking tests (following directions and budgeting time). Objective and essay test techniques and strategies. Managing test anxiety.

- *On Your Own*: Erase to Remember; Following Directions; Budgeting Your Time on Tests; Matching Quiz; Write Your Own Midterm
- *Collaborate*: Classmate Quiz; Test Each Other; Test Each Other Again
- *Tips*: Math and Science Aversion; Preparing for Tests; Forming an Effective Study Group; Preparing for Tests; Curbing Test Anxiety
- *Sidebars*: Cheating; What Instructors Look for in the Test; Irrational Progression

Part III Soaring On

Chapter 9
College After Class

Commuting challenges and strategies. Residence hall living (roommate rights, negotiating conflicts). Fraternities and sororities. Apartment living. Getting involved in clubs and organizations.

- *On Your Own*: Conflict Can Be Beneficial; Interview; Campus Organizations
- *Collaborate*: Negotiating Roommate Issues (Roommate Questionnaire); Resolving Conflicts; Negotiate a Solution
- *Tips*: For Car Commuters Only; Buying a Place to Live
- *Sidebars*: A Roommate's Bill of Rights; Frats Can Be Fatal

Chapter 10
Values, Culture, and Relationships

Developing strong values. Passive, assertive, aggressive. Relationships. American cultures and subcultures. Ethnocentrism and multiculturalism. Prejudice and stereotyping. Gender discrimination. Stages of cultural growth. Why change? Labeling is disabling. Safer sex. Acquaintance rape.

- *On Your Own*: Where Do Our Values Come From?; How Do I Relate to Others?; The Qualities of a Friend; Cultural Interview; Gender Bias in the Language; Labeling in the Media; How Do Others See Me?; Reviewing My Personal Pledge

- *Collaborate*: Comparing Our Value Systems; Role Playing; How Others Perceive Me; Cultures and Subcultures; You Be the Judge; Gender Issues; Experiencing Prejudice; Stereotypes; Team Names and Mascots
- *Tips*: Sexual Harassment; Put the Person First; About HIV and AIDS; Strategies for Safer Sex
- *Sidebars*: "I" Messages and "You" Messages; Shyness; A Quiz

Chapter 11
Staying Healthy, Stressing Less
The wellness concept. Nutrition and weight management. Getting enough sleep. Getting and staying in shape. Making good use of leisure time. Handling stress (sixteen stressbusters). Alcohol, smoking, and other drugs.

- *On Your Own*: Do I Have an Eating Disorder?; A Tally
- *Collaborate*: List Brainstorm
- *Tips*: Intoxicated People
- *Sidebars*: Fanatic About Food; *Dolce far niente*?

Chapter 12
Planning for Success
Graduating in four years. Academic planning, advising, course scheduling. Making the most of an academic advising session. Choosing a major. Thinking about a career. Developing a resumé. Co-ops and internships.

- *On Your Own*: Choosing a Major; Identifying Your Work Values; Plotting Your Lifemap
- *Collaborate*: My Schedule; Role Playing; Lifemap Exhibit
- *Tips*: What Documents Should You Save?; Will It Look Good on My Resumé?
- *Sidebars*: Transfer Tips for Community College Students; Ten Reasons to Attend a Summer Session; See Your Adviser Whenever You . . .

Appendix: Activity Report

Format and instructions for an assigned report on a campus event.

Glossary

Definition of 85 common (but sometimes puzzling) campus terms.

INSTRUCTOR SUPPORT

Orientation instructors are rarely developmental specialists or trained guidance counselors; more commonly they are drafted (as we were) from an academic department or student affairs area. As a result, those teaching the course for the first time may feel insecure and apprehensive. A brief survey of the contents of *Right from the Start: Taking Charge of Your College Success* should put many of these fears to rest.

Exercises, small-group activities, and discussion topics are embedded in the text at the point where they are most relevant and useful. Instructions to the student are clear and succinct. And the *Instructor's Manual*—completely revised for the Third Edition—provides suggestions on how to structure the course, sample syllabi for courses of semester or quarter length, chapter-by-chapter summary and teaching tips, and transparency masters for classroom use. Wadsworth Publishing Company provides additional support for this text as part of the Wadsworth College Success™ Series. Please contact your telesales or local marketing representative for information.

ACKNOWLEDGMENTS

Early editions of the text were reviewed and improved by dozens of student users and faculty adapters. I am deeply grateful to them, and to the following manuscript reviewers for the Third Edition: Jennifer L. Baker, Harrisburg Area Community College; Ancilla F. Coleman, Jackson State University; Arlene Jellinek, Palm Beach Community College; John S. Mulka, Bloomsburg University; and Carol A Rosenthal, Utah State University.

This Third Edition is not only much improved but would not have been possible without the ministrations of co-author Laurie Walker, who brings to the text many years of experience as a writer, developmental educator, orientation-course instructor, and administrator. She painstakingly reviewed every word of the text and made many salutary changes. She also completely revised the Instructor's Resource Manual and created several original cases for the case learning section.

Making textbooks is a team sport, and much of what is good about *Right from the Start: Taking Charge of Your College Success* must be credited to an outstanding team at Wadsworth.

Many people made felicitous contributions to this new edition and did their best to rid the book of error. If some mistakes remain, they are entirely my own.

As always, I invite everyone who uses this text to help write future editions. Tell me what you liked and disliked, what worked or didn't work. Write to me at this address:

Right from the Start
Wadsworth Publishing Company
Ten Davis Drive
Belmont, CA 94002

—Robert Holkeboer

A Student's Guide to Learning

Right from the Start: Taking Charge of Your College Success is the only college orientation text with an emphasis on self-management and strategic planning. It can help you acquire the tools and skills you need to make the most of your college experience. Take a few minutes to review the selected excerpts on the following six pages. They'll give you a quick overview of the Third Edition's main features.

In *Right from the Start: Taking Charge of Your College Success*, you will learn how to evaluate yourself in several areas vital to college (and career) success. You'll learn how to change and grow through a variety of hands-on activities and exercises. You'll learn how to collaborate effectively within a group. And you'll learn how to make strategic plans that will help you integrate all this newly acquired knowledge into your life.

Immerse yourself in this interactive workbook, and the insights and practical self-management tools you gain from it will serve you far beyond your college years.

A DYNAMIC THREE-STEP FRAMEWORK

The format of each chapter reflects the philosophy of Continuous Quality Improvement (or CQI), a long-acclaimed corporate tool that can be applied to your college experience with equally satisfying results. It's a methodical, hands-on approach that brings about positive change and growth in three steps by helping you (1) assess your behavior, (2) learn through hands-on activities, and (3) use what you've learned to plan your next step. The sample excerpts shown here are all from Chapter 5, "Going to Class" a crucial element in achieving college success.

Step 1: Diagnostic

Every chapter begins with a "Self-Assessment" activity that will help you begin to think about yourself and your habits and how they relate to the topic of that chapter. This activity is followed by a writing exercise where you broadly address the chapter content.

"I found this book very helpful, dealing with problems [that occur at] all colleges. It showed me how important participation is, managing time, etc. It's great and resourceful!"

Laura Blair
Student, Washington State Community College

Self-Assessment

Check the statements that apply to you.

- ☐ **1.** I haven't skipped one class since starting college.
- ☐ **2.** I tend to sit up front, where I am most likely to be involved in class conversation.
- ☐ **3.** I'm rarely drowsy in class.
- ☐ **4.** Most lectures interest me, make sense, and are memorable.
- ☐ **5.** I write down everything the instructor says and can usually keep up.
- ☐ **6.** My notes are thorough and useful; I occasionally swap them with a friend.
- ☐ **7.** I take detailed notes, review them immediately, and scan them periodically.
- ☐ **8.** I frequently ask questions and make comments in class.
- ☐ **9.** Speaking in front of a group is not difficult for me.
- ☐ **10.** I speak freely in class; I also listen carefully to others when they speak.

If you checked fewer than half, this chapter will be especially valuable to you.

Step 2: Instructional

The core of each chapter is packed with instructional devices, from brief discussions of the topic to numerous hands-on activities for both groups and individuals, illuminating exercises, helpful tips, journal ideas, and informative sidebars.

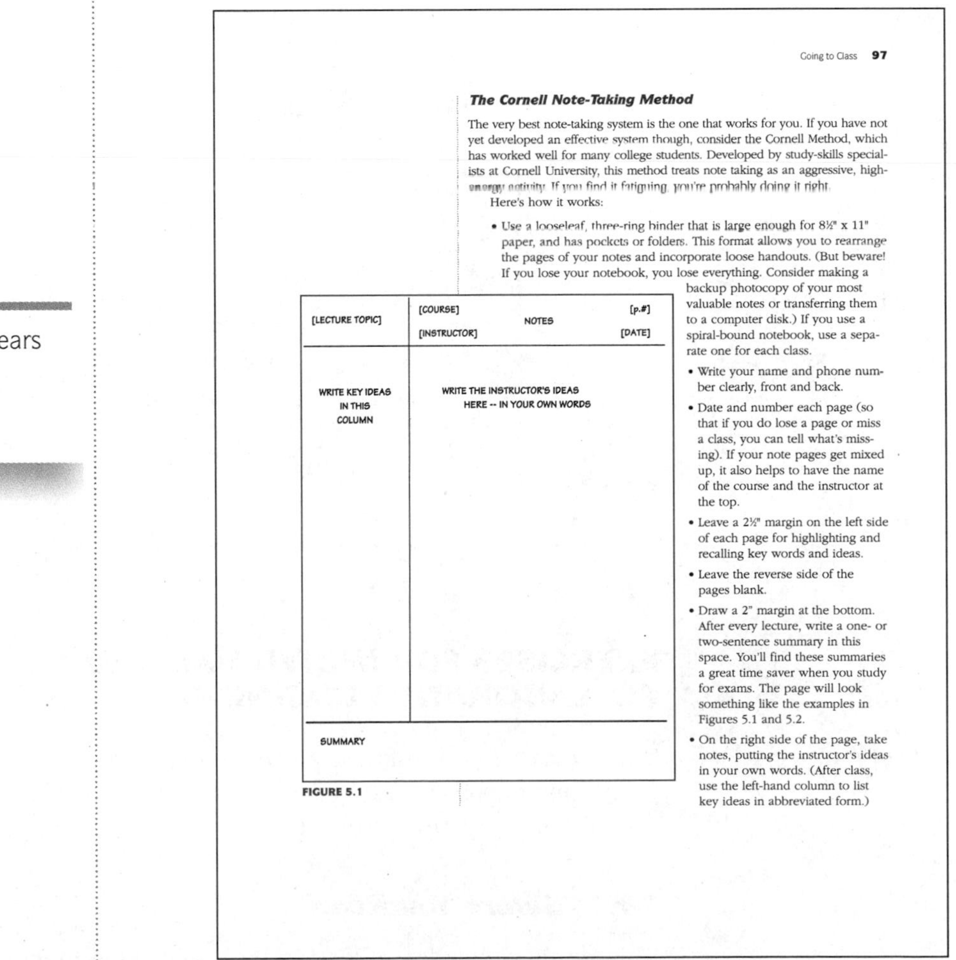

Going to Class **97**

The Cornell Note-Taking Method

The very best note-taking system is the one that works for you. If you have not yet developed an effective system though, consider the Cornell Method, which has worked well for many college students. Developed by study-skills specialists at Cornell University, this method treats note taking as an aggressive, high-energy activity. If you find it fatiguing, you're probably doing it right.

Here's how it works:

- Use a looseleaf, three-ring binder that is large enough for 8½" x 11" paper, and has pockets or folders. This format allows you to rearrange the pages of your notes and incorporate loose handouts. (But beware! If you lose your notebook, you lose everything. Consider making a backup photocopy of your most valuable notes or transferring them to a computer disk.) If you use a spiral-bound notebook, use a separate one for each class.
- Write your name and phone number clearly, front and back.
- Date and number each page (so that if you do lose a page or miss a class, you can tell what's missing). If your note pages get mixed up, it also helps to have the name of the course and the instructor at the top.
- Leave a 2½" margin on the left side of each page for highlighting and recalling key words and ideas.
- Leave the reverse side of the pages blank.
- Draw a 2" margin at the bottom. After every lecture, write a one- or two-sentence summary in this space. You'll find these summaries a great time saver when you study for exams. The page will look something like the examples in Figures 5.1 and 5.2.
- On the right side of the page, take notes, putting the instructor's ideas in your own words. (After class, use the left-hand column to list key ideas in abbreviated form.)

FIGURE 5.1

Nature has given us two ears and only one mouth.

Benjamin Disraeli
English politician

Step 3: Strategic

The final step is important. Here, you take what you've learned about yourself and the topic at hand, and come up with a strategic plan to effect positive change. The three-part exercise begins with a situation analysis; proceeds to goals, objectives, deadlines, and indicators; and concludes with a self-test.

Strategic *Plan*

Look over your Self-Assessment at the beginning of the chapter and identify an area in which you'd like to make a change. Then develop a Strategic Plan, using the format below.

I. Situation analysis

A. One problem I'm having in class is ______________________

____

B. One change I think I could make is ______________________

____

continued on next page

Strategic *Plan* *continued from previous page*

C. The benefits of making the change are ______________________

____

D. The consequences of not changing are ______________________

____

E. Some obstacles I'll have to overcome are ______________________

____

F. Some resources I'll need are ______________________

____

II. Goals, objectives, deadlines, and indicators

A. My goal is to ______________________

____

Deadline: ______________________

Indicators of success: ______________________

____

B. Here's what I'm going to do to achieve my goal, along with a reasonable deadline for each task:

	Objective	Deadline
1.		
2.		
3.		
4.		
5.		

III. Self-Test

YES	NO	
☐	☐	**A.** Are my goals and objectives stated simply and clearly?
☐	☐	**B.** Does each one have a single focus?
☐	☐	**C.** Are they stated in a positive way?
☐	☐	**D.** Are they realistic?
☐	☐	**E.** Can I achieve them by the deadline?
☐	☐	**F.** Will I know if I've achieved them?

EXERCISES FOR INDIVIDUAL AND COLLABORATIVE LEARNING

Throughout *Right from the Start: Taking Charge of Your College Success* are numerous exercises and activities you and your classmates will find involving, illuminating, and relevant.

Write Before You Read

This writing exercise following the "Self-Assessment" activity at the start of each chapter gives you the opportunity, after briefly skimming the chapter, to write your thoughts on some of the general areas the chapter addresses. It's an excellent activity for practicing writing and gathering your thoughts for the material that follows. This "Write Before You Read" is from Chapter 3, "Taking Stock."

"This book was so great! It's really an invaluable book to help guide students toward success in college. It's really helped me to organize. . . . All of the activities and exercises are totally practical. The 'study time' activity was most valuable."

Tuan Pham
Student, Lamar University

Write **Before** *You Read*

A. Spend about a minute surveying this chapter. Then write three questions you expect to find answers to in this chapter.

1. ____________________

2. ____________________

3. ____________________

B. Spend another minute writing down any thoughts that come to mind about the topics below. Write freely and rapidly.

1. My academic preparation for college: ____________________

2. Adjustments I need to make: ____________________

3. My biggest concerns: ____________________

Exercises: On Your Own

The varied and original exercises you'll find throughout this text encourage your participation and will hold your interest through the last chapter of the text. You'll learn lessons, gain insights, and experiment with new tools. This exercise from Chapter 8, "Test Management," teaches an important lesson about following directions.

I took a course in speed reading and was able to read *War and Peace* in twenty minutes. It's about Russia.

Woody Allen
Writer/filmmaker

On **Your** *Own*

Following Directions

Before you begin to write, read all ten of the directions below slowly and carefully.

1. Write your name here. ____________
2. Add 2 and 3 and write the answer here. ________
3. Draw a circle around your answer.
4. Multiply that answer by 2; write the product here. ________
5. Subtract 2 from the last answer and write it here. ________
6. Divide the last answer by 4; write the answer here. ________
7. Add 10 and write it here. ________
8. Multiply by 3 and write it here. ________
9. Subtract 10 and write the answer here. ________
10. Subtract 1 from 2, place it in the first blank, and do not complete any of the other nine items above.

Now follow the instructions in number 10.

Finished? If you followed directions, the number 1—not your name—should appear in the first blank.

Collaborate

Every bit as varied and innovative as the individual exercises, the numerous "Collaborate" boxes engage you and a few of your classmates in a social interaction that's crucial to achieving both personal and professional success. This "Collaborate" from Chapter 10, "Values, Culture, and Relationships," is an opportunity for a stimulating exchange of ideas and opinions.

Collaborate

Comparing Our Value Systems

A. **Comparing Values.** Take a few minutes to indicate how you feel about the statements below.
When you've finished, take turns explaining how you came to hold your view and how strongly you feel about it. Which would you consider very strong values, based on the criteria described on page 000. Which are weak values? Tell why.

What Are Your Values?

Statement	Agree	Unsure	Disagree
1. There is no such thing as a holy or just war.	☐	☐	☐
2. It's a dog-eat-dog world; everybody's out for themselves.	☐	☐	☐
3. My country, right or wrong!	☐	☐	☐
4. Abortion is murder.	☐	☐	☐
5. Homosexuality is immoral.	☐	☐	☐
6. Desire is the root of all evil.	☐	☐	☐
7. Eat, drink, and be merry, for tomorrow we die.	☐	☐	☐
8. Do unto others as you would have them do unto you.	☐	☐	☐
9. Do unto others before they do it to you.	☐	☐	☐
10. The meek shall inherit the earth.	☐	☐	☐

B. **Rules for Living.** List five values you were taught by authorities (parents, teachers, government, religious teaching), for example, wash your hands before you eat, don't work on the Sabbath, be kind to strangers.

1. __________
2. __________
3. __________
4. __________
5. __________

Read your list to your group. Then say which, if any, you still practice and why.

Web Search

New to this edition, at the end of every chapter, are Web Searches that will get you logged on, investigating key topics of this course and interesting issues. From using online catalogs at university libraries, to researching topics of interest, to evaluating the information you find—these exercises introduce you to online searching techniques that will help you use the Internet and the World Wide Web as tools for your college and career success.

Web Search

Search the last ten years of *USA Today* for news stories about sexual harassment, using *USA Today*'s own search tool (http://search.usatoday.com/). For much of this ten-year period, the legal definition of sexual harassment operated on the assumption that sexual harassment always involved members of the opposite sex. On what date did the Supreme Court rule that federal law also applies to same-sex harassment?

Journal Ideas

Another valuable writing exercise is keeping a journal. "Journal Ideas" provide you with several thought-provoking questions and an opportunity to organize your thoughts and put them into words. This list of "Journal Ideas" from Chapter 9, "College After Class," will help you evaluate and articulate your personal situation and how it may affect your college success.

Journal **Ideas**

1. Describe your living situation. What do you like about it? What would you change about it if you could?
2. Describe a conflict you recently faced—and resolved—with one other person. How was it resolved? Were both parties satisfied? Explain.
3. Describe your ideal place to live while attending college.
4. If you commute, what kinds of problems has this presented for you? What do you plan to do about them? What advantages to commuting have you found?
5. If you work part-time or are involved with a campus organization, describe your involvement. To what extent does it interfere with your academic success? How has it helped you so far?

Tips

"... very valuable. [This book] helped me get myself on track. It set my study habits for my college career."

Melinda Anderson,
Student, Spelman College

Gathered over 30 years from colleagues and classroom experiences, the author's helpful tips found throughout each chapter offer practical, sound, and detailed advice on everything from managing test anxiety to planning ahead for an effective first resumé. This "Tip" from Chapter 4, "Time and Money," offers several suggestions for getting organized.

Tips

Getting Organized

- Learn to be a list-maker.
- Wear or carry a watch.
- Each night before you turn in, check your schedule for the next day and make a prioritized list of what you need to do. Do the same for each upcoming week and month.
- Buy some manila files and a file box at the bookstore. Keep "slush files" (idea files) for major projects such as term papers or class projects. When ideas occur to you, jot them down and put them in the appropriate folder. Likewise, file relevant clippings, articles, and artifacts such as notes, photos, and so on.
- Use your daily planner to schedule "appointments with yourself." Block out large chunks of time to think, plan, or work on a major project.
- Schedule the unexpected. Leave some blank spaces in your calendar for emergencies and unpredictable events.
- Evaluate "emergencies." Think before dropping everything. Ask: Is this a real crisis? What would happen if I did nothing?
- Above all, get in the habit of asking yourself: What is the best use of my time right now?

HOLKEBOER'S "FIVE PRINCIPLES OF LEARNING"

Shown here excerpted from Chapter 1, "You're in Charge!" are five principles believed to be crucial to successful learning. In this edition, each principle has been given its own identifying icon or symbol. These symbols appear throughout the text to call attention to material that is relevant to a particular principle. See p. 17 for further explanation of these principles.

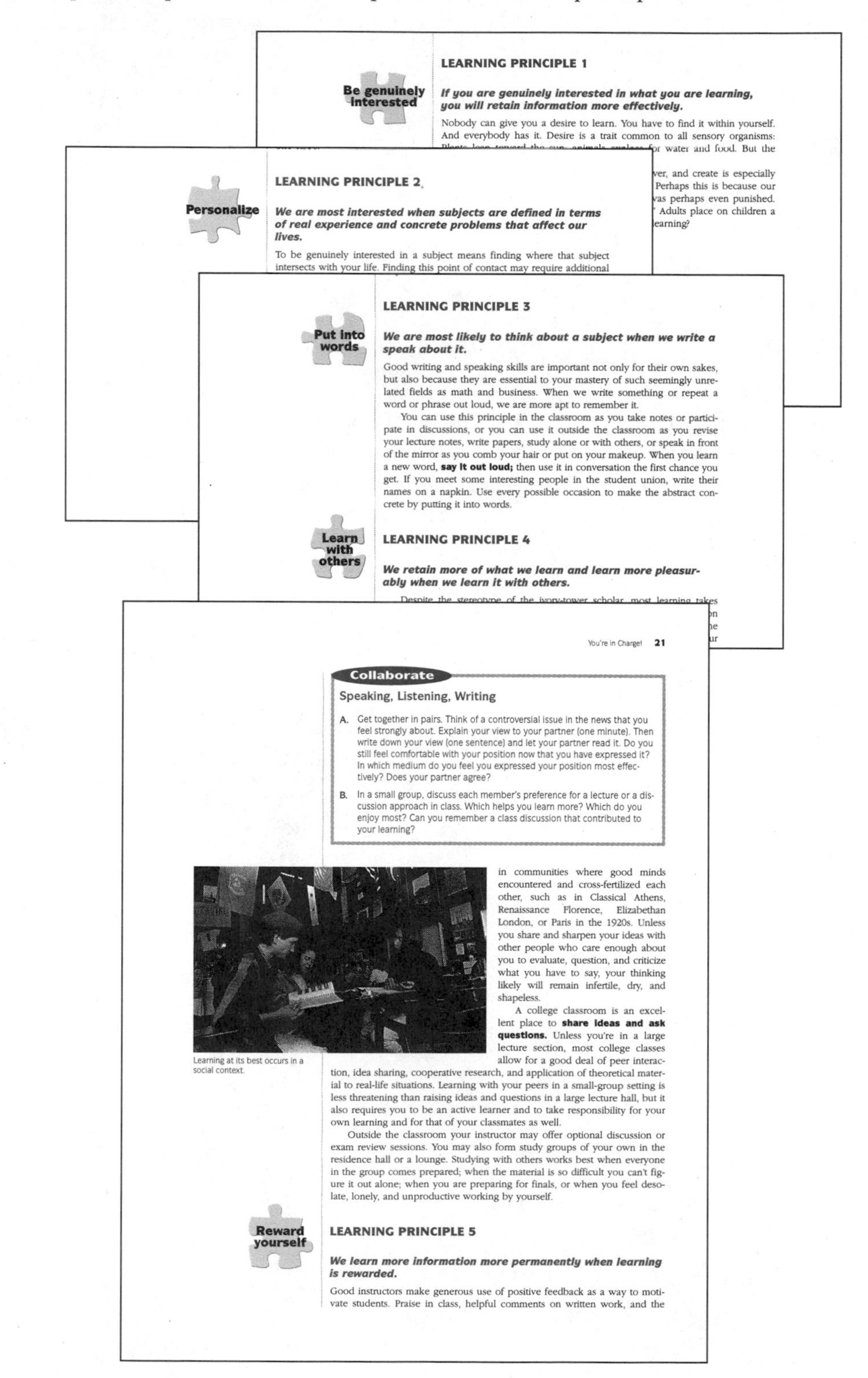

Be genuinely interested

LEARNING PRINCIPLE 1

If you are genuinely interested in what you are learning, you will retain information more effectively.

Nobody can give you a desire to learn. You have to find it within yourself. And everybody has it. Desire is a trait common to all sensory organisms:

Personalize

LEARNING PRINCIPLE 2

We are most interested when subjects are defined in terms of real experience and concrete problems that affect our lives.

To be genuinely interested in a subject means finding where that subject intersects with your life. Finding this point of contact may require additional

Put into words

LEARNING PRINCIPLE 3

We are most likely to think about a subject when we write a speak about it.

Good writing and speaking skills are important not only for their own sakes, but also because they are essential to your mastery of such seemingly unrelated fields as math and business. When we write something or repeat a word or phrase out loud, we are more apt to remember it.

You can use this principle in the classroom as you take notes or participate in discussions, or you can use it outside the classroom as you revise your lecture notes, write papers, study alone or with others, or speak in front of the mirror as you comb your hair or put on your makeup. When you learn a new word, **say it out loud;** then use it in conversation the first chance you get. If you meet some interesting people in the student union, write their names on a napkin. Use every possible occasion to make the abstract concrete by putting it into words.

Learn with others

LEARNING PRINCIPLE 4

We retain more of what we learn and learn more pleasurably when we learn it with others.

You're in Charge! **21**

Collaborate

Speaking, Listening, Writing

A. Get together in pairs. Think of a controversial issue in the news that you feel strongly about. Explain your view to your partner (one minute). Then write down your view (one sentence) and let your partner read it. Do you still feel comfortable with your position now that you have expressed it? In which medium do you feel you expressed your position most effectively? Does your partner agree?

B. In a small group, discuss each member's preference for a lecture or a discussion approach in class. Which helps you learn more? Which do you enjoy most? Can you remember a class discussion that contributed to your learning?

Learning at its best occurs in a social context.

in communities where good minds encountered and cross-fertilized each other, such as in Classical Athens, Renaissance Florence, Elizabethan London, or Paris in the 1920s. Unless you share and sharpen your ideas with other people who care enough about you to evaluate, question, and criticize what you have to say, your thinking likely will remain infertile, dry, and shapeless.

A college classroom is an excellent place to **share ideas and ask questions.** Unless you're in a large lecture section, most college classes allow for a good deal of peer interaction, idea sharing, cooperative research, and application of theoretical material to real-life situations. Learning with your peers in a small-group setting is less threatening than raising ideas and questions in a large lecture hall, but it also requires you to be an active learner and to take responsibility for your own learning and for that of your classmates as well.

Outside the classroom your instructor may offer optional discussion or exam review sessions. You may also form study groups of your own in the residence hall or a lounge. Studying with others works best when everyone in the group comes prepared; when the material is so difficult you can't figure it out alone; when you are preparing for finals, or when you feel desolate, lonely, and unproductive working by yourself.

Reward yourself

LEARNING PRINCIPLE 5

We learn more information more permanently when learning is rewarded.

Good instructors make generous use of positive feedback as a way to motivate students. Praise in class, helpful comments on written work, and the

1

You're in Charge!

Self-*Assessment*

Check the statements that apply to you.

☐ **1.** I feel in control of the decisions and events that shape my life.

☐ **2.** For all the money I'm spending on tuition and fees, I want more than just a diploma.

☐ **3.** I have a pretty good idea of what other people think of me.

☐ **4.** I'm confident that I will earn a college degree.

☐ **5.** Both my life and my education have been enriched by close relationships with teachers.

☐ **6.** I learn as much from my classmates as I do from my instructors.

☐ **7.** When I complete a difficult job, I remind myself to take time out and celebrate.

☐ **8.** I want an education that prepares me for successful employment, but I also want to learn just for the sake of learning.

☐ **9.** I'm constantly making connections between what I learn in the classroom and what I already know about life.

☐ **10.** I've made reading and writing a regular habit.

If you checked fewer than half, this chapter will be especially valuable to you.

Write **Before** *You Read*

A. Spend about a minute surveying the Table of Contents. Then write three questions you expect to find answers to in this course.

1. ______________________________

2. ______________________________

3. ______________________________

B. Spend another minute writing down any thoughts that come to mind about the topics below. Write freely and rapidly.

1. Initial impressions of my instructor: ______________________________

2. Initial impressions of my classmates: ______________________________

3. Initial impressions of my textbook: ______________________________

PREVIEW

A good way to begin a new venture is to do an inventory. In this chapter you'll be asked, first, to take stock: Who am I and what am I doing here? Second, you'll be encouraged to learn as much about your instructor as possible: What does your instructor expect of you in this course? Third, you'll have a chance to meet some people who may have a greater influence on your learning than your textbooks or instructors: your fellow students. By the end of the term, some of them may have become your friends for life. Finally, you'll be given a brief tour of your textbook and be introduced to Five Principles of Learning. If you remember and practice these principles, you will experience success in college beyond anything you thought possible.

YOU'RE IN CHARGE

ight from the Start operates on a single, overriding premise: **You are the chief executive officer of your life.**

You will be faced with many complex management tasks in the years ahead: using your study time effectively, writing papers, taking tests, learning to use campus resources, staying afloat financially, making good use of your time, balancing school with work, and staying physically and mentally healthy in an atmosphere of continual stress. Your success will depend on your ability to manage yourself and your situation.

All of us are called on to manage something every day. Doing the laundry, balancing a checkbook, getting the kids off to school, tuning an engine, giving a party—all are complex tasks requiring sharp managerial skills such as

- knowledge of yourself and your situation
- a clearheaded assessment of a problem and a desire to solve it
- knowing where to look for help and mobilizing support
- a vision of success and a realistic plan for achieving it.

Your success in college will depend on your ability to manage yourself and your situation.

To manage your college career successfully, you'll need to find your own answers to the following questions:

Where am I?
Where do I want to go?
How do I get there?

To start finding these answers, you (and this book) will begin where every good manager begins—with a **"situation analysis."** You will be called on to ask—and answer—some tough questions:

"Who am I and what am I doing here?"
"What are my strengths and weaknesses?"
"What are the strategic advantages and risks of my situation?"
"What challenges will I have to face?"
"What resources are going to be available to me?"

You get to know yourself better by getting to know others.

GETTING TO KNOW YOURSELF

The ancient Greek philosopher Socrates put it bluntly: "The unexamined life is not worth living." According to Socrates, the most important and difficult task humans face is to "Know yourself."

On the surface, knowing yourself isn't so difficult. All you have to do is make a list:

My name is Pat.
I am 26 years old.
I am a first-year student at Central State.
I have three older brothers.
My parents are divorced.
I like horseback riding and swimming.
I have experience in retail sales.
I am undecided about my major.

We could go on forever listing such neutral facts about ourselves. They're all true, but they're not the *whole* truth.

Real self-knowledge requires **careful self-analysis** followed by **complete, unconditional self-acceptance.** It means not only identifying and accepting our weaknesses but also discovering and taking pride in our strengths. It even includes our fervent hopes for the future—the person we want someday to become.

Begin your college career by getting to know yourself, practicing self-discovery. Self-analysis can make you aware of talents you didn't know you had, talents that you can build on. It may also uncover some areas where you may want to make a change.

> It isn't until you come to a spiritual understanding of who you are—not necessarily a religious feeling, but deep down, the spirit within—that you can begin to take control.
>
> Oprah Winfrey
> *Talk show host/actor*

On **Your** *Own*

Who Am I?

Spend about an hour outside of class on the following lists. If you run out of ideas, just move on to the next list. These lists should be confidential—"for your eyes only."

A. List the ten most important facts about yourself. If you were introducing yourself to a new pen pal in a foreign country or meeting someone for the first time, list the facts you would share about yourself in order of their importance to you.

1. ______________________________

____

2. ______________________________

____

continued on next page

On Your Own *continued from previous page*

3. ______________________________

4. ______________________________

5. ______________________________

6. ______________________________

7. ______________________________

8. ______________________________

9. ______________________________

10. ______________________________

B. Now make a list of "prouds"—things you really like about yourself. For example:

I'm involved in Special Olympics.
I always return calls and pass along messages.
I won a blue ribbon for flower arranging at the county fair.
I always remember Mom's birthday.
I can program a VCR.

Try to come up with at least ten "prouds" and write them in the following spaces.

1. I'm proud that ______________________________

2. I'm proud that ______________________________

3. I'm proud that ______________________________

4. I'm proud that ______________________________

5. I'm proud that ______________________________

6. I'm proud that ______________________________

7. I'm proud that ______________________________

continued on next page

On Your Own *continued from previous page*

8. I'm proud that ______________________________

____

9. I'm proud that ______________________________

____

10. I'm proud that ______________________________

____

C. Next, make a list of things you feel bad about. For example:

I once cheated on a quiz in government.
Sometimes I can be moody.
I am really prejudiced toward certain ethnic groups.
I watch too much TV.
I'm terrified about speaking in front of a group.

1. I feel bad that ______________________________

____

2. I feel bad that ______________________________

____

3. I feel bad that ______________________________

____

4. I feel bad that ______________________________

____

5. I feel bad that ______________________________

____

6. I feel bad that ______________________________

____

7. I feel bad that ______________________________

____

8. I feel bad that ______________________________

____

9. I feel bad that ______________________________

____

10. I feel bad that ______________________________

____

D. Finally, make a list of statements expressing the type of person you want to be. These should be realistic, attainable goals. Try to state them positively, not negatively—that is, "I want to get at least a C in math," rather than "I don't want to fail math." Examples:

I want to take responsibility for my academic work.
I want to feel comfortable around people who are different from me.
I want to learn how to use the Internet.

continued on next page

On Your Own *continued from previous page*

1. I want to ______________________________
____
2. I want to ______________________________
____
3. I want to ______________________________
____
4. I want to ______________________________
____
5. I want to ______________________________
____
6. I want to ______________________________
____
7. I want to ______________________________
____
8. I want to ______________________________
____
9. I want to ______________________________
____
10. I want to ______________________________
____

Sign and date your lists and keep them in a safe place. They'll make interesting reading on graduation day!

____
SIGNATURE

____
DATE

Answer the questions below by placing a check under the appropriate list name:

	A. **Facts**	B. **I feel good about**	C. **I feel bad about**	D. **Goals**
Which list was the easiest?	☐	☐	☐	☐
Which was the most difficult?	☐	☐	☐	☐
Which list is the shortest?	☐	☐	☐	☐
Which list is the longest?	☐	☐	☐	☐
Which list is closest to the real you?	☐	☐	☐	☐

GETTING TO KNOW YOUR INSTRUCTOR

A Middle Eastern expression, roughly translated, means "Take good care of your camel." A camel is an ungainly, unlovely beast of burden whose stubbornness may at times invite insult and abuse. But in the desert, a good camel can save your life. Take care of your camel, and it will take care of you.

Think of your instructor or group leader as your camel, your trustworthy guide through your first semester of college. College instructors know the territory. You don't. By training and experience, they have adapted to the sometimes bewildering environment of a college campus. You haven't. If you get into trouble, your instructor will be there to help.

It's therefore important to **get to know your instructors,** not only because they evaluate your work but also because (with proper handling) they can become valuable **mentors,** guides, and even friends to you.

Collaborate

Interview Your Instructor

A. A good reporter gets the essential facts first. As a class, ask your instructor to help you fill in the blanks below:

Real name:

____

Prefers to be called:

____

Title and department:

____

Office location:

____

Office hours:

____

Office phone:

____

Office e-mail and fax:

____

____

My instructor's three major expectations of me:

1. ______________________________

____

2. ______________________________

____

3. ______________________________

____

continued on next page

Collaborate *continued from previous page*

B. A reporter's next job, after getting the important facts, is uncovering interesting information. First, take a guess as to how your instructor will answer the following questions and write your guesses in the blanks. Then ask the questions as a class and see if you guessed correctly. (There are a few blanks at the end so you can add some questions of your own.)

1. What kind of car do you drive?

My guess

____

Instructor's answer

____

2. Who is your favorite performing artist?

My guess

____

Instructor's answer

____

3. What TV show do you watch most often?

My guess

____

Instructor's answer

____

4. What do you do for fun?

My guess

____

Instructor's answer

____

5. What political issue are you most concerned about?

My guess

____

Instructor's answer

____

6. Are you a tough or an easy grader?

My guess

____

Instructor's answer

____

7. Do you have any brothers or sisters?

My guess

____

continued on next page

Collaborate *continued from previous page*

Instructor's answer

______

8. Where would you go on a dream vacation?

My guess

______

Instructor's answer

______

9. What was your childhood ambition?

My guess

______

Instructor's answer

______

10. What was your major in college?

My guess

______

Instructor's answer

______

11. Why did you decide to teach?

My guess

______

Instructor's answer

______

12. ______

______

My guess

______

Instructor's answer

______

13. ______

______

My guess

______

Instructor's answer

______

continued on next page

Collaborate *continued from previous page*

14. ____

____

My guess

____

Instructor's answer

____

15. ____

____

My guess

____

Instructor's answer

____

C. Although this exercise is designed for this class, you may want to interview your other instructors as well. Some of them may be reluctant to answer some of the questions in part B, but try to obtain the information in part A from *all* your instructors. Record the information on the grid in Figure 1.1.

COURSE	INSTRUCTOR	OFFICE LOCATION	OFFICE HOURS	PHONE	E-MAIL	FAX

FIGURE 1.1 Instructor information

GETTING TO KNOW YOUR CLASSMATES

Research shows that **students learn more from each other** than they do from authorities (instructors or textbooks) and value the opinions of their peers more than the opinions of "experts." What you learn from your classmates will likely have a profound effect on your life. That's why *Right From the Start* has lots of collaborative group work: it is vital to get to know your classmates as well and as soon as possible.

As you get acquainted with your classmates, you'll find that you and they share many concerns. College students have always felt the pressure of grades and relationships, but today's students also face new sources of

It is important to get to know your classmates as well and as soon as possible.

stress: violence and sexual violence, sexually transmitted diseases, and rising college costs.

When first-year college students were asked, in 1997, why they chose to attend college, the number one reason given was "college grads get good jobs."[1] But they had other motivations as well. Volunteerism and engagement in human service professions are on the rise; environmental activism is widely practiced. Even though most college students place a premium on personal financial security, they also want careers that allow them to make a contribution to society.

Today's traditional-aged college student, whose coming-of-age was marked by low unemployment and a robust economy, rampant technological and communications innovation, post-Cold War politics, a Democrat in the White House, and a nominally balanced federal budget, struggles with whether to pursue a "generalist's" or a "specialist's" education. Meanwhile, global warming, mammal cloning, and the ongoing threats of AIDS and of international violence all serve to undermine this generation's sense of security, stability, or invulnerability.

Although students of all ages may have experienced these events, not all reacted in the same way. Discovering experiences and viewpoints you share with your classmates, as well as the unique value of your own perspective, is the opportunity that awaits you in college.

Facts About First-Year Students

1. At Dartmouth, which in 1972 became the last Ivy League school to go coed, the majority of students in the class of '99 are women.

2. Despite the 43-point gender gap favoring males on SATs, females get better grades in identical courses.

3. In 1965, male premedical students outnumbered women 4 to 1. Today, more women than men enter college with plans to pursue a medical degree.

4. The percentage of first-year students who smoke cigarettes rose from 9.1 percent in 1985 to 12 percent in 1995.

5. The number of first-year students who drink beer was at its lowest in 1995—53 percent.

6. Support for outlawing homosexuality reached an all-time low of about 34 percent in 1995, compared with 53 percent in 1987.

7. At the University of California, Berkeley, 42 percent of the first-year class is Asian-American. In 1997, because of a 1996 law banning affirmative action and mandating admission solely on the basis of grades and test scores, that number is expected to be 53 percent.[2]

[1] To obtain a copy of this unpublished survey, write the Division of University Marketing and Student Affairs, Eastern Michigan University, Ypsilanti, MI 48197.

[2] *The New York Times Magazine*, Sept. 10, 1995, p. 22.

Generation 2001

The "Chelsea Clinton class," which graduates in 2001, will be the first generation of young adults in the new millennium. A recent Lou Harris and Associates survey describes this group of college students as respectful of their parents and less so of their peers. Survey director Deanna Tillisch says the respondents "show a certain sense and sensibility" coupled with "idealism, optimism, and a vision of a better world."

Survey findings indicate the class of 2001 think they have technological and educational advantages over previous generations and look up to the moral integrity and honesty of older folks. Survey results indicated 68 percent said they trust their parents' age group "a lot," 79 percent trust their grandparents' generation, but only 25 percent feel this way about their peers. Two-thirds believe it will be their responsibility to care for elderly parents. Mothers are the most admired by Generation 2001, followed by fathers.[3]

Collaborate

Getting Acquainted

Here are four get-acquainted activities. Your instructor may use these or other activities. After class, try to recall the first names of at least five of your classmates and something about each of them.

A. Pair off and spend five minutes interviewing your partner, after which time your partner interviews you. Then everyone introduces his or her partner to the class.

Before you begin, take a few minutes to think of some questions you'd like to ask and use the lines here to write them down.

1. ______________________________
2. ______________________________
3. ______________________________
4. ______________________________
5. ______________________________
6. ______________________________
7. ______________________________

continued on next page

[3] *The Eastern Echo*, Eastern Michigan University, Ypsilanti, MI, Feb. 6, 1998, p. 3. Survey of "Generation 2001" students conducted at 101 colleges and universities nationwide between Nov. 11, 1997, and Jan. 12, 1998, for Northwestern Mutual Life Insurance Co. Margin of error: plus or minus 2 percent (UPI).

Collaborate *continued from previous page*

8. ____

____

9. ____

____

10. ____

____

B. Form a large circle and, one by one, introduce yourselves using this formula:

I'm ______________________ and I like ______________________.

The thing you like should start with the same letter as your name. For example, I might start by saying, "I'm Bob and I like bowling." Then the next person might say, "He's Bob and he likes bowling. I'm Pat and I like to party." Each person repeats all the introductions to that point (or, in a large class, the previous five or ten).

C. Form a circle and take turns introducing yourselves by showing the group an item from your wallet or purse that expresses an important part of your identity. Tell why the item is important to you.

D. This exercise works best with a large group. Figure 1.2 shows a tic-tac-toe game. Walk around the room and try to find someone who meets one of the nine conditions in the squares. When you find someone who, for example, was born in the same month as you, have that person sign the square. When you have three signed squares in a row, return to your seat. You're a winner!

Was born in the same month	Plays golf	Is bilingual
Owns a pair of cowboy boots	Is a vegetarian	Once attended a Phish concert
Has an unusual pet	Is over 21	Was born outside the U.S.

FIGURE 1.2 Get-acquainted tic-tac-toe

GETTING TO KNOW YOUR TEXTBOOK

Throughout *Right from the Start* you'll notice some special features that are separate from the rest of the text.

- Tips offer inside information that will give you an instant advantage.
- Sidebars give parenthetical information or may be addressed to students with special needs.
- Quotations—sometimes serious, sometimes funny—tie in with the passage you're reading.
- Group collaboration stimulates discussion and teamwork, usually in small groups of four or five people. Try to vary the composition of your groups so you get to know different people. And before everyone starts talking, appoint a "reporter" to take notes and report afterward.
- Exercises ("On Your Own") get you actively involved in learning. Some involve making lists or filling in blanks. Others require more substantial activity outside class.
- Each chapter contains a Web Search exercise. Some of them allow you to take advantage of your InfoTrac College Edition© subscription.
- Some instructors ask their students to attend one or more campus events and turn in a written report. You'll find an Activity Report form and instructions for this purpose in the Appendix. Feel free to make copies of the form if you have to do more than one of these.
- At the end of the book, there is a Glossary of campus terminology, which takes some of the mystery out of academic jargon. You may find it helpful just to read it straight through.
- Each chapter begins with a Self-Assessment—ten questions that will help you analyze your situation. This is followed by an exercise called Write Before You Read, in which you are asked to survey the chapter, formulate questions about the likely subject mater, and brainstorm some ideas about it.
- The Self-Assessment exercise is followed by a Preview of the chapter's contents.
- Each chapter ends with a Summary followed by a Strategic Plan, which is a simple, step-by-step procedure for identifying and achieving your personal goals.

One problem with an extended college orientation course is that first-year students need to know everything right away. Here are two suggestions for dealing with this problem.

First, *survey your text.* Scan the Table of Contents and the Index and leaf through the entire book, noting any chapters or sections you think may be useful to you later on. Place a check mark or star next to these items. Later, if you run into a problem, you'll know where to get help.

Creating a Journal

Most college orientation courses require a weekly journal. The journal is not only an opportunity to develop your writing skills but also a place to record:

- the changes taking place in your life
- reactions to courses and instructors
- significant social, cultural, and learning experiences
- difficulties you encounter that may interfere with your college success.

Use lined, three-hole paper for your journal so you can hand in individual entries and later store them in a binder.

Your instructor may assign one of the five Journal Ideas at the end of each chapter or let you write about anything you wish.

Journals should be handwritten and freeform. Write legibly but don't worry too much about spelling, grammar, or neatness—let it flow.

If something is weighing on your mind, write about that. The purpose of the journal is to express your feelings and ideas about what's happening to you during your first year in college. Because journals are personal, you can trust your instructor to keep what you have to say confidential.

Life has been hectic and I'm sure looking forward to the weekend although my boss wants me to work extra hours. I have so much homework I'll have to tell him no way—hope I don't get fired!

My roommate Carrie goes home every weekend so I'm all alone and there's not that much to do on campus except study. (I'm not really into football games and frat parties, although this guy in my psych class invited me to a keg party at the Sig house on Saturday night. He's kind of cute so I may just check it out.)

I'm doing good in all my courses except philosophy. I can't understand a word the prof says. I think it's too late to switch to another section and anyhow I don't want to make waves. He's a nice guy and all but he talks way over my head.

On Wednesday we had Officer Bowles from campus police talk to us about crime and safety. He said drug arrests on campus increased and murders, rapes, and burglaries decreased. I don't really see a lot of drug use at this school. He said the figures were not reliable since it may be that enforcement has increased, also that schools don't all report their figures accurately. I thought he had some good ideas, like how to find phone boxes on campus and to always go out in pairs at night. He seemed like a pretty nice man who cared about students, not the way people usually think about the police. I am thinking about majoring in criminology myself, so I thought it was interesting.

You asked about problems we might have in school and I wrote down taking tests. I try to never skip class and take good notes but when it comes time to take a test I get really stressed out and I can't think straight. I could use some help in this matter, getting nervous before and during tests.

On the personal side, things are going pretty well, although I miss my friends at home and my parents. I don't make friends that easily—I'm sort of shy. I usually wait for people to come to me, especially guys. Sometimes they think I'm arrogant but I'm really not, just timid I guess. My sister is very outgoing and flirtatious but I'm more reserved, like my father who is an electronic engineer. My mother is a homemaker but she is thinking about going back to school. Maybe she will come here and we can be roommates!

On **Your** Own

Need to Know

Intelligence agencies like the CIA operate on a "need to know" basis: They tell their agents only what they need to know to do a job. In our everyday tasks, most of us prefer to operate on the same basis: Just tell me what I need to know in order to get the job done.

The diagram below represents the buttons on a standard touch-tone phone. Your job is to fill in the numbers, letters of the alphabet, and symbols from memory. Do it now.

Is your drawing accurate? Did you begin the alphabet on numeral 2? Did you omit the letters *q* and *z*? Did you include the * and # signs?

Even though all of us have looked at and used the telephone thousands of times, few people are able to reconstruct a phone console accurately from memory. Why? Because we don't *need to know*.

Second, if a question occurs to you outside of class, *jot it down* in your notebook or journal and ask your instructor during the next class session.

There is no such thing as a "typical" college student. Because college students today represent many different cultures, age groups, ability levels, and learning styles, parts of this book won't apply to you. But **you should find something in every chapter** that strikes a chord, answers a need, and helps you manage your college career successfully—"right from the start."

FIVE PRINCIPLES OF LEARNING

You're not in college to study. You're here to learn. Study skills are important, of course, but **studying isn't the only way to learn.** And what you learn from studying isn't all you need to know.

Some students spend all their free time studying, and usually their grades show it. But grades are no more a measure of true learning than a pair of designer jeans is a measure of personal wealth or social status.

Remember: If you know how to study, you'll be prepared for class. But if you know how to learn, you'll be prepared for *life*.

Before you attend your next class, take a few moments to reflect on learning itself: What is real learning, exactly? What makes a lesson stick? What's the best way to learn? How did I come to learn the things I know for sure? How can I internalize what I learn so that it stays with me for the rest of my life?

Much valuable research has been done over the last two decades on how people learn. Much of it can be reduced to Five Principles of Learning. These principles are stressed throughout this text, and we've flagged them for you with special symbols?

Learning Principle 1

If you are genuinely interested in what you are learning, you will retain information more effectively.

Nobody can give you a desire to learn. You have to find it within yourself. And everybody has it. Desire is a trait common to all sensory organisms: Plants lean toward the sun; animals explore for water and food. But the desire to know is unique to the human species.

The desire to ask questions, explore, discover, and create is especially obvious in children and often less so in adults. Perhaps this is because our desire to learn was not properly rewarded or was perhaps even punished. "Curiosity," we tell our children, "killed the cat." Adults place on children a heavy yoke of rules and regulations that inhibit learning:

"Don't ask questions, just do it!"
"Speak only when spoken to!"
"Don't contradict your elders!"
"Why are you always getting into everything?"

Television has also played a part, inviting viewers to be passively entertained rather than actively exploring. If this has happened to you, it's time to rekindle the child in you. Fortunately, you'll find that most instructors are pleased when you ask questions and take intellectual risks.

Remember too that, with some effort on your part, it's possible to get interested in a subject even if it doesn't seem interesting at first. You may, for example, hear a song on the radio that holds no interest for you. Later you may be speaking to a friend who really likes the song ("Check out the bass line—it's really fresh"). At the music store you get a chance to read the CD jacket and learn more about the group that performed the song. You hear it again on the way home and kind of like it. Before long you've bought the

On Your Own

How I Learn

A. List three things that motivate you to *study*.

1. ______
2. ______
3. ______

Now list three things that motivate you to *learn*.

1. ______
2. ______
3. ______

Are they the same? Should they be?

______
______
______

B. Write two paragraphs describing an incident in your life when something you know in the abstract took on concrete significance. (Examples: My parents really do love me. You can't judge people on the basis of appearances. It's important to get a good education.) First describe the incident, and then explain its significance. Use a separate sheet of paper if you need more space.

______
______
______
______

CD and are recommending it to friends. In other words, the more you know about a subject, the more interesting it gets. Research stimulates interest: **interest stimulates learning.**

Stop for a moment and ask yourself why you study. If your reasons are to pass the test, to get a good grade, to fulfill a requirement, to satisfy a prerequisite, to graduate—take another look at Learning Principle 1. The paraphernalia of college (tests, grades, degrees) will never inspire real learning. Whatever you learn for these short-term reasons will be quickly forgotten. Only if you are genuinely interested will you really learn.

Some of what you will be asked to learn in college may be downright boring. Sometimes this is the fault of the instructor or the textbook. But by the time you get to college, learning has become your responsibility—no one else's.

Learning Principle 2

We are most interested when subjects are defined in terms of real experience and concrete problems that affect our lives.

To be genuinely interested in a subject means finding where that subject intersects with your life. Finding this point of contact may require additional background reading on your own initiative; it may require a few meetings with your instructor; it will certainly require imagination, critical thinking, and possibly some painful self-analysis on your part. But until you find the connection between the subject you are studying and your own life, whatever you learn will quickly evaporate.

Information that is imparted by an authority (a parent, professor, textbook) does not become part of us as readily as the information we search for, make personally meaningful, and share with others. It is when we take this last step—writing or speaking about what we have learned—that we are likely to retain it for the rest of our lives.

Much of what you read in your textbooks and hear in lectures will be abstract. For example, a sociology lecture may deal with prison conditions in the United States. Because all prisons are slightly different, the instructor may generalize by saying, "Most American prisons are overcrowded." This general statement may be supported by statistical data (for example, "68 percent of all prison wardens surveyed indicated a need for more space"). Unless you're planning to go into criminal justice, this may seem like pretty dry stuff. How do you make it interesting?

Somehow you will need to **connect the lecture with your own life.** You've probably never been in jail, but maybe you know someone who has. Maybe you've visited a prison or read a novel or seen a movie about prison life. Find a way to connect the material with something that really matters to you.

Learning Principle 3

Put into words

We are most likely to think about a subject when we write and speak about it.

Good writing and speaking skills are important not only for their own sakes, but also because they are essential to your mastery of such seemingly unrelated fields as math and business. When we write something or repeat a word or phrase out loud, we are more apt to remember it.

You can use this principle in the classroom as you take notes or participate in discussions, or you can use it outside the classroom as you revise your lecture notes, write papers, study alone or with others, or speak in front of the mirror as you comb your hair or put on your makeup. When you learn a new word, **say it out loud;** then use it in conversation the first chance you get. If you meet some interesting people in the student union, write their names on a napkin. Use every possible occasion to make the abstract concrete by putting it into words.

Learning Principle 4

We retain more of what we learn and learn more pleasurably when we learn it with others.

Despite the stereotype of the ivory-tower scholar, most learning takes place in a social context. Studies show that cooperation—not competition among students or between professors and students—leads to learning. The great intellectual, cultural, and scientific events in history have tended to occur in communities where good minds encountered and cross-fertilized each other,

Learning, at its best, occurs in a social context.

such as in Classical Athens, Renaissance Florence, Elizabethan London, or Paris in the 1920s. Unless you share and sharpen your ideas with other people who care enough about you to evaluate, question, and criticize what you have to say, your thinking likely will remain infertile, dry, and shapeless.

A college classroom is an excellent place to **share ideas and ask questions.** Unless you're in a large lecture section, most college classes allow for a good deal of peer interaction, idea sharing, cooperative research, and application of theoretical material to real-life situations. Learning with your peers in a small-group setting is less threatening than raising ideas and questions in a large lecture hall, but it also requires you to be an active learner and to take responsibility for your own learning and for that of your classmates as well.

Outside the classroom your instructor may offer optional discussion or exam review sessions. You may also form study groups of your own in the residence hall or a lounge. Studying with others works best when everyone in the group comes prepared; when the material is so difficult you can't figure it out alone; when you are preparing for finals, or when you feel desolate, lonely, and unproductive working by yourself.

Collaborate

Speaking, Listening, Writing

A. Get together in pairs. Think of a controversial issue in the news that you feel strongly about. Explain your view to your partner (one minute). Then write down your view (one sentence) and let your partner read it. Do you still feel comfortable with your position now that you have expressed it? In which medium do you feel you expressed your position most effectively? Does your partner agree?

B. In a small group, discuss each member's preference for a lecture or a discussion approach in class. Which helps you learn more? Which do you enjoy most? Can you remember a class discussion that contributed to your learning?

Learning Principle 5

We learn more information more permanently when learning is rewarded.

Good instructors make generous use of positive feedback as a way to motivate students. Praise in class, helpful comments on written work, and the reward of a good grade are wonderful spurs to greater achievement. But how often do you reward yourself when you've done a good job or completed a difficult task?

As you plan your reading and studying, break the work up into manageable segments of fifty minutes or so and **plan a reward** for yourself at the end of each segment. It doesn't have to be much—just something to look forward to, like a call home or fifteen minutes of MTV.

You should also reward yourself when you have an academic success. Get an A on your psychology midterm? Take a break from cafeteria food or preparing dinner for one night; take the family out to dinner or invite a few friends in for pizza and a video!

The Five Principles of Learning are stressed throughout *Right from the Start.* When you become bored in class or find yourself drifting during a study session, remember the Five Principles and use them to get yourself back on track.

SUMMARY

Self-discovery and self-discipline are the first steps in managing the changes you'll face in college. It's what this course is all about. Get off on the right foot by doing a candid inventory of your strengths and weaknesses. Then, familiarize yourself with your surroundings, including your instructor, your classmates, and your textbook. Finally, make sure you understand the difference between studying and learning. Memorize the Five Principles of Learning and practice them in all your classes and study sessions.

Strategic *Plan*

Look over your Self-Assessment at the beginning of the chapter and identify an area in which you'd like to make a change. Then develop a Strategic Plan, using the format below.

I. Situation Analysis.

A. One problem I'm having with setting my goals is ______________________________

____

B. One change I think I could make is ______________________________

____

C. The benefits of making the change are ______________________________

____

D. The consequences of not changing are ______________________________

____

E. Some obstacles I'll have to overcome are ______________________________

____

F. Some resources I'll need are ______________________________

____

continued on next page

Strategic *Plan*

continued from previous page

II. Goals, objectives, deadlines, and indicators

A. My goal is to ______________________________

____

Deadline: ______________________________

Indicators of success: ______________________________

____

B. Here's what I'm going to do to achieve my goal, along with a reasonable deadline for each task:

	Objective	Deadline
1.	______________________	__________
2.	______________________	__________
3.	______________________	__________
4.	______________________	__________
5.	______________________	__________

III. Self-test

YES	NO	
☐	☐	**A.** Are my goals and objectives stated simply and clearly?
☐	☐	**B.** Does each one have a single focus?
☐	☐	**C.** Are they stated in a positive way?
☐	☐	**D.** Are they realistic?
☐	☐	**E.** Can I achieve them by the deadline?
☐	☐	**F.** Will I know if I've achieved them?

Journal Ideas

1. Imagine a portrait of yourself hanging in an art gallery and describe it.
2. How would your roommate, spouse, or living partner describe you in a letter to someone else?
3. If you've worked for a boss you really admired, describe his or her management style. How would your life be better if you managed it the same way?
4. Think of yourself as your own boss. Tell this person how you would like to be treated.
5. After the first day of class, what was your initial reaction to your instructor? Your fellow students? The course? The textbook?

Web **Search**

Log on to your college Web site. Spend about an hour visiting as many home pages within your college or university as you can. You may want to:

- Find out if any of your instructors have their own home pages.
- Check out the library's home page and survey the resources it provides that might be useful to you.
- See if you can find a home page for a club or organization you might be interested in joining.

At the end of the hour, choose five sites you think will be the most valuable to you and bookmark each of them. In class, compare your list of sites with sites chosen by others in your class or group. To what extent did you and your classmates agree on which sites were most important?

A New Chapter

Self-*Assessment*

Check the statements that apply to you.

☐ **1.** I'm meeting lots of new and interesting people from varied backgrounds.

☐ **2.** I'm missing home, but I'm not homesick.

☐ **3.** I've been out of school for a while and am eager to return.

☐ **4.** I really want to be here—for me, not for my parents or anyone else.

☐ **5.** I've succeeded before. Why should college be any different?

☐ **6.** I expect my values and beliefs to change, and I look forward to that.

☐ **7.** I have made friends here at school.

☐ **8.** My life is shaped mostly by me; I control my destiny.

☐ **9.** I do not generally fear change.

☐ **10.** I consider strangers to be friends I've not yet met.

If you checked fewer than half, this chapter will be especially valuable to you.

Write **Before** *You Read*

A. Spend about a minute surveying this chapter. Then write three questions you expect to find answers to in this chapter.

1. ______________________________

2. ______________________________

3. ______________________________

B. Spend another minute writing down any thoughts that come to mind about the topics below. Write freely and rapidly.

1. Initial impressions of college: ______________________________

____

____

____

____

2. How I cope with new people and places: ______________________________

____

____

____

____

3. My hopes for the coming year: ______________________________

____

____

____

____

PREVIEW

The next few weeks of your life will be exciting and maddening at once. You'll be dealing with some complex emotions as you begin a new chapter in your life's story. Your values will be challenged daily, both by your peers and your instructors. You'll be adjusting to a new campus and its vast array of services and resources. Your instructors may expect you to work much harder than you've ever worked before, and all these challenges will be complicated by part-time jobs, responsibilities at home, adjusting to roommates and new friends, and extracurricular commitments. You may even fall in (or out of) love.

This chapter will help you anticipate, appreciate, and prepare for the changes that are likely to occur during your first year in college. It will show you how to manage them and take control of your life by developing a clear vision of success, a critical-thinking process for problem solving, and a strategic plan that works. In short, you'll learn how to channel change effectively.

ANTICIPATING CHANGE

Whether you're a recent high school graduate or an older adult, living on campus or commuting from home, your decision to attend college will mean some major changes in your life.

When faced with unfamiliar faces, places, new situations, and unusual ideas, most people feel a powerful urge to rush back into the arms of the familiar. It may be comforting to know this feeling is so universal that scholars have given it a name: cognitive dissonance, or "culture shock." Although stressful, the encounter between the known and the unknown can produce an excited, creative state of mind that is highly conducive to learning. You'll encounter this state of mind again and again throughout life. Each time you do, you'll be better equipped to use it to your advantage.

Remind yourself of your strengths.

Traditional Student Adjustments

If you've left home to attend college, you may be feeling a little displaced, disconnected. The good thing about feeling homesick is that it may mean you had a good relationship with your family and were happy at home. The bad thing is that homesickness can blind you to the possible pleasures of new friends and affiliations.

Your parents are probably feeling some unaccustomed emotions too, particularly if you are their oldest, youngest, or only child. If the former, your birth was perhaps the most significant and emotionally moving event of your parents' lives. If you're the youngest, you're their baby, the last to go, the "end of an era." Even if you're commuting from home, this is a time for "letting go," which can be a wrenching experience for parents.

If you're an only child, or if you've had to function as comforter, caretaker, and confidant to a parent who has been divorced, separated, or ill, the separation anxiety may be even more intense for both you and your parents. If they are hovering, fussing, and pressuring, take it as a sign of love, however clumsily expressed. Try to maintain a positive, caring relationship. Let

Collaborate

Adjusting

A. Get together in a small group and have one person read aloud the following list of common fears and anxieties of first-year college students. As a group, come up with five more. Put a check mark next to the ones you feel are most common among your peers. Discuss some possible coping strategies or steps toward resolution.

1. I won't have enough money.
2. I'll party too much and fall behind in my studies.
3. I won't make friends.
4. I won't know what I want to do in life.
5. My health will suffer.
6. Everybody will be smarter than I am.
7. People I care about will be disappointed in me.
8. I won't have time to do everything I have to do.
9. Instructors will talk over my head.
10. I'll make a fool of myself around more sophisticated people.

[add five more]

11. ______________________________
12. ______________________________
13. ______________________________
14. ______________________________
15. ______________________________

B. In your small group, brainstorm a list of differences you've noticed between college and high school.

College	High School

Mark the positives with an X and the negatives with an O. Which column got the most X's? On balance, has college represented a change for the worse or for the better?

Seek out opportunities to meet people. Practice introducing yourself.

You can't go home again.

Thomas Wolfe
American novelist

Collaborate

Ask the Class

On a half-sheet of paper, write down one or two questions you would like to ask, anonymously, of your classmates. These questions might be discussion starters (for instance, "Are you feeling homesick? What helps?") or requests for information ("Where is there live music nearby?"). Pass a hat to collect the questions from each class member. Then, designate a facilitator to pull several questions randomly from the hat and pose these to the class—one by one—for consideration and discussion.

them know you appreciate their concern but insist on your right to make important decisions about your life.

Students living away from home often feel especially disoriented when they first return home for a weekend or a holiday. Things have changed in mysterious ways: What did they do with your posters? Why is your mom's computer on your desk? Why does your dog seem to favor your little sister? Why does Dad get upset when you use a simple word like *psychosexual* at the dinner table? Other things that should have changed will be the same as ever: Why do you still have to take out the garbage and be home by curfew?

For some people, the result of this cognitive dissonance is not so much homesickness as a feeling of homelessness—that is, "My home is no longer my home, but neither is my new home at college. Where am I? Who am I? What is going on?"

It's hard to see yourself as others see you.

As humans, we derive our sense of identity, in part, by comparing ourselves with others. But it's hard to get honest feedback from your peers during the first few days of college, when the campus atmosphere is a little unreal. Your fellow students may seem to be feeling very different from the way you do. They may appear to have lots of friends; you hardly know anyone. They may seem smart and sophisticated; you may feel ignorant and naïve.

In reality, this cool demeanor is often a façade masking fears common to all human beings faced with new and threatening situations. Many first-year students play a role: "I'm not smart so I'd better act smart" or "I'm not sophisticated so I'll pretend I am" or "Personally, I find alcohol disgusting but I want to fit in, so I guess I'm going to have to get used to drinking it." It's hard to get honest feedback when so many people are bluffing.

First-year students are also concerned about whether they can make it academically: "Everyone around me uses big words. They talk about things I don't know anything about. I don't think my high school was very good. It's three weeks into the term, and I still haven't gotten any grades. I want to know how I'm doing!"

> Every body continues in its state of rest or of uniform motion in a right line, unless it is compelled to change that state by forces impressed upon it.
>
> Sir Isaac Newton
> *English physicist (1687)*

> The only people who like change are wet babies.
>
> Anonymous

You may feel tense, depressed, anxious. You can't sleep. Your stomach hurts. You have migraines. You long for the familiar landscape of home, the predictable place of no surprises, where what you are is OK and what you do is what everybody does. Yet (in your heart of hearts) you know that home has vanished. The time has come to create a new one.

Well, so be it. Look around. Take stock. Remind yourself of your strengths; you've got the right stuff. With a little help from your friends, you can make it. Reach out. Meet somebody. Find a friend willing to be as honest as you are.

And if you get really scared, make an appointment with a counselor and talk it over or approach an instructor or a resident adviser who seems especially understanding. You'll be comforted to learn that you are not alone, that all human beings make their way through similar passages into the warm sunshine of adulthood.

What will this passage be like? What is in store for you in the months and years ahead?

Ways You Can Expect to Change

Returning adult students face unique challenges.

Your values will be tested. Your encounters with instructors and students from widely divergent backgrounds will challenge you to consider new ideas and attitudes that may be radically different from those generally accepted by your family and community. Your belief system will undergo many alterations but they likely will be for the better. You will begin to create **your own values** rather than simply depending on "authorities" for answers to difficult questions. As you submit your beliefs to critical scrutiny and test them in action, they may become more meaningful to you.

You will become more sophisticated. Your political and social ideas may become less intractable, or at least more tolerant, than before. You will interact more comfortably with people of widely divergent backgrounds and cultures and may come to think of yourself increasingly as a citizen of the world.

Your intellect will be engaged. You will grow more confident in your ability to think for yourself by examining evidence and drawing reasonable conclusions. You will begin to see connections between ideas. You may develop a deeper appreciation of beauty and goodness or become more skilled at applying theoretical knowledge to practical situations.

You will become more self-confident. Although your fundamental spiritual values are not likely to change drastically, some college students find they are gradually less inclined to identify with the religious institutions, creeds, and rituals with which they were raised. You may learn to trust your feelings more and draw on them as sources of power and insight. Chances are you will become more self-reliant and like yourself better as you acquire communication skills and increased knowledge.

Your life will be richer and fuller. Most importantly, you will enjoy life more as you continue to learn, even beyond your college years. The more you see and understand, the more interesting and satisfying your life will become.

Re-Entry Student Adjustments

Some students in your classes may be older and more experienced; you may be one of these students yourself. In fact, if you're a "traditional student" (aged 18–22, living on campus), you're in the minority: Less than 40 percent of today's college population fit this category.

Over half of all adult students have been out of school for at least ten years. Many interrupted their educations to do other work, serve in the armed forces, raise a family. Statistically, a large majority are women pursuing college degrees while continuing to work (70 percent work full-time). These students resume their educations for many reasons—to learn new skills for professional advancement, or just for the personal satisfaction of completing a degree.

If you're returning to school after an absence, you face numerous adjustments. Some are no different than the adjustments faced by younger college students, such as grappling with new ideas and changing values. But others are very different. Take comfort in the fact that hundreds of thousands of adults like you return every year to continue their educations, and this number continues to rise. With similar challenges, re-entry students are finding—and sharing—workable coping strategies.

Re-Entry Student Challenges and Strategies

Challenge:
You've been out of school for so long you now lack confidence in your ability to compete academically with students fresh from high school.

Strategies:

- Be patient—this feeling may pass after a few weeks as you gain confidence in the classroom.
- "Prime the pump" by starting out slowly (one or two courses the first semester) and accelerate your progress as you feel yourself gaining strength.
- Take a "refresher" course if you feel you've forgotten what you learned years ago.
- Meet with instructors early in the semester, share your concerns, and ask for additional help.
- Sign up for a study skills course.
- Take advantage of tutors, labs, and the resources of peer groups—the women's center or the veterans' office, for instance. Make connections between what you learn in class and what you've learned in life.

- Remember, it may take a while to get "primed." Most adult re-entry students have high expectations, which is desirable and good "role modeling" for younger peers. Unfortunately, high standards can also produce disappointment. Don't be discouraged if your initial grades are not what you'd hoped.

Challenge:
You feel out of place in a classroom full of students who may be the same age as your own exasperating teenagers and whose developmental concerns differ from your own.

Strategies:
- Your life experiences enable you to make a real contribution to these students' learning and growth. Enjoy the pleasure an aunt or uncle feels in being a mentor to young nieces and nephews without having to be responsible for them.
- Be willing to share your stories with these students, keeping in mind that their youthful curiosity and exuberance can teach you something too.
- Meanwhile, get connected with other adult learners—even just a few—and form a network of mutual support.

Challenge:
- You feel alienated from your family, friends, and community and resent their chronic demands on your time.

Strategies:
- Learn to say "No" without apology. Don't back down.
- Set aside time for study and time to be with family or friends. Let them know which is which. When it's family time, be totally there for them, with no school distractions. Similarly, let them know you are not to be disturbed during study time.
- Hold regular family meetings in which concerns can be raised and discussed. Negotiate and agree on mutual expectations regarding meals, dishes, laundry, yard work, and transportation.
- Eat out as often as your budget permits. Simplify meal preparation and share responsibility for shopping, cooking, and cleaning up.
- Most teenagers have messy bedrooms; accept it and ask them to keep their doors closed. Adult students often put off schoolwork by cleaning furiously.
- Resign yourself to letting go of certain expectations. You can't be Supermom or Superdad or Superspouse and Superstudent at the same time. Wear a button that says, "Give me a break!"
- Make a list of what is important to you and rank all items by priority, for example:

  ____ school work

  ____ household chores

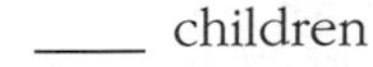

____ children

____ relatives

____ spouse

____ community service

____ relaxation

____ employment

____ extracurricular involvement

(add your own items)

____ ____

____ ____

- Remind yourself continually of your priorities; stick to them and take responsibility for them. Above all, keep your eyes on the prize.

Challenge:
Scheduling classes at times convenient for your busy work schedule is an ongoing headache.

Strategies:

- See an adviser (many advising offices have evening hours for adults who work in the daytime).
- Try to get overrides into closed classes by attending the first class and explaining your situation to the instructor.
- If you're enrolled at a four-year college, consider taking some of your required courses at a two-year school in the area, where tuition is cheaper and classes are more often scheduled with adult learners in mind.
- Explore distance-learning opportunities—high-tech versions of the old "correspondence course" that use compressed video, the Internet, faxed handouts and exams, and e-mail consultation with the instructor.

Challenge:
You'd like to take advantage of all the campus has to offer: attend special events, get involved in a club—do the things you never had a chance to do before. But you just don't have time.

Strategies:

- Consider the commitments you've made away from campus. Keep a log of just how you spend your time hour by hour. See if you can find some nonessential activities you might temporarily forgo in order to try something new.
- Accept that your college experience will be different from what it would have been had you gone the traditional route. Take responsibility for your life decisions.

Challenge:
With some financial assistance, you could reduce your work hours, take more classes, and get your degree sooner.

Strategies:

- Meet with a financial aid counselor to discuss your needs. Is your part-time status an obstacle to obtaining certain forms of aid?
- If you don't qualify for need-based aid, ask about endowed scholarships based on major, home town, age, ethnicity, and so on. Do you have to fill out a scholarship application? When is the deadline? Where can you get a list of scholarships offered by your school, women's or benevolent fraternal organizations, local businesses, and other groups?

Many college administrators have taken note of the personal and educational needs of re-entry students and have responded: commuter lounges, lockers, additional parking, weekend and evening classes, and distance-learning opportunities are increasingly available. If these services are inadequate or simply unavailable on your campus, make some noise! Write letters to your dean of students, academic vice president, and campus paper or work up a petition.

BECOMING A CHANGE AGENT

Some people don't like change at all. They avoid it or fight it or insulate themselves from it. They bury their heads in the sand. Others are just the opposite. Lacking a strong sense of self and coherent values, they are vulnerable to every passing fad, like leaves blown by the wind, believing whatever they are told.

Successful people are change managers. They have learned to adapt to new ideas while maintaining their own identities and values. Although proud of their cultures and common ties, they respect and interact comfortably with others. Keeping open minds about ideas and values that differ from their own, they remain firm in their convictions.

Some things have to be believed to be seen.

Ralph Hodgson
English poet

Your success in college will depend on your ability to channel the changes that are bound to occur. To do that, you will need to **discover yourself, accept yourself, and discipline yourself.** These are probably the most important and the most potentially beneficial challenges a human being has to face. They require honesty, humility, courage, and wisdom.

Apply a strategic planning process to the important decisions you make in college—decisions about relationships, learning, health, time, and money. This will make you an effective change manager and bring you success beyond your wildest dreams. But it can happen only if you really want to make a change.

Motivation

Nobody can give you motivation. You can't buy or borrow it. You can't get it from self-help books and motivational tapes. You have to find motivation in yourself. Ask: What do I really want? How badly do I want it? What am I prepared to do to get it?

There is a direct relationship between hope and success. Dr. Charles Snyder, a psychologist at the University of Kansas, published a study of nearly 4,000 college students in the *Journal of Personality and Social Psychology* (November 1991). He concluded that the level of hope among first-year college students was a better predictor of academic success than grades or test scores.

Hopefulness, according to Dr. Snyder, has two essential components: both the *will* and the *means* to accomplish one's goals. Usually the two go hand in hand: "Where there's a will, there's a way." Hopeful people have histories of success. They find ways to get out of jams. They believe there is no such thing as an insurmountable problem.

People with low levels of hope have come to believe (usually from a very early age) that no matter how hard they try, they will fail. If this is true of you, figure out how you came to believe it. Is it really true, or is it just a label others hung on you? Make a conscious, personal decision to put aside all those negative forces. If you learned to fail, you can also learn to succeed.

Here's how:

Make small gains

Start right now to accumulate small successes. Success, like failure, is addictive. The way to overcome a harmful addiction is to replace negative behaviors with positive ones. Start immediately on the path to success by defining one small goal you know you can accomplish. Focus on your strengths. Refuse all negative thoughts. Forgive all the people who taught you to fail and forget the lessons they taught you. Become your own best friend; treat yourself with kindness and respect.

Visualize

As you carry out your plan, it's important to keep in your mind a clear image of success. Athletes use visualization strategies all the time. Before shooting a free throw, basketball players picture the ball just clearing the front of the rim. A remarkable example of the **power of visualization** involves an American airman who was shot down and held prisoner for seven years in North Vietnam. In civilian life he had been a passable weekend golfer (he had never scored under 90 for eighteen holes). In solitary confinement, he passed the time by mentally playing each hole of his home course, shot by shot, over and over. When he returned home after the war, in his very first outing on the home course, he shot a score of 70! If you can picture it happening, it probably will.

Be flexible

Water flowing down a mountain finds its way around a rock, and you will also find your way around unexpected obstacles. Strategies rarely work out exactly as planned. **Be flexible.** It's OK to adjust a deadline or restate an objective in light of altered circumstances.

Keep trying

If you fail to achieve your goals, pick yourself up and try again. (Things often turn out better the second time around because we learn from our mistakes.)

You don't deserve punishment or blame. Berating ourselves is self-destructive. Remember: failure is not what happens when you try and don't succeed. Failure is what happens when you never try anything.

Collaborate

What Am I Doing Here?

Write down three reasons you chose to attend college and circle the one most important to you.

1. ______________________________

2. ______________________________

3. ______________________________

Now write down three goals you hope to accomplish over the next few years and circle the one most important to you.

1. ______________________________

2. ______________________________

3. ______________________________

Discuss your reasons and goals in a group of four or five. What reason for attending college was most frequently mentioned?

____

What goals were expressed by more than one member of the group?

____

What significant differences emerged in the discussion?

____

> Something we were withholding made us weak,
> Until we found it was ourselves.
>
> Robert Frost
> *American poet*

Take responsibility

People who repeatedly blame outside circumstances or "bad luck" have what psychologists call an "external locus of control." When they get a low grade, they blame it on the instructor or the textbook or their roommate. When they get a good grade, they have a hard time taking credit for it: it was just dumb luck.

You can't control what happens or what others do. You can only control what you do. Having an "internal locus of control" means taking responsibility for whatever happens without assigning blame. For example, if you find your commitment was unrealistic or overly ambitious, take responsibility for your decisions instead of blaming yourself, knowing that next time you'll be wiser about making commitments you can keep.

> My life seems like one long obstacle course with me as the chief obstacle.
>
> Jack Paar
> *TV entertainer*

When you do achieve a "small gain," be sure to reward yourself and celebrate. It doesn't have to be much—a coffee break, a pizza, a call home. Celebrating accomplishments will motivate you to keep trying new things.

Reinventing who you are—your core attitudes, beliefs, and behaviors—takes time. Don't get down on yourself if you occasionally slip into an old habit; acknowledge the slip and let it go. Then move ahead.

Critical thinkers are always open to new ideas.

CRITICAL THINKING

Motivation—as important as it is—is not enough to ensure success. Wanting to do the right thing is important, but it's useless if you don't know what the right thing is. That's where critical thinking comes in.

Thinking has been defined as "active, purposeful, organized effort to make sense of the world."[1] It is the essential first step in planning for change. Critical thinking involves four basic steps:

1. **Identify the problem.** State the problem simply and clearly, eliminating pseudoproblems. If your car has broken down and you're going to be late for class, that is your problem, not "I need a new car" or "I don't understand engines" or "These things always happen to me." Those are pseudoproblems.

> Invention, in my opinion, arises directly from idleness, possibly also from laziness, to save oneself trouble.
>
> Agatha Christie
> *Mystery writer*

2. **Brainstorm possible solutions.** List as many as you can think of without regard to their merits (for example, "Kick the tires." "Swear." "Look under the hood."). Include the use of outside resources (your car manual, your neighbor, AAA).

[1] John Chaffee, *Thinking Critically* (Houghton-Mifflin, 1985); 1.

On Your Own

Distinguished Alumni Acceptance Speech

A. Travel in time thirty years into the future. You've been invited back to campus to accept a Distinguished Alumni Award. Write the five-minute speech someone else will make to introduce you at this event. (Such speeches list the person's life achievements in considerable detail; do the same in your speech.)

B. If this doesn't appeal to you, here's an alternative: Assume the voice of your grandchild. Write the story this child will tell about you and your significant life accomplishments.

Thinking is a momentary dismissal of irrelevancies.

Buckminster Fuller
Architect

3. **Evaluate the alternatives.** Some will be obviously bad. Others may offer advantages that need to be weighed.
4. **Choose the best alternative.** Make sure this is the correct solution for you, not one designed to please somebody else.

Notice that critical thinking and problem solving involve both logic and emotion, deduction and intuition. To solve problems, both sides of the brain—the analytic and the synthetic—must work in harmony. Uncontrolled emotions (such as panic) immobilize the brain and make thinking impossible. On the other hand, pure, logical thought can stymie imagination, blocking creative solutions to problems. Effective critical thinkers insist on evidence, reason, and dispassionate examination of a problem. But they also remain open to new ideas, differing viewpoints, and imaginative visions of possible outcomes.

Strategic Planning

Once you've identified the best solution to a problem, it's time to act. That's where strategic planning comes in.

What Critical Thinkers Do

Think actively. Critical thinkers question and explore. They take initiative, make decisions, and follow through on their commitments. Instead of sitting back and waiting for events to unfold, they shape the course of events. By paying attention to change, they are sometimes able to predict the future with uncanny accuracy.

Think for themselves. Although they draw on other people for ideas, critical thinkers take final responsibility for decisions that affect their own lives. They trust their experiences. They identify and reject prejudice and bias.

Look at all sides. Critical thinkers are skeptical. They probe patiently beneath the surface, consider all arguments, challenge assumptions, and collect as much data as time permits. What other people call "screwball ideas" and "irrelevant clues" are especially interesting to them.

Use their imaginations. Critical thinkers relax and let their unconscious minds work on the problem. They explore alternative scenarios. They often seem absentminded, idle, "lost in thought." Critical thinkers cultivate a state of "purposeful daydreaming," in which mind and body are alert but relaxed—a meditative state.

On Your Own

Challenging Assumptions

Using only four straight lines, and without lifting your pencil from the page, connect the nine dots below:

•   •   •

•   •   •

•   •   •

(Solution provided on page 40)

After finishing a job, a call home is a good way to reward yourself.

Effective change managers don't just react to changing events and circumstances. They have a plan designed to *shape* the future.

Strategic planning has been effective in bringing about desired change, not only at the global organizational level (in large corporations, government, and military planning) but also in the lives of individuals.

The basic steps are shown in the box on the next page.

Strategic planning is a way of creating your "preferred future" by empowering yourself to control what can be controlled in life, while developing the skills to adjust to forces beyond your control.

Every chapter in *Right from the Start* concludes with a Strategic Plan—a blueprint that you can use to take control of your life.

Fill out the form on page 44 right now.

Start by doing some critical thinking about an area of your life you'd like to change: What is the problem, exactly? What are some possible solutions? What is the best solution?

Then—develop your plan and carry it out.

And give yourself a new title: Change Agent.

On **Your** Own

Solution to Connect the Dots, page 39

Did you assume you had to stay within the square? When you challenge that assumption, the solution is easy:

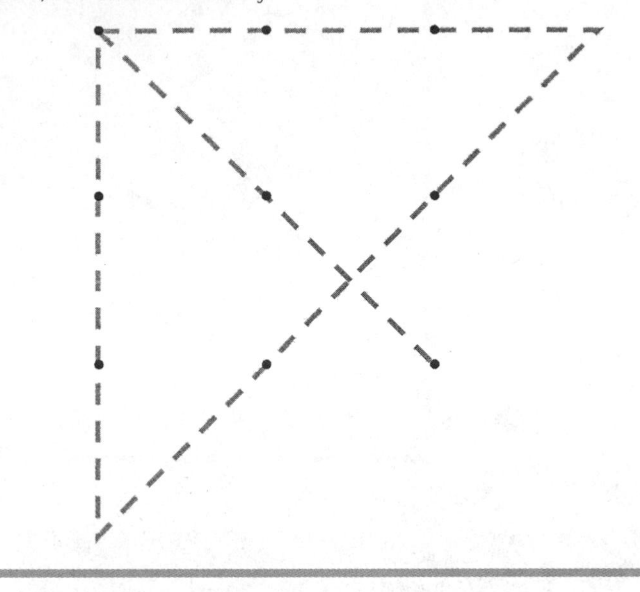

SUMMARY

College is a time of radical change. The first few weeks are especially stressful. Students new to college often feel homesick, or worse, homeless. Adult returning students have their own adjustments to make and can benefit from the experience of others traveling the same path. Many of the changes college students undergo are universal, and understanding these changes is the first step toward benefiting from them. Successful students enjoy change because they know how to channel it. They have thought critically and creatively about problems, made candid self-assessments, and contrived flexible, strategic plans designed to bring about the futures they want for themselves. You can do this, too! Motivation is the key.

Strategic Planning

1. **Assess your situation.** This first stage of the planning process is sometimes called a "situation analysis" or "information gathering." What is the problem? What changes are needed? What are the benefits of change and the consequences of not changing? What are possible obstacles to making the needed change? What resources are necessary to make the change?

2. **Define your goals and objectives.** Goals are global destinations expressing your preferred future situation. Goals are where you want to go. Objectives are the small-scale steps needed to get you there. For example, your goal might be to earn a final grade of at least B in calculus. Your objective might be: complete all assigned problems on time, visit the math clinic once a week, and go over each test with the instructor. Good goals require careful thought. Here are some guidelines for effective goal setting:

A. State your goals simply and clearly with a single focus.

Well-stated goal: Be ranked in the top 10 percent on the calculus midterm exam.

Poorly stated goal: Do better in calculus so my parents won't be so mad at me.

B. You'll be more motivated to accomplish your goals if you state them positively rather than negatively.

Positive goal: Attend class regularly.

Negative goal: Don't skip class.

C. Goals and objectives should be challenging but realistic. Creating impossible goals is a way of setting yourself up for failure. Make your goals consistent with your abilities and time constraints. Concentrate on "small gains."

Challenging but realistic goal: Earn at least a B in calculus.

Global and probably unrealistic goal: Graduate *summa cum laude,* win a Rhodes Scholarship, followed by a distinguished career as a Nobel Prize–winning mathematician.

3. **Establish timelines, accountability, and indicators of success.**

A. *Timelines.* You've already broken up the goal into a series of smaller steps (objectives). Now establish a reasonable timetable for each objective. Work backward from your deadline and decide on feasible "no later than" dates for each objective. This series of dates is your timeline. Obviously, you'll want to stick to it as much as possible.

B. *Accountability.* If your strategic plan is a personal one, you are the only responsible party. (Be careful about goals that depend on other people for success.) Accountability refers to the assignment of responsibility for each task, so if your goals are strictly personal, then you are the only responsible party. But if your goals require the cooperation of others, make sure they make the necessary commitments.

C. *Indicators of Success.* It's important to have some way of measuring or verifying whether a goal was actually accomplished. An indicator might consist of sales figures, for example, or a grade on a test. If your goal is vague (for instance, be a better friend, learn to play the piano), it's hard to know whether you've achieved your goal, so establish indicators that track your progress (call once a week, learn a new song each month). Numbers tend to give "indicators of success" precision.

On **Your** Own

It Helps to Have a Plan

Pair up with a partner and time each other on this exercise. You have sixty seconds to connect as many numbers as you can, in sequence, starting with #1.

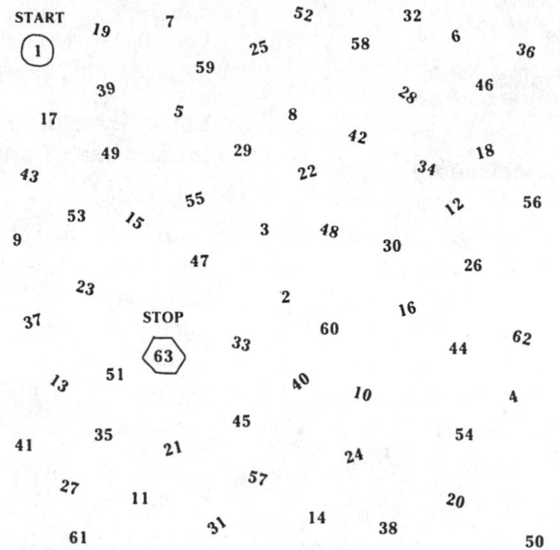

How far did you get? Take a closer look at the way the numbers are arranged. Notice anything unusual? All the odd numbers are on the left and the even numbers are on the right. Now try it again.

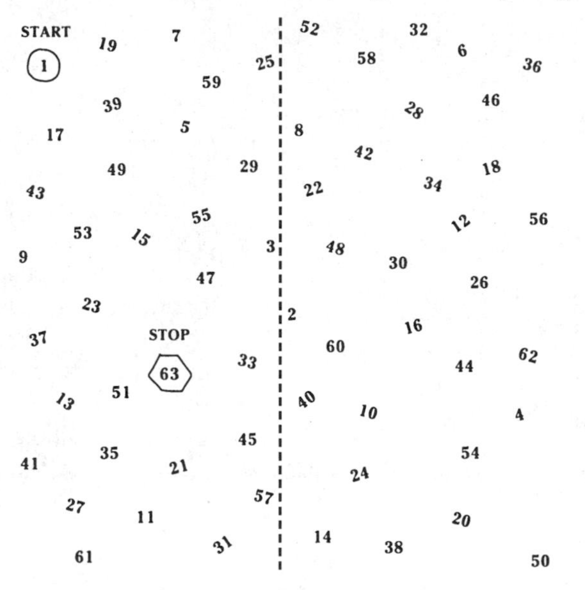

Did you get farther this time? Remember, you can accomplish more if you have a plan!

Collaborate

Problem Solving

Use the space below to state a problem in your life, for example, "I want to live on campus but my folks say we can't afford it." (The problem should be real but not so personal it will make others uncomfortable.)

Pass the exercise sheets around so each person has someone else's problem.

Form into groups of three or four. Have each student write down the first solution that comes to mind for the problem on his or her sheet, then pass the sheet to the next student. Repeat this until each sheet contains three or four solutions.

Taking each problem in turn, discuss and list one or two advantages and disadvantages of each solution, perhaps adding others agreed on by the group. Select the best solution to each problem; then report your findings to the class.

When it comes to problem solving, three or four heads are frequently better than one.

THE PROBLEM: ____________________

SOLUTION 1: ____________________

advantages: ____________________

disadvantages: ____________________

SOLUTION 2: ____________________

advantages: ____________________

disadvantages: ____________________

SOLUTION 3: ____________________

advantages: ____________________

disadvantages: ____________________

SOLUTION 4: ____________________

advantages: ____________________

disadvantages: ____________________

NOTES

____

Strategic *Plan*

Look over your Self-Assessment at the beginning of the chapter and identify an area in which you'd like to make a change. Then develop a Strategic Plan, using the format below.

I. Situation Analysis

A. One problem I'm having in adjusting to college is ______________________

____

B. One change I think I could make is ______________________

____

C. The benefits of making the change are ______________________

____

D. The consequences of not changing are ______________________

____

E. Some obstacles I'll have to overcome are ______________________

____

F. Some resources I'll need are ______________________

____

II. Goals, Objectives, Deadlines, and Indicators

A. My goal is to ______________________

____

Deadline: ______________________

Indicators of success: ______________________

____

B. Here's what I'm going to do to achieve my goal, along with a reasonable deadline for each task:

	OBJECTIVE	DEADLINE
1.	______________	______
2.	______________	______
3.	______________	______
4.	______________	______
5.	______________	______

III. Self-Test

YES	NO	
☐	☐	**A.** Are my goals and objectives stated simply and clearly?
☐	☐	**B.** Does each one have a single focus?
☐	☐	**C.** Are they stated in a positive way?
☐	☐	**D.** Are they realistic?
☐	☐	**E.** Can I achieve them by the deadline?
☐	☐	**F.** Will I know if I've achieved them?

Journal **Ideas**

1. Is college different than you expected or about what you expected? If different, describe your expectations in one paragraph and the reality you've encountered in another.
2. What adjustments have you had to make so far? Which adjustments have been most challenging?
3. What changes, if any, have you noticed at home?
4. Make a list of your reasons for attending college. Which do you think are most important? Which are least important? Explain.
5. Describe an unforgettable person you met when you first arrived on campus.
6. Describe two or three "pleasant surprises" you've had since your arrival.

Web **Search**

Visit the *Center for Critical Thinking* (http://www.sonoma.edu/cthink/) Web site from Sonoma State University. Click on the *College and University* section and go to the *Library,* where you will find a short article called "Universal Intellectual Standards" by Linda Elder and Richard Paul. Read the article. Then discuss in your group or class how your own thinking meets or falls short of the intellectual standards listed in the article.

3

Taking Stock

Self-Assessment

Check the statements that apply to you:

☐ **1.** I'm getting adequate sleep.

☐ **2.** College is no more difficult than I thought it would be.

☐ **3.** I'm enjoying the social scene and keeping up with assignments and class attendance.

☐ **4.** Freedom, for me, means rights coupled with responsibilities.

☐ **5.** I feel comfortable around my instructors.

☐ **6.** I expect to spend more time reading and studying than I did in high school.

☐ **7.** I have read my student handbook and understand my rights and responsibilities.

☐ **8.** I understand what academic probation involves.

☐ **9.** I understand the requirements for graduation from this college.

☐ **10.** I know my way around campus and am acquainted with most campus offices.

If you checked fewer than half, this chapter will be especially valuable to you.

Write **Before** *You Read*

A. Spend about a minute surveying this chapter. Then write three questions you expect to find answers to in this chapter.

1. ______________________________

2. ______________________________

3. ______________________________

B. Spend another minute writing down any thoughts that come to mind about the topics below. Write freely and rapidly.

1. My academic preparation for college: ______________________________

2. Adjustments I need to make: ______________________________

3. My biggest concerns: ______________________________

PREVIEW

Each day, as more students make the decision to enroll in one of the 3,500 colleges and universities in the United States, the percentage of those who graduate remains the same as it has for at least 100 years: about 50 percent. A baccalaureate degree is highly prized. Only 12 percent of American adults have reached this milestone. Statistically, students who attain a baccalaureate degree have higher average lifetime earnings and report greater satisfaction with their lives than do those with only a high school diploma.

You can tip the odds in your favor by finding a proper balance between personal freedom and public responsibility, by understanding what is expected of you academically, and by observing and practicing the behaviors of successful students.

COLLEGE: THEN AND NOW

First—a quiz. Take a guess about each of the statements below, then check your guesses against the correct answers.

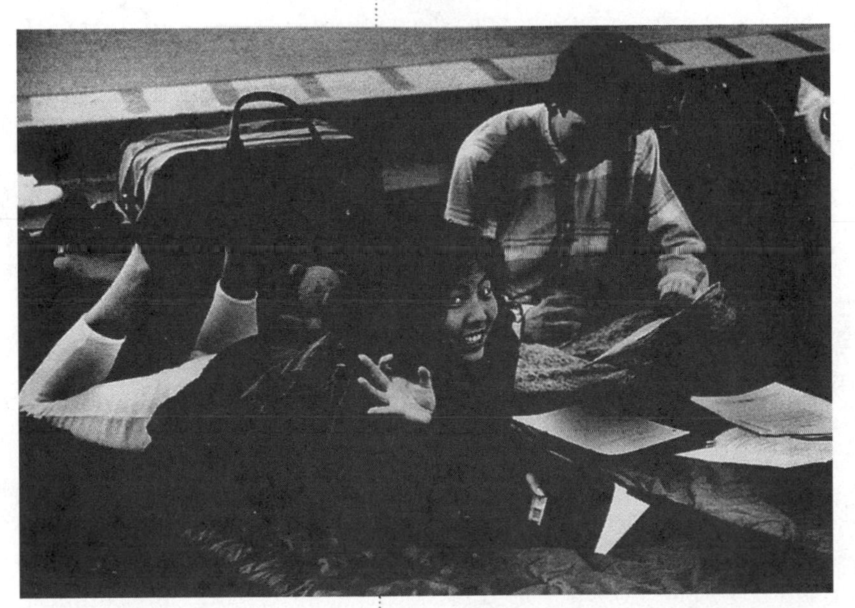

Here you are!

T/F

___ **1.** Today a much higher proportion of students eligible for high school actually attend and graduate than was the case 100 years ago.

___ **2.** Today a majority of high school graduates go on to attend college.

___ **3.** Because the pool of high school graduates is smaller, college enrollments have declined every year since 1984.

___ **4.** Ten percent of all college students are enrolled in two-year community colleges.

___ **5.** Most college students eventually graduate.

(*Answers: 1. T 2. T 3. F 4. F 5. F*)

A century ago, 200,000 students—only 7 percent of those eligible—were enrolled in American high schools. Of those who were not enrolled, most had dropped out by the end of eighth grade to work on the family farm or in a factory. In a high school graduating class of fifty students, only one—usually a white male—went on to college, where he became part of a tiny, privileged minority.

Today all that has changed. A majority of American young people earn a high school diploma; nearly 75 percent of them go on to college.

College enrollments rose annually from 1984 to 1998, despite declining numbers of high school graduates, to over 14,000,000. More than one-third of all college students attend two-year colleges with open admissions policies. If their academic work is acceptable, they may transfer to one of over 2,000 four-year institutions in the United States or abroad. In other words, any American with a high school diploma—or GED—now has the opportunity, if not necessarily the means, to get a college education.

Increased access to higher education has been a great victory for the democratic system. Unfortunately, many new college students—who would not have been admitted to college 25 years ago—are woefully unprepared for the academic rigors ahead. Over the last 25 years, the number of first-year college students who had ever checked out a book from the library declined by 40 percent. The number who had done nonrequired reading declined by 24 percent. The number who had argued with a teacher declined by 20 percent. The number who expected they would need tutoring in college doubled.

One grim statistic has not changed in the last 100 years: **Half of all students who enter college never graduate.** This means that, according to the statistics, either you or the student sitting next to you will never earn a college degree.

This statistic suggests factors other than academic ability may be to blame for the high attrition rate.

Economics is certainly one. Higher education is expensive, and the costs of tuition, books, and fees have been rising faster than the inflation rate for more than a decade. Many students drop out of college or never attend because they cannot meet their financial obligations.

But perhaps the major reason for this perennially high dropout rate—and the most difficult challenge first-year college students must face—is the task of managing freedom in a responsible way.

FREEDOM AND RESPONSIBILITY

The sudden freedom of college life, especially if you are living away from home for the first time, is intoxicating. It may take weeks, months, even years to **find the proper balance between freedom and responsibility.**

For the first time in your life, nobody tells you what to do. Your life, it appears, is your affair. You can take courses that appeal to you and as many or as few as you want. Some professors don't seem to know or care if you attend class (and some do). If you don't like a course, you can withdraw. You can stay up all night, drink till you pass out, pierce your nose, or dye your hair green. You can run barefoot in the snow, live in squalor, gorge yourself on junk food. You can do what you want, when you want.

Sooner or later, however, the intoxication of freedom gives way to the hangover of reality. You discover **your actions have consequences.** If you drink too much, you'll get sick. If you sleep in, you'll miss class, flunk the quiz. Your freedom could be the freedom of the goldfish that leaped out of its bowl and ended its days flopping miserably on the carpet.

> Someday I hope to enjoy enough of what the world calls success that someone will ask me, "What's the secret of it?" I shall say simply this: I get up when I fall down.
>
> Paul Harvey
> *Radio newscaster*

Collaborate

What Is a Successful Student?

Think about students you know who are successful. What do they do that makes them successful? Focus on their *behaviors* (verbs) rather than on who they are (nouns) or what they are like (adjectives). Express these *behaviors*, or habits, by using positive verbs ("studies") rather than negative verbs ("doesn't party every night").

In small groups, take five minutes to brainstorm anything that comes to mind (for example: "attends class regularly," "eats a good breakfast"). Write your group's ideas below. Then have the reporters from each group read these lists to the entire class.

SOME POSITIVE BEHAVIORS OF SUCCESSFUL STUDENTS

1. ______________________________
2. ______________________________
3. ______________________________
4. ______________________________
5. ______________________________
6. ______________________________
7. ______________________________

Add to your list any behaviors others thought of that weren't on your list.

Which three would your group agree are most important? Put a check mark next to these. Why are they important? Which are least important? Why?

Pick any three behaviors you could practice this semester. Write them below as "I will" statements ("I will attend class regularly," "I will review my notes for five minutes after each class"). Make only those commitments you know you can keep.

MY PERSONAL PLEDGE

1. I will ______________________________
2. I will ______________________________
3. I will ______________________________

______________________________ ______________________________

SIGNED DATE

This is a pledge to yourself, not to your instructor, parents, or anyone else. Sign and date your pledge. Every couple of weeks, reread it and recommit to it.

Freedom and responsibility, you'll discover, are brother and sister. The purpose of *Right from the Start* is not to tell you how to live your life, but to let you know what choices are available and help you strike a balance that works for you and your goals. Making **responsible choices** will help you make the most of your college years.

What Instructors Look For

In elementary school you may have been rewarded for keeping quiet, obeying the rules, or having neat penmanship. In college you are likely to find a different set of expectations that emphasize more active learning behaviors.

Listed below are the academic virtues most highly prized by college instructors. Put a check mark next to the descriptions that fit you:

- ☐ conscientious class attendance and preparation
- ☐ high-quality work
- ☐ effective written and oral communication skills
- ☐ patient inquiry, painstaking organization, and a respect for detail
- ☐ persistent effort
- ☐ critical-thinking and problem-solving skills
- ☐ a questioning, curious mind
- ☐ taking intellectual risks and asking tough questions
- ☐ taking responsibility for one's own work—not cheating, plagiarizing, or making excuses

YOUR INSTRUCTORS

Many students have a difficult time during their initial college semester adjusting to the personalities and expectations of college instructors, to a significantly increased workload, and to more exacting quality standards in their academic work.

Students can be easily intimidated by instructors. Because many are intelligent and well educated, you may feel ignorant by comparison. Some are internationally famous. Some are eccentric and enjoy challenging students with bizarre ideas and unconventional behavior. And, of course, they have nearly absolute power to assess and evaluate your performance in their class.

Instructors and students learn from each other.

As you gain experience as a college student, these fears will diminish. You will begin to think of instructors not as celebrities or monsters, but as **human beings well worth knowing.** Most professors are not highly paid (around $54,000 a year on average). Most love their jobs, sincerely care about students, and consider teaching to be their life's work. In a recent survey, a remarkable 83 percent indicated they would choose the same profession if they had to make the choice again.

Professors (as distinguished from teaching assistants, lecturers, and other instructors) have spent from five to ten years in graduate school taking advanced courses and doing specialized research in an academic discipline to earn an advanced degree. Even though some are organized, articulate, and entertaining teachers, most have had no formal training in how to teach. A few prefer to do only research and view teaching as a necessary sideline. You may encounter a few who are hopelessly ineffective in the classroom. It's worth remembering that **you can still get something valuable from every class,** even if you dislike the instructor, and that a dynamic, entertaining instructor is a bonus, not the rule. View your instructors as the experts and the resources that they are and be assertive in making their acquaintance.

Often, instructors are experts in a highly specialized field and may consider what they have to say more important and up-to-date than your textbook. They won't spend much time in class going over assigned readings. Some may speak disparagingly of the text or not refer to it at all in class, assuming you are reading it as a supplement to the lecture. So it's sometimes difficult, especially on the first exam, to guess how much you'll be tested on the textbook and how much on the lecture. When in doubt, ask!

How Faculty Spend Their Time

To earn tenure (a permanent appointment with job security) and promotion through the ranks (instructor, assistant professor, associate professor, full professor), faculty are expected to:

- Research and publish their findings
- Obtain outside funding from grants to conduct research
- Advise students
- Serve their department and college on faculty committees
- Maintain office hours each week
- Be effective classroom teachers (measured by student evaluations and peer observation); prepare for class by reading, updating lecture notes, revising course plans, creating and grading tests, and grading papers
- Keep up with their field by reading scholarly journals and recent publications
- Serve the community through consulting, speaking engagements, and service activities
- Participate in academic conferences in their discipline, preferably by presenting a paper or serving on a panel.

All this adds up to an exceptionally busy 60- to 80-hour week.

Most faculty agree that time pressures are their major sources of stress. Because instructors are busy people, they may not offer more than a generalized invitation to drop by the office for a visit. You will have to **take the initiative.** Be especially sensitive about chatting with your instructor before or after class, when he or she may be preoccupied or rushed. Make an appointment (or stop in) during the instructor's posted office hours.

Students who establish personal relationships with their instructors get better grades. A faculty mentor can provide you with job recommendations later on but, more importantly, can become an inspiring guide and sometimes a lifelong friend.

Successful students find out who the most highly regarded instructors are on campus and take courses with them. If you're lucky enough to study under a superb classroom teacher, let that teacher know how much you enjoyed the class. Applaud an instructor after a great lecture or after the last class of the semester. A teacher's highest reward is hearing a student say, "Thanks—I learned a lot!"

Tips

Professorial Protocol

1. Address your instructor as "Doctor" only if you use the last name too. Use "Dr. Smith," or "Professor Jones." Learn how to pronounce your instructor's last name and use it. Some like to be addressed by their first names, but wait until you're sure.
2. If you make an office appointment, show up on time. If you do show up on time and your instructor isn't there, wait ten minutes (you'd wait longer in a physician's office); then leave a note. If you miss an appointment, apologize in person and reschedule.
3. If an instructor is late for class, it's customary to wait ten minutes before leaving.
4. Many instructors have been teaching in certain time blocks (50 minutes, 90 minutes, 150 minutes) for so long that they know exactly when time is up without checking the clock. You won't hasten the event by standing up, rustling notes, slamming books, or leaning in the direction of the exit. This is not only maddening to instructors but may cause you to miss something important. Wait until you're dismissed.
5. Avoid saying, "I was absent last Friday. Did I miss anything important?" Instructors believe everything they say and do in class is important. (Some students go a step further and ask if they can borrow the instructor's notes—not a good idea!) If you do miss class, ask a classmate what transpired and if you might borrow his or her notes.

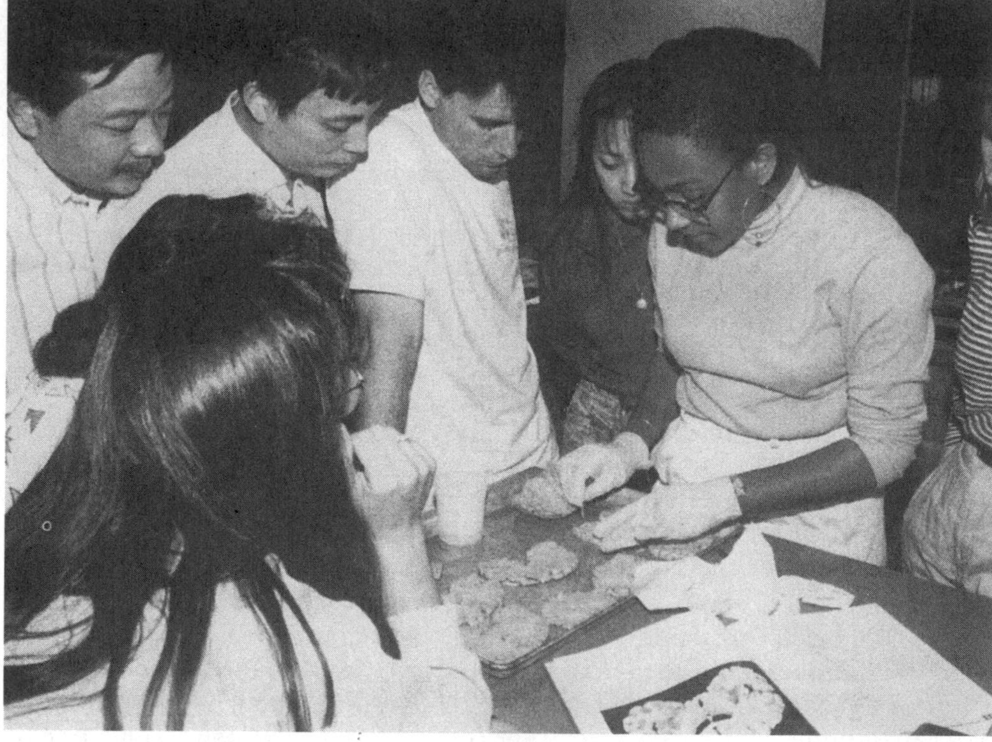
Lab work teaches critical-thinking and problem-solving skills.

GENERAL EDUCATION REQUIREMENTS

Because preparation for a career is one major reason we attend college, many first-year students are discouraged to learn they must now face yet another round of basic courses in mathematics, writing, social studies, lab science, and humanities.

Variously referred to as general education, basic studies, general studies, distribution requirements, liberal arts courses, or simply "the core," these foundation courses often constitute over one-third of the minimum hours required for graduation. Because many are prerequisites (courses you must take before enrolling in a higher-level course in your major field), some students see them as an annoying impediment to their real purpose for attending college—career preparation.

To assume that general education is something to be gotten "out of the way" is a serious mistake. Although the knowledge base needed to function in the workplace is constantly changing, the basic skills required for a successful professional career are stable. They are shown in the box below.

These essential job skills are precisely those taught in liberal arts courses. While you're doing math or logic problems or dissecting a frog, you acquire problem-solving and organizational skills. By participating in a debate about federal budget policy, you develop skills in creativity, communication, and leadership. In reviewing your psychology notes for an exam or writing a paper on a Keats poem, you develop organizational, critical thinking, and problem-solving skills.

Liberal arts courses (the word *liberal* comes from the Latin *liber*, meaning "free") are meant to "liberate" us from the intellectual bonds of ignorance, superstition, and prejudice. These classes help us understand ourselves, each other, and the world we live in.

Liberal arts courses traditionally include

- the humanities, which study the human search for beauty, truth, and goodness (literature, philosophy, religion, art, music, theater, dance)
- the social sciences, which study the behavior of individuals and groups (history, psychology, sociology, anthropology, economics, political science) quantitative courses, which teach us to think in a systematic, orderly fashion (mathematics, logic, economics, statistics, computer science)
- the sciences, which use the scientific method to observe and draw conclusions about the physical universe (chemistry, biology, physics, astronomy, geography, geology)

What Employers Expect of College Graduates

1. **Effective written and oral communication skills.** These include the ability to

- write rapidly, clearly, and succinctly
- communicate successfully, both at the interpersonal level and in small and large groups
- communicate goals to many people
- be a good listener and get along well with fellow employees
- use most common computer applications

2. **Creativity, critical thinking, and problem-solving skills.** These include the ability to

- analyze a problem quickly and work with colleagues to find a solution
- evaluate proposals and identify new ideas
- gather information
- make sound judgments under pressure
- make decisions on the basis of incomplete information
- understand a problem in the context of a broad base of knowledge

3. **Organizational skills.** These include the ability to

- analyze and synthesize complex material
- bring order out of chaos
- see the broad outlines of a problem
- find ways of incorporating new ideas

4. **Leadership skills.** These include all of the above plus the ability to

- generate widespread support for an idea and mobilize many people in a single direction
- inspire confidence and organizational pride
- spur people into action for the common good

Success in your major field will depend on a firm foundation in the liberal arts. **Such courses teach us not what to think but *how* to think.** In them, we acquire "higher order" cognitive skills: analysis and synthesis, induction and deduction, logic and imagination. These disciplines help us to distinguish between good and evil, truth and falsehood, beauty and ugliness; to make sound judgments; to feel kinship with the dead, responsibility

On **Your** *Own*

Design Your Own Degree

A. Review the graduation requirements, and the general studies requirements in particular, in your college catalog. If you could take any courses you wanted (as long as you completed the required number of hours), how would you redesign your course of study?

Fill in the eight-semester schedule below with the courses you would take (the total hours should equal or exceed the number required for graduation). If you are attending a two-year college, fill out only semesters I through IV.

Eight-Semester Schedule

I

Course	Hours
______________	______________
______________	______________
______________	______________
______________	______________
______________	______________
Total Hours	______________

II

Course	Hours
______________	______________
______________	______________
______________	______________
______________	______________
______________	______________
Total Hours	______________

III

Course	Hours
______________	______________
______________	______________
______________	______________
______________	______________
______________	______________
Total Hours	______________

IV

Course	Hours
______________	______________
______________	______________
______________	______________
______________	______________
______________	______________
Total Hours	______________

V

Course	Hours
______________	______________
______________	______________
______________	______________
______________	______________
______________	______________
Total Hours	______________

VI

Course	Hours
______________	______________
______________	______________
______________	______________
______________	______________
______________	______________
Total Hours	______________

continued on next page

On Your Own *continued from previous page*

VII Course	Hours	**VIII** Course	Hours
Total Hours		Total Hours	
Grand total number of hours		Hours required for graduation	

B. If you had the power to change your college's curriculum, what courses would you require of all students? What basic knowledge and skills do you think every college graduate should have today?

List these basic knowledge/skill areas along with the course in which these would be taught.

Knowledge/Skill	**Taught in This Course**

You can expect considerable required reading in college.

for the living, and commitment to the generations to come; to understand and control our emotions and be calm in a crisis; to cope with difficult people; and to make better use of our leisure hours.

Taking your general education requirements seriously and giving them your best effort will pay great dividends later on.

ACADEMIC ADJUSTMENTS

Workload

Most college students agree **the workload in college is much greater** than it was in high school. Expect more reading (you may be asked to complete a novel in a week, for example), more writing (weekly short papers of two to five pages and term papers of ten to twenty pages), more homework (two to three hours for every hour spent in class), and much higher grading standards. Research papers are no longer a matter of paraphrasing an entry from the encyclopedia; you will be expected to do primary-source research.

Self-Direction

There are fewer study halls in college, so you'll have to schedule your own study time. You won't be given constant reminders about assignments due, class attendance, or deadlines. Usually on the first day of class, an instructor will hand out a syllabus with this information, and that will be the last reminder you get. Hang on to this syllabus. It is, in many ways, an "academic compact" between you and your instructor. Some instructors simply don't accept work handed in late. Some will give you a failing grade if you miss the equivalent of two to three weeks' work, with or without a doctor's excuse. High school teachers may have told you to write something down because it's important, and you'll be tested on it. College instructors will generally assume you're taking notes all along, and **you may have to figure out what's important by yourself.**

Attendance

Attendance policies vary widely. Usually, they are explained in your course syllabus. Although some instructors allow you to miss some classes without penalty or never take roll at all, **there is a direct correlation between regular attendance and grades.** Make it a point of personal honor to attend every class. It's especially important not to miss certain classes—the first few days of the semester, for example, when expectations are announced, and the days before and after vacations. If you must miss a class, always let your instructor know, in advance if possible; this is both courteous and academically prudent.

Grades

Most colleges use the traditional A-B-C-D-F grading system, where A equals 4.00. If your high school GPA was in the 3.00 to 4.00 range, you can expect to achieve much the same in college, but you'll have to work harder to do it. If you're transferring from a two-year college, your GPA may stay the same or drop as much as a grade and a half, depending on the quality of your former school and your ability to adjust to the higher expectations and workload.

More and more, instructors are using a system of "contract grading." In contract grading, you're not competing on a class curve with other students for a finite number of A grades; any student who meets the terms of his or her contract can get an A. The contract itself may be worked out between you and your instructor. More commonly, you will be offered a menu of tasks and be asked to make a commitment to complete an agreed-upon number.

Some classes may require you to attend and review a campus event either for course credit or extra credit. A form for this activity is in the Appendix (pp. 259–260).

On **Your** *Own*

Computing Your GPA

GPA is figured differently at different schools. If your institution uses a standard four-point scale and factors in plusses and minuses, you can use the following system to calculate your own GPA.

1. In the table below, list the courses you are taking this semester in the first column. For each course, list the number of credit hours and the letter grade you expect to receive.

COURSE	CREDIT HOURS	LETTER GRADE	GRADE POINTS	TOTAL POINTS
TOTAL				

2. Using the table below, enter the grade points you will earn for each letter grade.

A+	4.30	B+	3.30	C+	2.30	D+	1.30
A	4.00	B	3.00	C	2.00	D	1.00
A–	3.70	B–	2.70	C–	1.70	D–	0.70

(a failing grade = 0.00)

3. For each course, multiply credit hours × grade points. Enter this figure in the far right column.
4. Add up the total credit hours you are taking and put this figure at the bottom of the column. Do the same with the total grade points.
5. Divide the total grade points figure (bottom right) by the total credit hours figure. That's your GPA.

________________ ÷ ________________ = ____________

Total grade points   Total credit hours   GPA

Tips

Digging Yourself Out

You've been a college student for three weeks, but already you're falling behind in your reading assignments. You've started skipping class because you're afraid the instructor may call on you and you won't know the answer. Before long, you've missed so many classes you're embarrassed to show up at all. You're in an academic hole. What should you do?

Step #1. Take responsibility. It'll be tempting to blame others for your dilemma—parents, friends, school. But the sooner you take responsibility for it, the sooner you'll get out of it.

Step #2. Get information. Make an appointment with an academic adviser to discuss your options, including complete withdrawal from the college (how much tuition would be refunded?), withdrawal from one or two courses, retaking courses to improve your grade, or remaining enrolled and salvaging what you can of the semester.

Step #3. Meet with your instructors. Make appointments with each of your instructors. (Tell them you'll need at least half an hour.) Tell them candidly what has happened and take full responsibility for it. Find out exactly what you've missed (make a written list on the spot) and what you would need to do to get back on track.

Step #4. Make a decision. Once you have all the information you need, make a decision and share it with someone you respect. Then take action.

Step #5. Make a plan. If you decide to stay in school, write out your commitment briefly, sign it, and tape it to your door or mirror. Then create a detailed "Comeback Plan" using the Strategic Plan format at the end of the chapter. Write out specific tasks and deadlines.

Step #6. Go to work. Make measurable progress, day by day, in the time remaining. Don't try to do everything overnight; accept that a D or C may be the best you can expect, even with maximum effort. Enlist the support of instructors. Show them your plan and ask them to help you achieve it.

YOUR ACADEMIC RIGHTS AND RESPONSIBILITIES

Your college's expectations of you are spelled out primarily in the college catalog, in the student conduct code, and in any contractual room-and-board agreements you may have signed. Make sure you have copies of these documents and that you know what they contain. The penalty for breaking the rules can run from a warning to probation to expulsion from the college to prosecution in a criminal court.

The following are general operating guidelines, but keep in mind that policies on your campus may differ somewhat and that you are responsible for *those* policies, not the generic ones sketched next.

Academically, **you are responsible for attending class regularly, completing assignments on time, and participating in all required class activities.** These are minimum expectations. Fulfilling them will not guarantee an A or even a passing grade if the quality of your work is unacceptable. If your work is acceptable (C quality or better) but you are prevented from completing the course by illness or necessary absence, you may, at your instructor's option, be awarded an Incomplete (I) grade. You may have anywhere from a few weeks to a full year to make up an Incomplete (check your catalog); if you don't, it is then converted to a failing grade.

When your GPA falls below 2.00 (a C average, the minimum required for graduation), you are automatically placed on academic warning or probation, during which time you may be barred from certain campus activities,

Collaborate

Probation Appeal Review Panel

This is a dramatization.

You are a group of experienced student leaders, faculty, and administrators meeting to hear probation appeals. Five students are waiting in the hall to speak with you, all very nervous. All have failed to meet the terms of academic probation; their GPAs remain below the 2.00 needed for graduation. They are here to appeal to you for one last chance to remain in college. As the court of appeal, you have two options: (1) to expel the student; or (2) to offer the student one last chance, providing he or she agrees in writing to fulfill certain contractual expectations.

Take turns playing the roles of student or panelist. First, the person playing the student reads one of the cases that follow. The panel then briefly questions the student and takes notes. Interview each student/actor in turn, spending about five minutes with each case. After the last student is finished, discuss each case in turn and agree as a group whether the student should be expelled or given a last chance. If the former, explain your reasons. If the latter, briefly list the contractual conditions this student will have to meet.

Cases

Dan: "I really let myself down last year. It's not that I'm stupid or anything—heck, I'm a National Merit Scholar! But here I am, a junior, and I don't know what I'm going to do with my life. I've changed my major six times. My folks cut me off because I quit pre-med. So I had to work thirty hours a week to make ends meet. Then my girlfriend dumped me and everything fell apart."

Gloria: "I was misadvised. My roommate told me I had to take calculus for my interior design program and it wasn't true. I can't even balance my checkbook. Then my English professor talked me into taking two courses with her—medieval lit. and linguistics—both way over my head. I was enrolled in eighteen hours and later found out only one of those courses counted for anything."

Gordon: "To be honest with you, I'm here to play football. My dream is to be in the NFL. I was never very good in school, but I was a Prep All-American. Football is all I really care about. Nobody ever told me that academics were so important. The coaches said to let them worry about that, they'd take care of things. Now they're kicking me out of college. If I miss a whole season, I won't ever get drafted. I'm pretty bitter."

Michele: "I'm a party animal. I love people and I love to have fun. My roommate says I party too much, but I can handle it. It's just that the classes I needed were all in the morning, and I'm really a night person."

Mario: "My parents got divorced last year. My mom didn't have any money and was crying all the time. Dad kept coming over, and sometimes they'd have major fights. All my little brothers and sisters would be crying and screaming. It was a madhouse! How was I supposed to study with all that going down?"

such as varsity athletics. Probationary status usually requires that you continue to achieve a GPA of at least 2.00. If you don't succeed in raising your GPA back up to the 2.00 standard by the stated time, you may have an opportunity to appeal before you are officially suspended.

The student conduct code explicitly states what you have the right to expect from your instructors and describes the grievance procedure you

Collaborate

Conduct a second dramatization as described above. This time, each class member writes one case (hypothetical or not) for probationary appeal, in 50–75 words. Student/actors then select cases from those composed by classmates to read aloud for panel consideration.

must follow to appeal a grade. As a first step in appealing a grade or complaining about inappropriate behavior, you will normally be expected to discuss your concern with the instructor.

THE SYLLABUS

Instructors typically hand out a syllabus on the first day of class; on some campuses they are required to do so. A syllabus (the plural is *syllabi*—pronounced "sill-a-bye") is a **guide to course requirements.** Sometimes a syllabus also contains a day-to-day schedule of topics and assignments. A sample syllabus is shown in Figure 3.1.

Your syllabus should contain the following information. If it doesn't, you have a right to ask.

1. The course name, number, and meeting times. Check to make sure you're in the right class.
2. Information about the instructor (name, office location and office hours, phone, e-mail address, fax number).
3. The textbook and other required or recommended readings (materials placed on reserve in the library, journals, articles, a coursepack). Make sure you have the correct edition of the text.
4. Reading assignments and due dates.
5. Writing assignments and their length, type, value, and due dates, as well as other special assignments, such as computer programs, class presentations, and construction projects.
6. Dates, type, and value of examinations. Find out if they are comprehensive—that is, covering everything up to that point. Find out the type of exam (objective, essay, or a combination) and whether exams will emphasize reading, lecture, or both.
7. Policy on attendance, class participation, cheating, and plagiarism.

Syllabi are seldom carved in stone. Your instructor may make changes in the syllabus from time to time. Transfer important dates (paper deadlines, exam dates) to your personal calendar and keep your syllabus in a safe place. It is a valuable document.

Humanities 152: From the Gay '90s to the Crash
MWF 10:00–10:50 a.m. 107 Rackham

Instructor

Dr. Dashing
Office: 701G McMillan Office phone: 497-0144
Office hours: MWF 11–12 and by appointment
E-mail: ddash@emich.edu

Texts

Tuchman, *The Proud Tower*
Doctorow, *Ragtime*
Remarque, *All Quiet on the Western Front*
Fitzgerald, *The Great Gatsby*
Allen, *Only Yesterday*
Coursepack (available in campus bookstore)

Expectations

1. Attendance. Expected at all class sessions. Grade lowered by one grade after three absences, failing grade after six. Missed quizzes and tests may be made up only upon instructor's acceptance of a valid, verifiable excuse.
2. Reading. It is essential that you have read and understood the assigned readings by the due dates indicated below. Quizzes will be given on the readings.
3. Grades. A midterm and a final exam will each constitute 25 percent of your final grade. A research paper (details below) will constitute 30 percent of your final grade. The balance of your grade will be based on quizzes and your contribution to the learning of your peers. Students who cheat or plagiarize will be asked to withdraw or be given a failing grade for the course.

Reading and schedules

September
9 *Ragtime* (3–146)
16 *Ragtime* (147–end)
23 *Proud Tower* (Chapters 1 and 2)
30 *Proud Tower* (Chapters 3 and 4)
October
6 *Proud Tower* (Chapters 5 and 6)
13 *Proud Tower* (Chapters 7 and 8)
18 Midterm examination
20 *All Quiet* (7–122)
27 *All Quiet* (123–end)
November
13 *Gatsby* (1–64)
20 *Gatsby* (65–end)
27 *Only Yesterday* (Chapters 1–4)
December
3 *Only Yesterday* (Chapters 5–8)
10 *Only Yesterday* (Chapters 9–14)
15 Research papers due
17 Final examination (comprehensive)

Research paper

A research paper of 10 to 20 pages will be required on or before Dec. 15. Topics to be selected and announced by second week of classes. Must be typed.

FIGURE 3.1 Sample Syllabus

The Privacy Act

The Family Education Rights and Privacy Act was passed into law in 1974. It bars your college from passing on information about you, even to your parents, without your permission. It ensures the confidentiality of your grades and other academic records, with the following conditions:

- Your college may release "directory information" (name, demographic data, major, and so forth) unless you declare your wish not to have this information released.
- Your academic records may be made available to authorized college personnel for advising purposes.
- Your parents have a right to your records only if they claim you as a dependent for income tax purposes; otherwise, they must have your signed permission.
- You have a right to see any written recommendations about you unless you waive this right by signing a form. It's advisable to waive this right for two reasons:

1. Some people will refuse to give you a recommendation unless you waive your right of access.

2. Many employers and admissions officials will discount or disregard altogether a recommendation if its privacy is not guaranteed.

In disciplinary cases, college officials are not allowed to inform your parents, but they may require you to tell your parents to call the Dean of Students' Office.

COMMAND RESPECT

As college costs continue to rise, students are increasingly taking a consumerist approach to their education. Learning, of course, is not a product that can be returned if defective, and instructors are not sales clerks. But you do have a right to **insist on fair and respectful treatment** by college personnel.

If you feel your rights have been violated, consider first the seriousness of the case: much time and energy can be misspent contesting insignificant matters. If the issue is important to you and the consequences are significant, by all means take your complaint to the top (how to do this is usually spelled out in the grade grievance procedure section of your catalog). However, always begin by trying to resolve the problem one-on-one with the person who you feel may have disregarded your rights.

A Student's Bill of Rights

1. You have a right to fair, impartial, and dignified treatment in the academic setting (this includes the instructor's office, the classroom, and field trips).
2. You have a right to express your ideas and ask questions.
3. You can't be forced to express your private, personal views in public.
4. You have a right to know in advance what work will be expected of you and when, the basis on which it will be evaluated, and the penalty for missing class.
5. Grading may never be capricious, arbitrary, or discriminatory.
6. Exams and written work should be returned to you promptly, with enough feedback to explain the grade.
7. Your instructor is contractually obligated to schedule and keep office hours and to be available at mutually convenient times for conferences and advising.
8. When possible, you should be told in advance of any cancellation of class or office hours.
9. During a course/instructor evaluation by students, you must be guaranteed anonymity.
10. You have a right to be heard, to say, "Yes," "No," or "I don't know," and to be treated with respect.

SUMMARY

More students than ever before have access to a college education. You can capitalize on this opportunity by using your newfound freedom wisely and enacting the behaviors of successful students; by getting to know your instructors and their expectations of you; by approaching general education requirements with an open mind. Be prepared for exacting academic standards; fully understand your rights and responsibilities as a college student; and have a comeback plan in case you start to fall behind. All the above will increase your familiarity with common college policies and procedures, helping you to create informed academic goals and objectives.

Strategic *Plan*

Look over your Self-Assessment at the beginning of the chapter and identify an area in which you'd like to make a change. Then develop a Strategic Plan, using the format below.

I. Situation Analysis

A. One problem I'm having adjusting to academic expectations in college is ______________________

____

B. One change I think I could make is ______________________

____

C. The benefits of making the change are ______________________

____

D. The consequences of not changing are ______________________

____

E. Some obstacles I'll have to overcome are ______________________

____

F. Some resources I'll need are ______________________

____

II. Goals, Objectives, Deadlines, and Indicators

A. My goal is to ______________________

____

Deadline: ______________________

Indicators of success: ______________________

____

continued on next page

Strategic *Plan*

continued from previous page

B. Here's what I'm going to do to achieve my goal, along with a reasonable deadline for each task:

OBJECTIVE	DEADLINE
1. ______________________________	______________
2. ______________________________	______________
3. ______________________________	______________
4. ______________________________	______________
5. ______________________________	______________

III. Self-Test

YES	NO	
☐	☐	**A.** Are my goals and objectives stated simply and clearly?
☐	☐	**B.** Does each one have a single focus?
☐	☐	**C.** Are they stated in a positive way?
☐	☐	**D.** Are they realistic?
☐	☐	**E.** Can I achieve them by the deadline?
☐	☐	**F.** Will I know if I've achieved them?

Journal Ideas

1. What qualities do you look for in an effective instructor? What does an ideal teacher-student relationship look like or include?
2. What courses do you think will be difficult for you? Why? What will you need to do to succeed in them?
3. How do expectations of you in college differ from what you imagined? Explain. How have *your* expectations been (or not been) met?
4. Students and instructors can both be frustrated by the grading system. What's right with it, wrong with it, and how would you change it?
5. What habits and behaviors will you need to acquire or give up to be successful academically?

Web Search

Using the keywords *college freshmen*, do a search using InfoTrac College Edition© or the search tool Lycos (http://www.lycos.com/) to find out as much as you can about this year's class of first-year college students. List at least ten statements that describe your class and that derive from sources you found in your search. Identify the source for each statement with the last name of the author and the date of publication in parentheses, like this: (Wolper, 1997).

Time and Money

Self-*Assessment*

Check the statements that apply to you.

☐ **1.** I almost always turn my work in on time.

☐ **2.** I am rarely late for class or for work.

☐ **3.** I am rarely absent from class or from work.

☐ **4.** I keep lists and calendars to help me plan my time.

☐ **5.** I have adequate financial resources for my needs.

☐ **6.** I am debt-free.

☐ **7.** I know where and how to find employment, if I need to.

☐ **8.** I receive financial aid to attend school.

☐ **9.** I have applied for grants and scholarships.

☐ **10.** I feel confident about my management of time and money.

If you checked fewer than half, this chapter will be especially valuable to you.

Write **Before** *You Read*

A. Spend about a minute surveying this chapter. Then write three questions you expect to find answers to in this chapter.

1. ______________________________

2. ______________________________

3. ______________________________

B. Spend another minute writing down any thoughts that come to mind about the topics below. Write freely and rapidly.

1. Managing my time: ______________________________

2. Managing my money: ______________________________

3. Working while attending college: ______________________________

PREVIEW

According to opinion polls, the two things that worry college students most are time and money. Both time and money are precious, available to us in a supply that may never seem quite adequate for our needs. Managing time and money successfully requires self-discipline and careful planning, especially if you're working your way through school.

> I must govern the clock, not be governed by it.
>
> Golda Meir
> *Former prime minister of Israel*

> Perhaps the most valuable result of all education is the ability to make yourself do the thing you have to do, when it ought to be done, whether you like it or not. . . . The great end of life is not knowledge but action.
>
> Thomas Huxley
> *English biologist*

> It's more important to do the right things than to do things right.
>
> Peter Drucker
> *Management expert*

MANAGING YOUR TIME

Some incursions on our time are beyond our control—a sick relative, an emergency at work, a broken fan belt, or a traffic jam.

Other **time wasters** only appear to be outside our control but are really a subtle form of rationalization, for example:

"Sue broke up with her boyfriend, and she really needed someone to talk to."
"The guys came over to watch the Super Bowl, and by the time they left, I only had one hour to write my paper."
"My family comes first."

Some professional writers use the phrase "cleaning the refrigerator" to describe the devious strategies they use when confronted with writer's block. To avoid the sometimes unpleasant task of writing, a writer will do almost anything—even a distasteful chore. Cleaning the refrigerator instead of writing a paper means substituting an unpleasant task for a somewhat less unpleasant task, thus soothing the stricken conscience.

The Solution: Prioritize

A major cause of procrastination is the absence of clearly defined goals. Without a clear sense of purpose, you may believe one activity as good as another.

The solution to the problem is prioritization. When you feel overwhelmed by personal and academic obligations, make a list of things you have to do and arrange them in priority order. Prioritizing simply means **doing first things first**. It may mean doing an easy, fun job first, if pleasure or relaxation is a high priority at the moment. Prioritizing also means doing jobs in a meaningful order rather than haphazardly.

Before you go to bed each night, or during breakfast each day, make a list in random order of things you need or want to do that day. Then look over your list and ask yourself:

- Have I included only things I have to do, or things I want to do as well?
- How important is this (to me, not to somebody else)?
- How difficult is this really?
- What would this involve, step by step?
- Do I really have to do this?
- What would happen if I didn't do this?

On Your Own

Twenty Time Wasters

Listed below in Column A are twenty common causes of wasted time.

A. Put a check mark next to the *time wasters* that affect your productivity.

B. Now think about how each time waster you checked keeps you from accomplishing everything you'd like. Describe its *effect* on your productivity in Column B.

C. Think about each time waster you checked. What is its major *cause*? Is this a cause you are able to control in any way? If so, write this cause in Column C. If not, leave it blank.

D. Finally, try to come up with an effective *cure* for each time waster and write the cure in Column D. If the cure is totally outside your control, leave Column D blank.

One item has been completed as an example.

	A Time Waster	B Effect	C Cause	D Cure
☐	1. Too many commitments			
☐	2. Inadequate resources			
☐	3. Daydreaming			
☑	4. Travel, commuting	often late	live 40 min. from school	move closer to campus
☐	5. Disorganization			
☐	6. Meetings			
☐	7. Unable to say "No"			
☐	8. Unable to delegate			
☐	9. Crisis management			
☐	10. Friends dropping in, phone calls, interruptions			
☐	11. Watching TV			
☐	12. Perfectionism			
☐	13. Snacking			
☐	14. Drowsiness			
☐	15. Partying			
☐	16. Busywork, cleaning			
☐	17. Stopping before a job is complete			
☐	18. Lack of self-discipline			
☐	19. Poor planning			
☐	20. Miscommunication			

Collaborate

Strategies for Avoiding Work

Take five minutes to list below three of your own favorite strategies for avoiding work. Then share your avoidance strategies with your small group. What suggestions can you offer as a group to help each other deal with the problem? Write down any solutions you think might work.

Avoidance Strategies	Possible Solutions
1. ______________________	______________________
	______________________
	______________________
	______________________
	______________________
2. ______________________	______________________
	______________________
	______________________
	______________________
	______________________
3. ______________________	______________________
	______________________
	______________________
	______________________
	______________________

- Is there someone else who could do this?
- Can I expect help on this?

Prioritize your list by putting a number next to each item and doing them in that order. An example is shown in Figure 4.1 (p. 73).

Reward yourself

If a task is too demanding to complete in one sitting, break it into smaller steps and only do part of it. If you find yourself assigning a low priority to things you want to do and a high priority to things you need to do, or vice versa, try alternating the two so you'll have something to look forward to after completing a difficult job. You'll also find it rewarding to check off tasks as you complete them.

To get a sense of the big picture, consider making weekly, monthly, and even yearly lists. They'll have to be adjusted as you go along but will help to keep you on track.

Post these "to-do" lists, syllabi, and calendars in prominent places, at eye level, as unavoidable visual reminders. Keep lists, clocks, or watches and calendars nearby to promote habitual, routine inspection. Finally, tell someone your plans. This may help to keep you accountable.

On **Your** Own

How Are You Spending Your Time?

Here is an incomplete list of ways college students spend their time (you can add more items at the end if you like). If you feel you spend too much time or too little time on the item, put a check mark in the appropriate blank. If the time you spend is just about right or the item doesn't apply, leave it blank.

Too much time	Activity	Too little time
________	Sleeping	________
________	Attending Class	________
________	Doing homework	________
________	Relaxing with friends	________
________	Relaxing alone	________
________	Doing chores	________
________	E-mail or Internet surfing	________
________	Volunteer work	________
________	Working for pay	________
________	Eating	________
________	Brooding, worrying, daydreaming	________
________	Transportation	________
________	Personal hygiene	________
________	Organized extracurricular activities	________
________	Playing sports or working out	________
________	Interacting with my family	________
________	Listening to music	________
________	Talking on the phone	________
________	Being with girl-/boyfriend, spouse	________
________	Caring for children	________
________	Watching TV	________
________	Playing video games	________
________	Drop-in visitors	________
________	Reading for pleasure	________
________	Working on hobbies	________
________	Partying	________

Look over the checklist and consider areas you might be willing to spend less time on in order to have more time for things that are more important to you. Circle the items you most enjoy and underline the ones you least enjoy. Then consider saving an enjoyable but low-priority activity as a reward for completing an unpleasant but important task.

Reward yourself

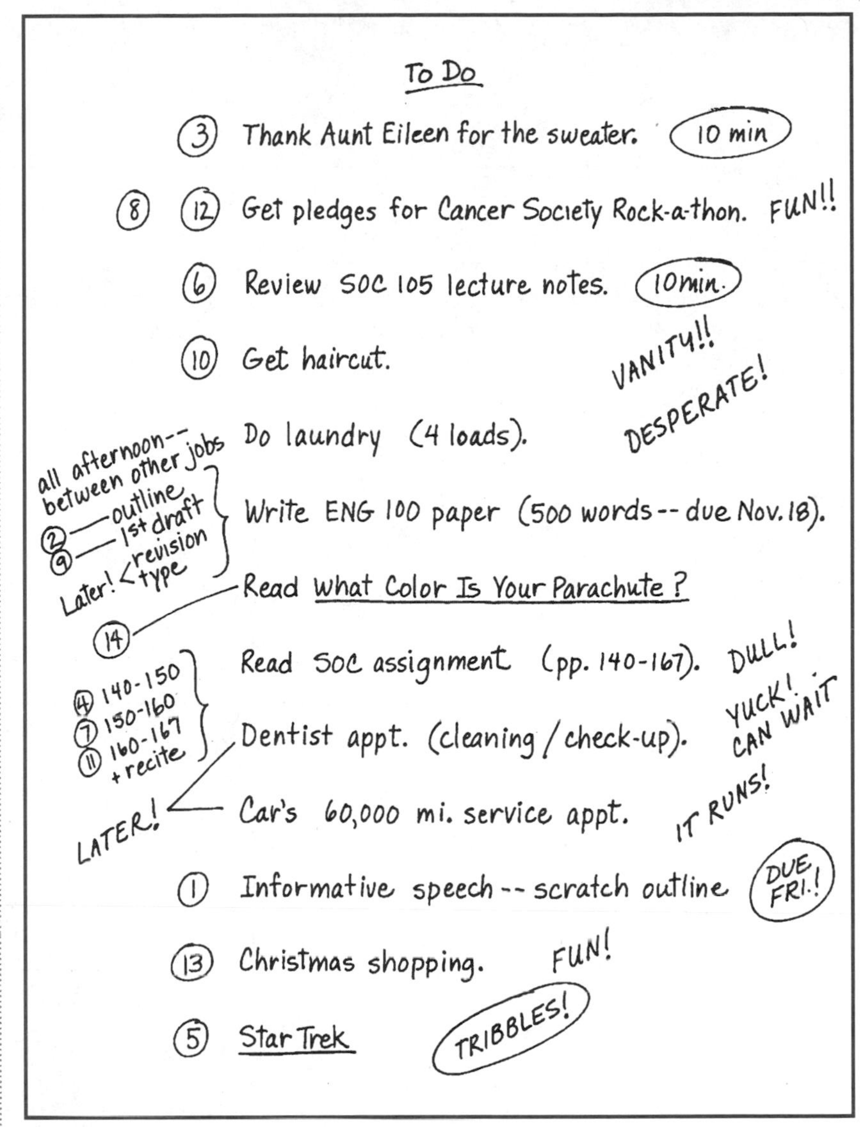

FIGURE 4.1 A prioritized to-do list

On **Your** *Own*

Prioritizing with a Scatterplot

In assigning priorities to a set of tasks, it's important to think about your prioritization criteria, that is, the basis for your decisions. These may include urgency, importance, cost, or complexity. When multiple criteria are at work, prioritizing is more complicated.

One way of assessing multiple options on the basis of two separate criteria is by using a *scatterplot*, or four-square grid. You may, for example, want to prioritize a set of tasks on the basis of *urgency* (things that need to be done right away; emphasis on *time*) or *importance* (things that must be done to avoid negative consequences; emphasis on *outcome*). Here's how:

A. List below five things you need to do during the next few weeks:

	Rank by urgency	Rank by importance
1. ______	______	______
2. ______	______	______

continued on next page

On Your Own *continued from previous page*

	Rank by urgency	Rank by importance
3. ____________	______	______
4. ____________	______	______
5. ____________	______	______

B. Next, assign a rank-order number to each item, both by urgency and by importance. For example, if Item 1 is the least urgent, place a 5 in the blank under urgency. If Item 5 is the most important, place a 1 in the blank under importance.

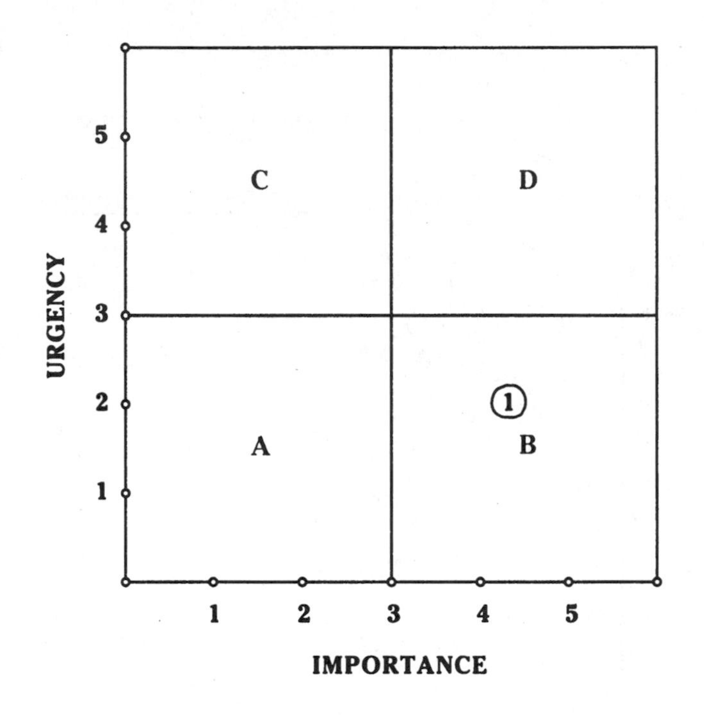

C. Finally, write all five numbers on the grid above, according to their vertical and horizontal rank. For example, if you ranked Item 1 the second most urgent priority but only the fourth most important, you would write the number 1 in Quadrant B, at the intersection of vertical 2 and horizontal 4, as indicated on the grid.

D. When you have finished, Quadrant A should contain the item(s) you consider most urgent and most important. Do these first. The activities in Quadrant D should be done last.

People who spend most of their time doing activities from Quadrant A (urgent and important) tend to be *reactive* rather than *proactive* managers. They spend a lot of time reacting to emergencies and putting out fires. As your management skills improve, you'll find more and more of your jobs are located in Quadrant B—important but not urgent.

On Your Own

Looking Forward, Looking Back

In Figures 4.2 and 4.3 on the following pages are two blank weekly schedules. Complete the form in Figure 4.2 before next week by stating how you plan to use your time for that week. Include such activities as going to class, studying, sleeping, eating, exercising, working, attending meetings, socializing, running errands, watching TV, fulfilling family and service commitments—everything you can think of. During that week, fill in each day on the form in Figure 4.3 with what you actually did, hour by hour. Then compare the two forms. Were the changes unavoidable, or did you make a conscious decision to stray from your plan?

On Your Own

Looking Forward, Once Again

Using Figure 4.4 on page 78, mock up an "ideal week" for next term or semester. Complete the form in detail, spelling out the classes you hope to take and when you hope to take them. Include all other commitments as in Figures 4.2 and 4.3. Write a brief statement to accompany this, explaining the contrasts between your current schedule and this ideal, and what preferences the schedule in Figure 4.4 reflects. It is best to complete this exercise during the week or two prior to your registration date for the coming semester.

Tips

Getting Organized

- Learn to be a list-maker.
- Wear or carry a watch.
- Each night before you turn in, check your schedule for the next day and make a prioritized list of what you need to do. Do the same for each upcoming week and month.
- Buy some manila files and a file box at the bookstore. Keep "slush files" (idea files) for major projects such as term papers or class projects. When ideas occur to you, jot them down and put them in the appropriate folder. Likewise, file relevant clippings, articles, and artifacts such as notes, photos, and so on.
- Use your daily planner to schedule "appointments with yourself." Block out large chunks of time to think, plan, or work on a major project.
- Schedule the unexpected. Leave some blank spaces in your calendar for emergencies and unpredictable events.
- Evaluate "emergencies." Think before dropping everything. Ask: Is this a real crisis? What would happen if I did nothing?
- Above all, get in the habit of asking yourself: What is the best use of my time right now?

	MON	TUES	WED	THUR	FRI	SAT	SUN
6:00							
7:00							
8:00							
9:00							
10:00							
11:00							
12:00							
1:00							
2:00							
3:00							
4:00							
5:00							
6:00							
7:00							
8:00							
9:00							
10:00							
11:00							
12:00							
1:00							
2:00							
3:00							
4:00							
5:00							

FIGURE 4.2 How I plan to use my time

	MON	TUES	WED	THUR	FRI	SAT	SUN
6:00							
7:00							
8:00							
9:00							
10:00							
11:00							
12:00							
1:00							
2:00							
3:00							
4:00							
5:00							
6:00							
7:00							
8:00							
9:00							
10:00							
11:00							
12:00							
1:00							
2:00							
3:00							
4:00							
5:00							

FIGURE 4.3 How I actually used my time

	MON	TUES	WED	THUR	FRI	SAT	SUN
6:00							
7:00							
8:00							
9:00							
10:00							
11:00							
12:00							
1:00							
2:00							
3:00							
4:00							
5:00							
6:00							
7:00							
8:00							
9:00							
10:00							
11:00							
12:00							
1:00							
2:00							
3:00							
4:00							
5:00							

FIGURE 4.4 How I plan to use my time next semester: the "ideal week."

Tips

A Time-Saving Strategy Sampler

- Do two tasks at once ("two-fers").
  - exercise/recite definitions
  - housework/watch TV
- Prepare ahead for hectic periods in the day (for example, morning routine).
  - select and lay out clothes the night before, pack lunches
- Know your "peak" performance periods, your most productive times of day (are you a morning, midday, or evening person?). Schedule study time during these, if possible.

- Establish a sleeping/eating pattern and stick as closely as possible to it each day to maintain stamina and energy.
- Overestimate the amount of time you will need to complete assignments.
- Break up study periods—one hour maximum for one subject at one time. Take a small break and allow "sink-in time"—do something pleasant during this break.

- If it is difficult to study at home or in your room, find a spot on campus that works, and *go there* to study.
- Try to do the same things at the same times every day, or every other day, to establish productive routines.
- Learn to say "No."
- Sacrifice perfection to get the job done.

A pocket-sized, **week-at-a-glance type of calendar** is a valuable time-management tool and can be carried with you wherever you go. Use it to record not only other people's demands on your time (exam dates and paper deadlines, religious commitments, residence hall government meetings, soccer practice, classes and labs, work) but also your own goals and objectives (do math assignment, lunch with Dave, take kids to dentist, debug program, attend concert, call home, weight workout). Write in due dates for assignments as well as your own deadlines for specific tasks required by the assignment. For a research paper due on December 12, for example, you could develop a timeline backward from that date for completing important steps:

Task	Complete by
Turn in paper	Dec. 12
Revision and final typing	Dec. 4
Rough draft	Nov. 24
Complete research, final bibliography	Nov. 17
Refine topic and thesis sentence	Nov. 7
Preliminary research	Nov. 4
Preliminary bibliography	Oct. 15
Define topic	Oct. 8

Balancing School with Work

There is some evidence that students who work part-time while attending college do better academically. This is especially true of on-campus jobs. Students who work are forced to make better use of their limited free time, and those who work on campus tend to feel more involved in the learning enterprise.

How Much Is Too Much?

Traditional full-time college students typically take twelve to sixteen credit hours per semester or quarter. A three-credit class normally meets three hours and requires six to nine hours of class preparation per week. A five-credit lab course normally requires seven hours in class and twelve to fifteen hours outside of class per week.

The time you spend on your schoolwork, both in and out of class, constitutes your *total academic commitment*. (Notice that a full academic load requires a 45–65-hour work week. If this were a job, you'd be getting overtime!) Add the hours you spend in class each week(___) to the hours of outside work they require (___) to determine your *weekly academic commitment (___ hours)*.

Next figure your *weekly nonacademic commitment* by adding the hours you spend each week on travel to campus and parking (if you commute), inescapable family commitments (for example, preparing meals, driving kids to school), and cocurricular involvement (clubs and organizations, volunteer work, and so forth).

Now determine your total weekly commitment as follows:

weekly academic commitment	___ hours
weekly nonacademic commitment	+ ___ hours
total weekly commitment	= ___ hours

If you take one day off per week and sleep eight hours a day, you'll have 96 hours available in your week. Subtract your total weekly commitment from 96. That figure is your discretionary time (___ hours)

Now subtract from your discretionary time the number of hours you spend each week working at a job (include time required for transportation to and from work). This figure (___ hours) is your *real* discretionary time—the time you have left to do precisely as you wish!

IF YOUR DISCRETIONARY TIME IS	YOU SHOULD
Below 15 hours	Reprioritize your activities and reconsider your commitments. You've taken on too much.
15–30 hours	Keep things as they are. Your schedule is about right.
Above 30 hours	Take on some new commitments. You have plenty of time to spare.

If you think education is expensive, try ignorance.

Derek Bok
Former Harvard University president

But there's a limit. If you're taking a full load of classes, ten to twenty hours of work per week is plenty. Students who work more than that have a dropout rate *five times higher* than those who work fewer hours.[1]

If your campus is located in an urban area, job opportunities may be more abundant off campus. If you have your own transportation, prior experience, or special skills (keyboard, clerical, and "people" skills), your chances of being hired are even better. Off-campus jobs tend to pay more than campus jobs.

However, if your job is some distance from campus, the extra income may be offset by transportation costs, added time constraints, and course-scheduling conflicts. Your Career Services, Placement, or Student Employment Office should provide lists of available jobs, but such lists are by no means exhaustive. Check the classified ads in the local newspaper, grocery-store bulletin boards, and your network of employed friends to identify additional opportunities for employment.

If your college is located in a small rural community, campus employment may be your only option. But many students prefer to work on cam-

[1] Martin Kramer, "Earning and Learning: Are Students Working Too Much?" *Change* (Jan.–Feb. 1994), 6–7.

pus, even at a reduced wage, because it's close to home and classes. It's also a good opportunity to learn how a college operates, to acquire a network of faculty and staff mentors, and to develop a personal stake in your education and school.

When looking for a campus job, ask, "What will I learn?"—not "What will I earn?"

The best time to apply for a campus job is before the fall quarter or semester begins. Many departments don't know how many student employees their budgets will allow until late summer. It helps to get your application in before the masses arrive.

Major campus employers are food services, housing, the student union, the library, and the athletic and intramural departments. Once you've identified the department or office you'd like to work in, go there and find out what jobs are available and who does the hiring. Arrange a meeting with that person if possible, so he or she can connect your face with your application. Some colleges hold "job fairs" during the first week of the fall quarter or semester; attend!

If you qualify for college work-study, your chances for a campus job will be better, because hiring you won't cost your employer anything. Many students don't take full advantage of federal or state work-study programs because the money they make reduces their total unmet financial need[2] or because they can make more money from an off-campus job.

However, top dollar doesn't always mean best benefit. If wages are not your major consideration, hold out for a job that will teach you something, give you a valuable skill, or introduce you to a career opportunity or to mentors who can help you later. View every job as a challenge and give it all you've got. Your work habits at minimum-wage employment will probably not be too different from the ones you practice in your professional career. Above all, **seek a reasonable balance between school and work** and put school first. The time you spend in college is an investment in more gainful employment to come (see Fig. 4.5). As long as you're in college, learning is "job one."

[2] *Unmet financial need* is the amount you need to cover your college expenses after all other available resources (family income, scholarships, home mortgage equity, personal savings, and so on) have been exhausted. The figure is determined by federal guidelines on the basis of the financial information you provide on your Financial Aid Form (FAF).

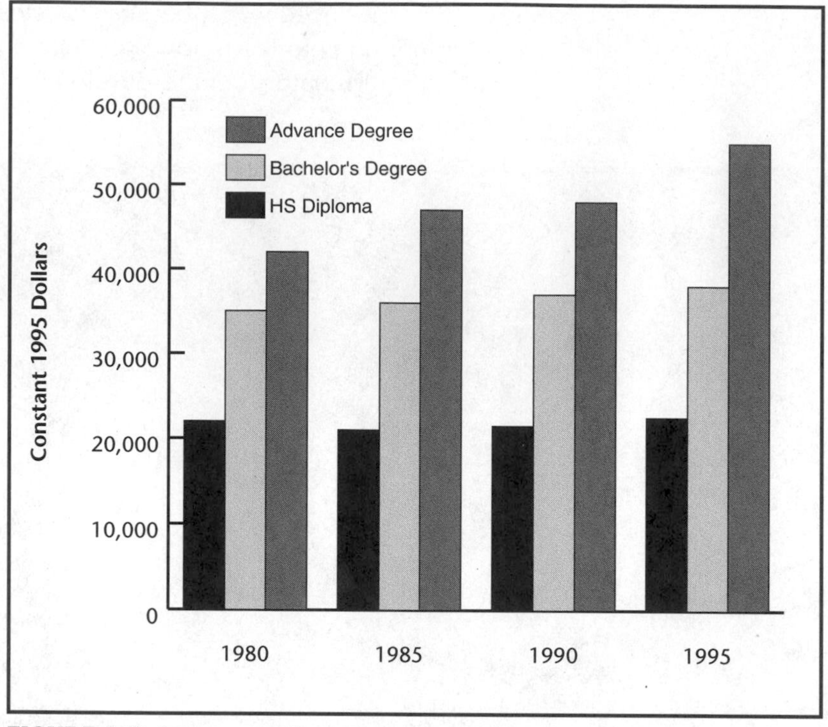

FIGURE 4.5 Average earnings of workers 18 years old or older, by educational attainment, 1980 to 1995

> A banker is a person who is willing to make you a loan if you can provide sufficient evidence to show you don't need it.
>
> Herbert V. Pronchnow
> *Author*

MANAGING YOUR MONEY

These days, hitting the books often means hitting the checkbook. Each year, college becomes more expensive, with costs for residential students exceeding $30,000 a year at some private institutions. During the first half of the 1990s, overall state support for higher education declined. Colleges have come to expect less money from their state legislatures and make up for these cuts in revenue by charging students increased tuition and fees.

Although federal and state aid for college students continues to rise, it is not keeping pace with either inflation or escalating college costs. These disparities have hit middle-income families especially hard. If you are partially or totally responsible for financing your education, you will need to **become a skilled money manager**. People who possess this skill enjoy tangible personal benefits throughout life, and they are highly prized employees.

> My problem lies in reconciling my gross habits with my net income.
>
> Errol Flynn
> *Film actor*

There is one simple rule for managing money: **Live within your means.** And, like the business axiom "buy low, sell high," there are two solutions to debt: increase money in and decrease money out. Of course, it's easy to know the rules but much more difficult to practice them, as our own staggering national debt attests.

Financial Aid

> If you've got the money, honey, I've got the time.
>
> Hank Williams
> *Country singer*

Financial aid is typically awarded on the basis of need or merit. If your resources are inadequate (and whose aren't?), make an appointment with a financial aid counselor to discuss possible additional sources of income. You may qualify for some form of federal or state aid based on need, or for a scholarship or grant.

Tips

ATMs, Credit Card, and Checks

1. ATMs (automated teller machines, sometimes called "the money god") should be approached with caution. If you're paying a fee for each transaction, try to anticipate your needs and make one withdrawal instead of several. Hang on to your receipts and record your withdrawal immediately.

2. A debit card (you deposit money in your student account, and the money is immediately debited—subtracted—when you make a purchase) makes it easy to buy shampoo or do your laundry without carrying around a lot of cash. Some debit cards can be used as keys to campus buildings and rooms, and some can be used at local merchants. Maintaining a large cash balance helps the college (they keep the interest) but it doesn't help you—and it encourages impulse buying.

3. College students represent a lucrative market for credit card companies—82 percent of all college students own at least one card. Most companies do not require a parent's cosignature and offer a credit line ranging from $500 to $2,000. Credit cards are handy in an emergency and allow you to make monthly payments for tuition, books, and rent. If you're able to pay off your entire unpaid balance every month, they are harmless and an important initial step in establishing a good credit history. But their purchasing power is intoxicating, and some students run up such huge debts that they are forced to declare bankruptcy. Start with the smallest credit line possible. Make sure you know how much interest you're paying for that "free" card and whether there's an annual fee.

4. If you're opening a checking account for the first time, call around, ask questions, and shop for the best deal. If fees apply, are they monthly or per check? Do fees depend on maintaining a minimum or average daily balance? If you're paying a per-check fee, think twice before you write a check for fifty cents or a dollar. How does the bank figure interest on an interest-bearing account? What does the bank charge for a bounced check? For check printing? For a certified check? For using an ATM? How close is the nearest branch? The nearest ATM? What are the bank's hours? Once you've opened a checking account, be sure to record all checks and ATM withdrawals immediately, and keep a running account balance. Use a calculator to avoid careless errors. As soon as your monthly statement arrives, balance your checkbook (you'll find step-by-step instructions on the statement).

Scholarships and grants don't have to be repaid, but they do require financial need (defined by the granting agency, not you) or merit—outstanding academic ability—or both.

Loans must be repaid, but often at low rates of interest and not until you graduate and start working.

Federal aid has historically come in three forms:

1. **Grants.** The amount varies on the basis of what the federal government considers to be your "unmet need" up to a legal maximum. A grant is the most attractive (and the most difficult) form of aid to obtain because it does not have to be repaid. Grants are deposited into your student account and can only be used for tuition and room and board.

2. **Loans.** Since the Reagan and Bush administrations, when severe cuts were made in the federal grant program, guaranteed loans have replaced grants as the principal source of student aid. A low-interest loan must be repaid after you graduate. It does not require a credit check or collateral, and a check is disbursed directly to you.

3. **College work-study.** You earn your award by working a part-time job, usually in a campus office at minimum wage. The federal gov-

ernment and your employer share the cost. College work-study accounts for only 3 percent of all federal financial aid.

Many forms of financial aid require a minimum GPA and enrollment in a minimum number of credit hours. Also, if you withdraw from classes, you may be required to repay federal aid received to that point.

Many students are unaware that they must apply (and reapply annually) for all need-based and some merit-based aid. Make sure you know and anticipate your campus deadline for application and, since the pool of aid is limited and applications are handled as they come in, **apply early**.

Millions of dollars in available aid go unclaimed each year. Many students simply aren't aware of available aid or were told by a friend that they wouldn't qualify because their family income was too high. Others are reluctant to do the paperwork. Some endowed scholarships are never claimed because they aren't advertised, so they just sit in a bank collecting interest. Many applications for aid are never considered because they are incomplete, incorrect, or late.

> I have enough money to last me the rest of my life—unless I buy something.
>
> Jackie Mason
> *Comedian*

As any seasoned fundraiser will tell you, the best way to get money is to ask for it. Don't let available aid go unclaimed by you because you didn't ask.

If you're applying close to the deadline, deliver the application in person.

Many students supplement outside support (from parents, spouse, savings, scholarships, grants, and loans) by working an average of 20 hours a week. If you can't find employment on campus or off, consider **going into business for yourself**.

Over the years, college students have found ingenious ways of financing their own educations: typing term papers; tutoring; selling candy bars in the residence halls; providing copying or desktop publishing services; or doing singing telegrams, nails, laundry, or hair. College students cut lawns, walk

Collaborate

Money Savers

Take five minutes to list below any ways you've found to reduce your expenses and increase your revenue while attending college. Then gather with your group and, in turn, share each person's ideas. Add these to your list. When everyone has finished, go around again and discuss which ideas would or would not work for you and why.

My ideas for saving money or increasing income:

1. ______________________ 3. ______________________
2. ______________________ 4. ______________________

Other people's ideas:

1. ______________________ 6. ______________________
2. ______________________ 7. ______________________
3. ______________________ 8. ______________________
4. ______________________ 9. ______________________
5. ______________________ 10. ______________________

Collaborate

Solicitation Simulation

With a partner, make some scrip (or play money) in varied denominations to total $200 each, or $400 together. Develop a solicitation pitch, an appeal for money, that you and your partner think will be effective with your classmates. You might ask for a donation for your favorite charity, take orders for product delivery (the product is up to you), promise a return on an investment, sell time-share weeks at a condo in Cancún. Be creative. You don't have to "come through"; this is a simulation. Ask yourself: For what would *I* pay or give money? During ten minutes of class time (with your teacher minding the clock), approach as many of your classmates as time allows, trying out your solicitation, asking each for cash.

They will do the same. You *must* give away *some* scrip, and you must keep some. How you decide to disburse your scrip will depend on the persuasiveness of your classmates' appeals. Partners who have amassed the most scrip after ten minutes are Superstar Solicitors. If you are one of those partners, congratulations! You are learning to ask for money—effectively.

dogs, clean gutters, and provide home care for children and the elderly. Resale shops buy used clothing, CDs, sporting goods, and computer equipment. With creativity, you too can be a thriving collegiate entrepreneur.

The other obvious way of managing money is by **reducing expenses**. You probably have a good idea by now of where your money is going, especially fixed expenses like car payments, tuition, fees, room and board. If you ought to have some money left over after paying your fixed expenses but don't, take a look at where your disposable cash is going. Keep a list of every expenditure, no matter how small: vending machine snacks, beer, cigarettes, newspapers and magazines, gas and car care, movies and video rentals, pizza, donations to worthy causes, clothing, makeup, haircuts, laundry. Try to anticipate major expenses during the coming year (travel over spring break, special course fees next semester, major purchases). Then make a budget that looks something like the one in Figure 4.6 (p. 76).

In Part II, add the monthly totals from Section C of your budget and divide by 12 to determine your average monthly anticipated expenses.

Now add up your monthly variable expenses (from Section A), your monthly fixed expenses (from Section B), and your average monthly anticipated expenses to get your total average monthly expenses.

Find the difference between the total average monthly expenses figure and your total monthly income figure. This represents your disposable cash.

Your disposable cash is the money you have available each month for additional savings and investments. If this is a negative figure, you've got a money problem.

To do something about it, study your budget carefully and **make some decisions** about generating additional income, reducing your variable expenses, and saving more. If you own a car, for example, can you save money by leaving it at home, selling it, trading it in for a less expensive model, or postponing a major repair? Can you cut down on beer or pizza or vending machine snacks? Can you rely on free or inexpensive campus

I. Income		
Income for the month of: ________		________
Net (take-home) wages	$	________
Gifts, grants, scholarships, loans		________
Other income		________
Total monthly income	$	
II. Expenses		
A. Actual expenses		
Food, beverages, sundries, incidentals	$	________
Car (operation and upkeep)		________
Utilities (electric, water, phone, cable)		________
Laundry, dry cleaning, shoe repair		________
Clothing		________
Medical, dental, prescriptions		________
Hair care, beauty treatments, hygiene		________
Entertainment (dining, hobbies, films, sports)		________
Child care		________
Books, supplies, newspapers, magazines, tapes		________
Gifts, dues, contributions		________
Miscellaneous		________
Subtotal monthly actual expenses	$	
B. Fixed expenses		
Rent, mortgage, or room and board	$	________
Tuition		________
Loan payments		________
Health insurance		________
Auto insurance		________
Homeowners/rental insurance		________
Savings		________
Subtotal monthly fixed expenses	$	

FIGURE 4.6 Budget

events for your entertainment? Can you save money by sharing an apartment? Buy used books instead of new?

Finally, create a Strategic Plan that clearly states your financial goals, both short-term and long-term, and the objectives you will use to achieve them.

C. Major anticipated expenses

	Taxes, fees	Vacation, other	Investments	Monthly totals
Jan				
Feb				
Mar				
Apr				
May				
Jun				
Jul				
Aug				
Sep				
Oct				
Nov				
Dec				

Total anticipated monthly expenses $ ________

Divide total by 12 to get ÷ 12 = ________

Subtotal average monthly anticipated expenses $ ________

Total monthly expenses (add up totals in gray boxes) $ ________

III. Calculate your disposable income

Total monthly income (Part I) $ ________

Less
Total monthly expenses (Part II) – ________

Disposable cash = $ ________

FIGURE 4.6 Budget (continued)

There are other ways to reduce expenses and save money. For instance:

- Don't go shopping. Take a long walk instead. All too often, we shop as a kind of emotional balm and buy things we neither need nor even particularly want.
- Instead of replacing a broken item, can you fix it yourself, or barter for goods or services? Do you cut hair? Is your friend a premier mechanic? *Swap* your skills and talents and don't pay another to perform tasks you can do yourself.
- Save money by paying cash rather than using credit. If you *wait* to make purchases until you have the cash in hand, you will pay less and save more.

- Can you buy it used? Ask for a discount? Shop around for the best price by telephone?
- Monitor your thoughts, especially; that voice in your head screaming "Buy, buy, buy!" might not have a clue about what is truly best for you.

SUMMARY

Effective management of our two most precious resources—time and money—is an essential life skill. And college is a good time to learn this skill. For most college students, both time and money are scarce commodities that are easily frittered away on nonessentials. Arranging our obligations in priority order and budgeting our money amount to the same thing: they are ways of bringing our actions in line with the goals we set for ourselves. Working at a part-time job while attending college is a good way to alleviate the money crunch, but working too many hours is self-defeating. Above all, making thoughtful, informed choices will yield many happy returns.

Strategic *Plan*

Look over your Self-Assessment at the beginning of the chapter and identify an area in which you'd like to make a change. Then develop a Strategic Plan, using the format below.

I. Situation Analysis

A. One problem I'm having with managing my time (or my money) is ______________________

____

B. One change I think I could make is ______________________

____

C. The benefits of making the change are ______________________

____

D. The consequences of not changing are ______________________

____

E. Some obstacles I'll have to overcome are ______________________

____

F. Some resources I'll need are ______________________

____

continued on next page

Strategic Plan

continued from previous page

II. Goals, objectives, deadlines, and indicators

A. My goal is to ______________________________

____

Deadline: ______________________________

Indicators of success: ______________________________

____

B. Here's what I'm going to do to achieve my goal, along with a reasonable deadline for each task:

	OBJECTIVE	DEADLINE
1.	______________	________
2.	______________	________
3.	______________	________
4.	______________	________
5.	______________	________

III. Self-Test

YES	NO	
☐	☐	**A.** Are my goals and objectives stated simply and clearly?
☐	☐	**B.** Does each one have a single focus?
☐	☐	**C.** Are they stated in a positive way?
☐	☐	**D.** Are they realistic?
☐	☐	**E.** Can I achieve them by the deadline?
☐	☐	**F.** Will I know if I've achieved them?

Journal Ideas

1. Brainstorm a list of ten to twelve free (or low-cost) things to do for fun by yourself or with others. Exchange lists with a classmate; rank ideas according to your own preferences.
2. Are you a procrastinator? What kinds of things most often prevent you from getting work done?
3. Do you think you'll be overly busy this semester? Have you taken on too much? Where do you think you could cut back?
4. Do you have a lot of leisure time on your hands? Make a list of ways you could use this time profitably.
5. What kinds of money problems do you anticipate this year? Are you worried about them? Brainstorm some possible solutions.
6. Describe your spending habits. Are you an impulsive spender, or a careful money planner? What would you like to change?

Web Search

Here is a list of Web sites that offer free advice about financial aid and money management:

1. www.collegenet.com
2. www.signet.com/collegemoney/toc1.html
3. www.easi.ed.gov
4. www.fastweb.com
5. www.finaid.org
6. www.kaplan.com
7. www.mapping-your-future.org
8. www.mastercard.com/students
9. www.petersons.com
10. www.review.com
11. www.inet.ed.gov/prog_info/SFA/StudentGuide
12. www.visa.com/cgi-bin/vee/ff/tips/choices/choices.html

Browse as many of the above sites as you have time for or make a list of your own. Then select three sites that look interesting to you and study them more closely. Finally, write three paragraphs—one per site—describing the site (source, contents) and stating what you learned from the site.

5

Going to Class

Self-Assessment

Check the statements that apply to you.

- ☐ **1.** I haven't skipped one class since starting college.
- ☐ **2.** I tend to sit up front, where I am most likely to be involved in class conversation.
- ☐ **3.** I'm rarely drowsy in class.
- ☐ **4.** Most lectures interest me, make sense, and are memorable.
- ☐ **5.** I write down everything the instructor says and can usually keep up.
- ☐ **6.** My notes are thorough and useful; I occasionally swap them with a friend.
- ☐ **7.** I take detailed notes, review them immediately, and scan them periodically.
- ☐ **8.** I frequently ask questions and make comments in class.
- ☐ **9.** Speaking in front of a group is not difficult for me.
- ☐ **10.** I speak freely in class; I also listen carefully to others when they speak.

If you checked fewer than half, this chapter will be especially valuable to you.

Write **Before** *You Read*

A. Spend about a minute surveying this chapter. Then write three questions you expect to find answers to in this chapter.

1. ______________________________

2. ______________________________

3. ______________________________

B. Spend another minute writing down any thoughts that come to mind about the topics below. Write freely and rapidly.

1. Taking lecture notes: ______________________________

2. Other students' classroom behavior: ______________________________

3. Speaking in class: ______________________________

PREVIEW

Academic success begins in the classroom. Classroom habits that characterize the successful student are:

- eager and regular attendance
- careful preparation
- positive regard for instructor, classmates, and school
- active listening
- a rapid and aggressive system of note taking
- a brief, after-class review of notes
- full participation in discussions and group activities
- a willingness to question

This chapter concludes with some tips on how to meet a challenge many students fear: speaking in front of the class.

BEING THERE

Research shows that students who attend class regularly get better grades than those who do not. In one college study, 85 percent of the students who attended class regularly earned at least a B average. Attending class is like sticking to a diet or an exercise regimen: It's something you make a commitment to because you want the results.

There's no sugar-coating the fact that learning demands effort. People don't learn by absorption or osmosis; **learning requires the active involvement of the brain.**

The word "attend" means not only to be present but also to be alert, to listen. Attending in class means being there, body and soul. Here's how:

> Ninety percent of success is showing up.
>
> Woody Allen
> *Writer/Filmmaker*

- Get plenty of sleep the night before.
- Wear clothing you associate with work, not with sports, pleasure, or attracting attention.
- Arrive a few minutes early to review your reading assignment and notes from the last class.
- Sit where you have a good view of the instructor and the board.
- Sit up straight.
- Watch the instructor's eyes.
- Be aware of other people around you, but don't let your concentration be diverted by them.
- Pay attention. If your mind wanders, note that, then guide yourself back to the speaker. Find his or her eyes, and when you do, what he or she says will follow.

Learning is an intentional activity. Good learners **resolve to listen**; they **expect to learn**. Intentionality is an important ingredient in achieving success in any enterprise. Intending to listen or expecting to be bored are both self-fulfilling prophecies; what you think is going to happen is usually what happens. Even if the instructor is uninspired or the subject matter is tedious, if you resolve in advance to learn something, you will.

Tips

If You Have to Miss Class

1. Take the first opportunity (before class, if possible) to tell your instructor you have a conflict. If you can't reach him or her, leave a message.
2. Find out what you missed, preferably from a classmate you trust, otherwise from the instructor. Instructors often get upset when students ask, "Did I miss anything important?" or "Could I copy your lecture notes?" Also, they don't have time to repeat the entire lecture for your personal benefit.
3. Nobody's notes are absolutely trustworthy. Your friend may have dozed during class and missed the announcement about the midterm. Talk to as many sources as possible. If you know in advance that you must miss a class, get someone to tape the class for you. (Always ask the instructor for permission in advance.)
4. Few instructors will accept Greek activities (rush, pledge, "hell week") as legitimate excuses for missing class. School-sponsored activities (varsity athletics, forensics competitions, field trips) may be excused, but check with your instructor in advance.
5. Never skip class because you haven't read the assignment. If the instructor calls on you, it's embarrassing, of course, to admit you're unprepared, but missing an entire lecture has far greater consequences. If you skip class for this reason, it can become chronic and, when it does, the damage is irreversible.

On **Your** *Own*

Instant Recall

Try to remember as much as you can of a lecture you heard 24 hours ago. On a clean sheet of lined paper, jot down the main ideas and as many supporting details as you can.

When you have finished, compare what you wrote to your actual lecture notes for that class.

How much were you able to remember? Did you leave out any major ideas or key facts? Did you do a quick review of your notes after class? If so, do you think it helped you remember more? If not, try doing one after a lecture tomorrow. Then repeat this exercise.

Collaborate

Listening and Remembering

In a small group, take turns giving a brief (two-minute) descriptive narrative about your family while the others listen and take notes. After all have finished, have each person designate, in turn, any other person in the group to repeat back what was said. Were important details left out? Which details were easiest to remember? Which were more difficult? Why?

Now, repeat the activity without taking notes. This time, the narrative should be a detailed description of your sleeping quarters and its contents. As you repeat back the narratives, how much forgetting occurred when you didn't take notes? Did people concentrate harder or not as hard when they weren't taking notes?

ACTIVE LISTENING

Many people have a harder time remembering what they hear than what they read. We acquire 83 percent of our information from seeing and only 11 percent from hearing. And we remember only 20 percent of what we hear, compared to 30 percent of what we see and 50 percent when we both hear and see something.

Most of our forgetting occurs almost immediately. Researchers tested one group of students on how much they could remember from a lecture: within 24 hours, most had forgotten more than half.

Hearing and listening are not the same thing. Hearing is what the ears do when sound waves vibrate against the eardrums. Stop a moment as you read this and listen carefully to the sounds around you: can you hear traffic noise? Birds chirping? Voices outside your window? Those same sounds were there before you looked up from your book, but you weren't listening to them, so they made no impact on you. **Listening is a deliberate activity** of the brain that interprets and stores those sound vibrations. If your brain is not actively listening to what your ears hear, you will rapidly forget what you heard, or never hear it in the first place.

> There is no substitute for paying attention.
>
> Diane Sawyer
> *TV news anchor*

Listening is a skill that requires mindful involvement. In the classroom, your mind must be fully engaged in listening for key words and important ideas. It needs to ask questions—silently or out loud—and probe for answers. **Active listening gives you a tremendous advantage** over passive hearing, because human beings can think at least four times faster than we can speak. This means you will have at least three-quarters of every class period to process what the speaker says into a coherent set of notes, think about and evaluate what is said, and relate it to your own experience and learning.

Being an active listener means anticipating the lecture by showing up early to review the reading assignment and check the day's topic on your syllabus. It means being alert for key ideas, important points, and verbal cues, triggered by such phrases as:

"There are three reasons why . . . "
"A good example of . . . "
"The most significant development . . . "
"The important thing to remember here is . . . "

Lean forward and tell yourself to concentrate. Relate what's being said to your own life, and to what you're learning in your other classes. Start taking notes as soon as the instructor starts speaking. If they prove to be unimportant, you can recycle them later. **The important thing is to *stay active***, and taking notes helps you listen better.

Read the assignment and understand it before coming to class. Take your textbook to class and mark the sections of the text emphasized by the lecture. This will help you be a better listener because you can then relate the lecture to a familiar context.

ACTIVE NOTE TAKING

Good notes come from active listening. They contain both the instructor's key points and your own thoughts, questions, and reactions. However, if note taking prevents you from listening, take fewer notes.

Put into words

Writing down everything an instructor says, word for word, is one way to stay involved, but it's not necessarily an effective use of class time. Students who record everything may be getting the words, but missing the gist. Taking notes is not like court reporting, which involves transcription of every word of a trial. Court reporters often have no idea what is actually happening in court. In fact, they try not to think about what is said because it interferes with their recording accuracy.

Good notes contain both the instructor's key points and your own ideas.

Listen and make sure you understand. Then write it down in your own words. The best lecture notes will include some of the instructor's language, his or her key ideas (paraphrased by you, in your language) and your own reactions to what is said. Active note taking is an investment you make in yourself. If you were being *paid* to take notes, what would yours be worth? Minimum wage? Top dollar? Raise your wage!

The Cornell Note-Taking Method

The very best note-taking system is the one that works for you. If you have not yet developed an effective system, though, consider the Cornell Method, which has worked well for many college students. Developed by study-skills specialists at Cornell University, this method treats note taking as an aggressive, high-energy activity. If you find it fatiguing, you're probably doing it right.

Here's how it works:

- Use a looseleaf, three-ring binder that is large enough for 8½″ x 11″ paper, and has pockets or folders. This format allows you to rearrange the pages of your notes and incorporate loose handouts. (But beware!

Nature has given us two ears and only one mouth.

Benjamin Disraeli
English politician

If you lose your notebook, you lose everything. Consider making a backup photocopy of your most valuable notes or transferring them to a computer disk.) If you use a spiral-bound notebook, use a separate one for each class.

- Write your name and phone number clearly, front and back.
- Date and number each page (so that if you do lose a page or miss a class, you can tell what's missing). If your note pages get mixed up, it also helps to have the name of the course and the instructor at the top.
- Leave a 2½″ margin on the left side of each page for highlighting and recalling key words and ideas.
- Leave the reverse side of the pages blank.
- Draw a 2″ margin at the bottom. After every lecture, write a one- or two-sentence summary in this space. You'll find these summaries a great time saver when you study for exams. The page will look something like the examples in Figures 5.1 and 5.2.

[LECTURE TOPIC]

[COURSE]

NOTES

[p.#]

[INSTRUCTOR]

[DATE]

WRITE KEY IDEAS IN THIS COLUMN

WRITE THE INSTRUCTOR'S IDEAS HERE -- IN YOUR OWN WORDS

SUMMARY

FIGURE 5.1

- On the right side of the page, take notes, putting the instructor's ideas in your own words. (After class, use the left-hand column to list key ideas in abbreviated form.)

LAWS OF ENERGY	GEO 118 DR. HANSEN	p. 12 9-27

LAW #I
INPUT = OUTPUT
"THERE'S NO FREE LUNCH"
	TWO LAWS OF ENERGY
	① Matter ~ created ~ destroyed. (but may change form)
	Exception: Nuclear reactions
		AKA
		• law of conservation of energy
		• 1st law of energy
		• 1st law of thermodynamics

LAW #II IN AN ENERGY TRANSACTION, YOU'LL NEVER BREAK EVEN!	② ENERGY QUALITY may be lost (degraded energy -- fuel converted to heat → dispersed)	
EX ⟶	EXAMPLE: 10% of gas actually runs a car Light bulb: 5% light, 95% heat THEREFORE: Can't recycle high-quality energy to perform useful work	
Q: Is LAW #2 the reason perpetual-motion machines don't work? ☺	84% of all commercial energy in the U.S. is wasted.	
VOCAB "Entropy" — ? (look up) ☆	SOLUTION: Increase energy efficiency	

Proposals for improving environmental quality must take into account the TWO LAWS OF ENERGY: Although it may change forms, ① it can neither be created nor destroyed, and ② its quality (usefulness) will diminish when it is converted from one form to another.

FIGURE 5.2

On Your Own

Practicing the Cornell Method

Select two pages of notes you took in another class and rewrite them using the Cornell Method. Then compare the two versions side by side. Which would be easier to study from? Can you combine the best features of both into an even more effective style of note taking? How?

Collaborate

Swap both sets of notes (see above) with a classmate to critique. Each partner should identify two strengths and two shortcomings of the other's notes. Write these down, then share your observations orally.

- Write today's lecture topic at the top of the key ideas column (example: Laws of Energy).
- Copy anything your instructor writes on the board. Often these are names, dates, and terms you will need to remember for a test.
- If your instructor gets excited about something, put a big exclamation mark (!) in the left-hand column. If you hear what sounds like the main idea for the lecture, draw a box around it with a star at the left. If you see a connection between two points, draw an arrow from one to the other. If you get lost or confused, put a big question mark (?) in the column.
- Listen for verbal cues that indicate how the instructor will organize the lecture. "Today we'll be talking about the Civil War and looking at the combustible materials that brought it about, some of the significant developments of the war itself, and the aftermath—what happened as a result of this terrible conflict in our nation." The simple outline of this lecture will be: The Causes, Main Events, and Effects of the American Civil War.
- Some instructors don't lecture in outline form; others stray from an outline without warning. Use a modified, flexible outline format. Forget about A, B, C, 1, 2, 3. Just spread items out on the page, indent subpoints, and leave plenty of white space to tuck in details later.
- Take notes on examples, illustrations, and supporting data as well as key ideas. These will be useful later to support your generalizations on an essay exam.
- Write down even the obvious. Otherwise, three weeks down the road, you'll have forgotten what was so "obvious" and have nothing to study from.
- Listen for words you don't understand that seem important and useful. Circle these in your notes and look them up after class. Concentrate on the specialized vocabulary of the academic discipline but also note words that will be generally useful to you. Remember, successful stu-

dents have deep, powerful vocabularies, and they don't get them by accident.

- If you're writing down questions and opinions of your own (and you should), find a way to distinguish these from the instructor's views (like drawing your initials or writing "mine" in the left column). This will give you ideas for paper topics and essay/exam questions later.
- If your instructor is a fast talker or speaks with a heavy accent, review the suggestions in the box on page 101.
- Take notes during discussions, too. If you're too busy talking, record the main points of the discussion right after class.

All aspects of the Cornell Method may not work for everybody. Experiment with your note taking until you **find a system that works for you**. If you're a visual learner, for example, you may find it helpful to make a map or diagram of the lecture, color-code your notes, or create graphic images of abstract concepts.

Pay especially close attention during the first and last five minutes of class. The beginning is important because the instructor may give an assignment, remind you of a deadline, briefly review key ideas from the last lecture, or announce key ideas for today. The end is important because an instructor may be running short of time and feel the need to squeeze in several final, important points.

Reviewing class notes saves study time later.

When taking notes in math and science classes, copy everything the instructor writes on the board—each step of an experiment or a math problem—but write down his or her explanations for the steps, as well. Be careful with the shorthand symbols you've been using in your other classes: they may have a different or more specific meaning in math or science. In fact, because math and science use a lot of symbols, it's a good idea to reverse the shorthand process by writing down the word for the symbol.

Some students who have difficulty taking good notes, staying awake, or hearing the instructor should bring a tape recorder to class. (It's a courtesy to ask an instructor in advance for permission to tape.) Auditory learners might benefit by hearing the lecture a second time, and the stop-start function can't be used to slow down a fast lecturer. But remember: Tape record-

When Instructors Talk Fast

1. **Preview material** at greater length. Read ahead. Familiarity with a subject makes it easier to identify points of emphasis when they're coming at you rapidly.

2. **Record selectively.** Focus on getting the main ideas down clearly in your notes; examples and elaboration can be added later.

3. **Leave blank space** in your notes for material you miss. Take advantage of breaks in the lecture to revisit these and fill in the gaps.

4. **Trade notes with a classmate** after class. Even if neither of you feels confident your notes are complete, two heads are better than one, and two sets of notes will be more comprehensive than one.

5. **Tape record the lecture**—with permission. Do this not as an alternative to active listening or note taking, but to supplement the original exchange, as a backup. Also, this may enable you to "start-stop" delivery at will.

6. **Attend again.** If there are multiple sections of the same class, attend the lecture a second time.

7. **Devise a personal shorthand system** that will allow you to write (take notes) more rapidly.

8. **Ask the speaker to slow down.** Visit your instructor after class. Ask questions, lots of questions, and invite his or her response to your notes.

9. **Don't give up!** Keep writing. Even sketchy notes are better than none. If you are persistent and your intention to understand the speaker is sincere, you will eventually create useful, comprehensive notes to study from.

ing is no substitute for active listening and note taking. If you're using a recording in this way you're still a passive listener and will have a hard time remembering what was said. Also, relying on tape recordings instead of notes doubles or triples study time. Can you afford it?

Reviewing After Class

Right after class, if possible, or within hours at the latest, spend five to ten minutes reviewing your notes. Reviewing notes immediately after class will significantly decrease the amount of time you will need later to prepare for exams. **A brief review after class increases long-term retention of the materials by 50 percent**. You can increase your retention even more by reciting aloud or discussing a difficult concept with a classmate. It's like setting your ideas in quick-drying cement: you have to act fast or lose the chance.

During review, make sure you understand your shorthand abbreviations and hasty scrawls. Some students rewrite (or type) their notes completely after each class: this clarifies illegible notes and facilitates recall. Some students highlight their own notes or tape record themselves reading notes or text material aloud, then listen to these tapes (while driving, for instance).

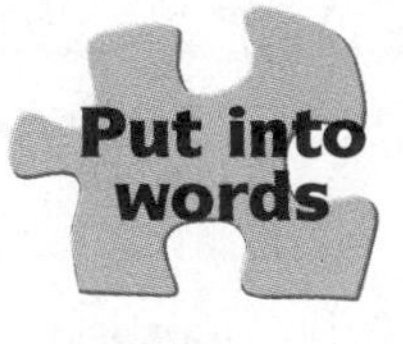

During after-class review, use the reverse side of the page for additional comments, reactions, and questions that occur to you. As you review, recite to yourself: cover up your notes and try to recall what was said by referring to the key words you wrote in the left-hand column.

The Cornell note-taking format—with its left-hand "recall" column—can function much as flashcards do for self-test purposes.

Tips

Design Your Own Shorthand

You can save time taking notes by developing a personal shorthand for frequently used words. This will free up class time for active listening. Take care not to make your shorthand so dense that later you won't understand what you wrote. You should be able to read it as rapidly as longhand.

1. Spell our short words (in, on, but, too) but disregard articles (a, an, the).
2. Use common symbols such as
   not (~)
   and, also, moreover (+ or &)
   therefore, thus (∴)
   between (/)
   with or without (w/ or w/o)
   against (vs)
   less than (<)
   more than (>)
   equals, is similar to (=)
   does not equal (≠)
   the relationship between x and y (x:y or x/y)
   same as above (")
   frequency (f)
3. Create your own symbols, for example:
   world (O)
   psychological (psyl)
   It's important to remember that (!)
   Example: St. Augustine's view of time differed radically from that of the pre-Socratic philosophers (Aug's vw:tm diff/! presoc)
4. Use standard abbreviations:
   compare (cf)
   department (dept)
   the United States (US)
   that is (ie)
   for example (eg or ex)
   background (bg)
   World War I (WWI)
   New York City (NYC)
5. Use just enough of a word to recall the whole:
   William Shakespeare (W.S.)
   distribution system (dist sys)
   zygote (zyg)
   literature (lit)
   introduction (intro)
6. Omit vowels:
   estimate (estmt)
   confused (cnfsd)
   doubletalk (dbltk)
7. If the lecture topic is parliamentary procedure, spell it out the first time and use (PP) thereafter.

If you use a lot of shorthand, it's especially important to review your notes right after class. Fill in gaps and spell out, in longhand, any abbreviations that might later be unclear.

On **Your** *Own*

Practicing Shorthand

Select two or three pages of notes you took in another class and rewrite them using your own shorthand. Set the shorthand version aside for 24 hours, then take another look. Can you read the shorthand notes rapidly with full comprehension? Can you see ways of condensing the material still further?

ACTIVE PARTICIPATION

A poll of business and industry leaders asked the question, "What is the most important skill you look for in an employee?" The almost universal answer was effective communication skills.

A college classroom provides an excellent opportunity to become a better communicator. Some instructors formally evaluate your class participation and factor it into your final grade. Remember, too, that you have a responsibility not only for your own learning but also for the learning of your classmates. Questions you raise or comments you make in class often echo what your classmates are thinking, too.

When you do have a question or comment, it's not a good idea to rehearse it over and over in your mind: by the time you raise your hand, it may no longer be appropriate. Just raise your hand and say what's on your

Collaborate

Practice Paraphrasing

Select two sequential paragraphs from any chapter in *Right From the Start* that you have not yet read. With a partner, read your selections aloud to one another in turn. As you read, your partner will listen carefully. Then when you have finished, your partner will write down—in his or her own words—what you said. Spend no more than three minutes composing these paraphrased passages. To critique, compare paraphrased versions with the originals.

Build a Powerful Vocabulary

The English language contains over 600,000 words. According to linguist William Safire, a well-educated person has a reading and writing vocabulary of about 20,000 words but uses only 2,000 of these when speaking. Twenty-five percent of our spoken vocabulary consists of only 10 words. ("I" ranks first; "you" ranks second.) Our vocabulary increases by hundreds of words a year while we are in school; after we leave, it increases by only 25–50 words a year—proof that constant and active reading and learning are the keys to building a strong vocabulary.

One reason for developing a strong vocabulary is to understand more of what we read and hear. Words are tools for thinking about and understanding the world around us. Another reason is to express ourselves clearly and to be understood. One research study of successful Americans in all walks of life indicated a direct correlation between vocabulary range and salary within a profession. Language gives us power and mastery within our environment. When you add a new word to your vocabulary, you acquire a new idea, way of seeing, avenue of thought. In your other courses, you are being introduced to an academic discipline primarily through its essential vocabulary.

A good way to increase your vocabulary is to listen actively for useful, new words in lectures and look actively for them in your reading. When you encounter a word you'd like to know, circle the word and, at your first opportunity, write it in a special notebook used only for that purpose.

- Write down both the word and the context in which it appeared.
- Ask your instructor or a friend to define the word for you.
- Look it up in a good dictionary (most paperback dictionaries are inadequate because they don't give alternate meanings and word origins) and write the definition.
- Note the etymology (origins of the word) and any alternate meanings.
- Note how the word is pronounced; say it out loud.
- At your first opportunity, use the new word in a conversation or paper. Actually using the word yourself is a crucial step toward making it your own.

Be on the lookout for new words; heighten your awareness. As you do, be selective. Choose words you've heard before, but whose meanings elude you (vocabulary experts call these "frontier words"). Sometimes you'll hear a new word in a lecture and then see it again in your reading a day later. These are good words to zero in on. Pick words that interest you and that you think might be useful. Unless they're related to your major interest, avoid technical terms you may never see again. Limit your vocabulary-building program to about 10 words a week. Review all your words once a week (use 3" x 5" flashcards if you like) or have someone test you on them. Read widely. Learn to enjoy the acquisition of language. Make it a hobby and a habit.

If you don't understand, ask.

mind—the earlier the better. Listen carefully and react to what the instructor says. If you disagree with something your instructor says, do it with tact.

Be sensitive to the proper timing of questions in class. Some instructors encourage questions during a lecture; others discourage them or provide a time at the beginning or end of class for questions. A lot of hand waving can disrupt the momentum of a lecture; if you have a question and don't want to interrupt the speaker, mark it in your notes and ask it after class.

Students who make up questions just to score points waste everybody's time. But don't hold back just because you think your questions might sound stupid. There is no such thing as a stupid question if you really want to know the answer. If people try to make you feel stupid, that's their problem, not yours. If they succeed, then it's your problem.

When you are called on to speak, respond promptly. If you're taken by surprise, begin by rephrasing the question in your own words. This will give you time to think. If you didn't hear or didn't understand the question, just say, "I'm sorry, could you repeat the question?" When you do speak in class, be brief (especially if you're recounting a personal experience) and stick to the point. Try not to dominate a discussion—give others a chance to have their say. If someone else is talking too much and wasting class time, speak to the instructor privately about it.

On **Your** *Own*

Start a Vocabulary Notebook

Buy a small notebook that you will use exclusively for vocabulary building. Over the next week, find ten new words that you want to add to your vocabulary. For each word, write

1. The word itself (in capital letters)
2. The pronunciation of the word (unless it's obvious)
3. The preferred (first) dictionary definition
4. The etymology (only if it's interesting or helpful to you)
5. The context in which you heard or read the word

Bring your notebook to class a week from now and show your instructor or share with your group your first ten words. After that, keep it up—ten words a week.

Collaborate

Word Games

Play language games! Scrabble, Boggle, Magnetic Poetry—all are fun and will enrich your vocabulary. Try out new words first in e-mail or in letters home or to friends; then introduce them in your everyday conversation. Building a bigger vocabulary can be fascinating; it won't be a chore unless you approach it as one.

Participate actively in small group discussions. You'll find some of your most valuable learning will take place in these sessions, and you'll be developing leadership, listening, and small group communication skills, too. Most decisions in both the public and private sector, in and beyond academe, are made collaboratively, in small groups. The more you participate, the better team member—and communicator—you will be.

Some students view group discussions as a chance to relax and just rap for a while, not realizing they are being carefully observed and evaluated by their instructor and their peers. **Make a meaningful contribution**. To do so, be well read and thoroughly prepared.

> Nobody can make you feel inferior without your consent.
>
> Eleanor Roosevelt

Group Projects

In some classes you may be asked to give a more formal presentation in front of class in the form of a debate, panel discussion, or group presentation. If you are working with others, you may need to arrange preparation meetings outside of class. If you are being graded as a group, make it a point of honor to **contribute actively to the team's success**. Be prepared and on time for meetings. Make only those commitments you know you can keep. If someone in your group is not contributing, discuss it with the group before going to the instructor with the problem.

Tips

Small Group Discussions

Here are some practical tips for successful participation in class and small group discussions:

- Respect the ideas of your classmates and expect them to do the same.
- Make sure you understand what another student is saying before you respond. If you're unsure, say, "What you're saying is interesting. Could you talk a little more about that?"
- Let others know when they've made an important point.
- Concentrate on following the discussion rather than waiting for an opening to make your point.
- Try not to dominate a discussion. If there are five people in the group, talk about one-fifth of the time.
- Avoid one-on-one debates that cause nonparticipants to feel left out.
- If the discussion gets derailed, exercise leadership to get the group back on track.

Giving a Speech

Because the best way to learn something is to teach it, instructors occasionally ask students to prepare and present information in front of the class. Here are some tips that may make this assignment a little less threatening.

1. It's possible to control audience response. Audiences respond warmly to speakers who:
   - know their subjects thoroughly
   - are believable
   - are enthusiastic
   - have similar values, beliefs, and interests

Controlling Stage Fright

The Transformation of Communication Energy

Sometimes people refer to the very valuable source of energy present in a public speaker with a host of negatively associated words like *stage fright, speech anxiety, communication apprehension* or *logophobia*. This reminds us that of all phobias, stage fright ranks number one, outranking the fear of spiders, snakes, dentists, and even death. It is better, by far, to think of public speaking in more positive terms and remind yourself that the preperformance burst of adrenaline is, first, a very natural physiological response when something is important to you. In fact, this **communication energy** can be transformed into communication behaviors, like gestures and vocal variety, to make your message more meaningful for your audience.

Transform Your Mind

Self-confidence, your belief that you can speak well, is an excellent starting point for a public speaker. Of course, nothing fosters self-confidence more than systematic practice. The Rev. Jesse Jackson once said, "We do best what we do most." Videotape your practice performances and practice in front of live audiences whenever possible. Most of all, start strong! Practice the beginning of your speech (all the way through the introduction and your transition into your first main point), so that you can deliver it automatically. A smooth beginning involves your audience and gives your body time to channel communication energy positively.

Transform Your Body

Many of us wouldn't think of going jogging or golfing without a few stretching exercises or practice swings. Too frequently, we ignore the physical dimensions of public speaking. Both **physical** and **vocal warm-ups** are advisable. In a private place, as close to your performance time as possible, sing a song, try a tongue twister, or practice the first few minutes of your speech aloud. Warm up the muscles involved in vocalization. Gently shake the muscles in your arms and legs, assume your finest public-speaking posture, and practice your introduction. Remember, your whole body is involved in the speaking interaction; see and hear yourself successfully communicating with your audience.

- **Be confident** Believe you can establish a connection with your audience.
- **Prepare** Have a firm grasp of the subject matter, your audience, and the speaking occasion.
- **Practice** Rehearse your speech many times, and you will really feel reassured; allow the muscles involved in the vocalization and physicalization of your speech performance to develop a *memory* of their own.
- **Repeat** Practice, practice, practice. Repetition is a valuable learning strategy and confidence booster. Take advantage of opportunities to practice your public speaking; make a toast, answer questions in class, take a stand and express your view in a university and/or public forum.
- **Start strong** Audiences love great beginnings! Pay particular attention to the writing, arrangement, and presentation of your introduction.

2. "Hook" your audience at the very beginning of your speech. Find an imaginative way to engage their interest. Keep audience interest throughout by getting them actively involved. Call on specific individuals to share their views on an issue. Listen and respond to your audience: getting interested in them will help you forget about yourself.
3. Your audience is likely to remember only two or three main points, not the details. Limit the scope of the information you present; use details only to underscore the main points. Reinforce these main ideas by clearly identifying them and by repeating them in the middle and at the end of your speech.

4. Audiences retain information that is personally meaningful to them. Relate new information to something they already know. Use illustrations and examples to turn the abstract into the concrete. Show your audience how they can use the information you're presenting. If possible, ask them to apply it in a practical way during your presentation. Be sure you understand how this information is important and communicate its relevance clearly to them.
5. Because people remember what they see better than what they hear, use visual aids (posters, overheads, handouts, physical objects) and write on the board.
6. Organize your presentation in a simple way: introduction, body, conclusion. Use your introduction to establish rapport, get attention, show how the topic relates to your audience, and give a sneak preview of the body of your speech. Limit the body to three main points. Use your conclusion to remind the audience of your main points. End your speech in an upbeat fashion.
7. All the physical and vocal aspects of effective public speaking—vocal pitch, rate, and volume; clear enunciation; gestures, facial expression; eye contact; body movement—are the products of relaxation. Stay relaxed by breathing slowly and deeply before you speak. Concentrate on relaxing individual muscles. Once on stage, force yourself to move around, use hand gestures, and look individuals in the eye.

Practice your speech—including gestures and facial expressions—in front of a mirror, or videotape rehearsals.

The best way to manage performance anxiety is to prepare thoroughly. Know your subject inside and out, videotape rehearsals, or **practice your presentation in front of a full-length mirror**. If you've been given a time limit, time yourself repeatedly: your audience will love you for it!

Collaborate

Design Your Own Class Session

Apply what you have learned about strategic planning to create a special class period devoted to an issue of current interest on your campus.

First, agree as a class on a date for the special session that will allow everyone plenty of time to prepare.

Second, agree on a topic for the session. One way of doing this is to brainstorm (either in small groups or as a whole class) a list of major campus issues (for example, alcohol-related vandalism, racism, abuses in student government, bad teaching, stress). Try to come up with at least ten. List all of these where everyone can see them on the board. Have each class member draw a star next to the five issues they consider most important. Choose the topic that gets the most stars.

Third, discuss what kind of activities (guest speaker? survey research? panel discussion? debate? field trip?) would help the class best learn about the issue. What resources are available? What obstacles might be encountered? What will the session look like, ideally? What are some desirable outcomes? What sorts of tasks will need to be accomplished to ensure a high-quality learning experience for all? Who will take responsibility for each? What is a reasonable deadline for the accomplishment of each task?

Finally, execute your plan.

SUMMARY

Class time is precious. You may be spending anywhere from $50 to $150 an hour for the opportunity to learn from an expert—your instructor. Students who skip class, daydream, or even sleep through class are throwing their money away. You'll get the full value of your tuition dollar, and your time, by showing up for every class awake, alert, and prepared; by listening actively and developing an effective system for taking good notes; and by participating in class. Even the sometimes scary prospect of giving a speech or class presentation can be a positive experience, a chance to grow.

Strategic *Plan*

Look over your Self-Assessment at the beginning of the chapter and identify an area in which you'd like to make a change. Then develop a Strategic Plan, using the format below.

I. Situation analysis

A. One problem I'm having in class is ______________________________

____

B. One change I think I could make is ______________________________

____

continued on next page

Strategic *Plan* *continued from previous page*

C. The benefits of making the change are ______________________________

____

D. The consequences of not changing are ______________________________

____

E. Some obstacles I'll have to overcome are ______________________________

____

F. Some resources I'll need are ______________________________

____

II. Goals, objectives, deadlines, and indicators

A. My goal is to ______________________________

____

Deadline: ______________________________

Indicators of success: ______________________________

____

B. Here's what I'm going to do to achieve my goal, along with a reasonable deadline for each task:

	OBJECTIVE	DEADLINE
1.	______________________	__________
2.	______________________	__________
3.	______________________	__________
4.	______________________	__________
5.	______________________	__________

III. Self-Test

YES	NO	
☐	☐	**A.** Are my goals and objectives stated simply and clearly?
☐	☐	**B.** Does each one have a single focus?
☐	☐	**C.** Are they stated in a positive way?
☐	☐	**D.** Are they realistic?
☐	☐	**E.** Can I achieve them by the deadline?
☐	☐	**F.** Will I know if I've achieved them?

Journal Ideas

1. In school, do you most often prefer to work alone or with a group? Why?
2. Which class are you enjoying most at the moment? Why?
3. Describe your listening behavior in class.
4. Describe your way of taking notes.
5. Have you had to speak in any class so far? How did it go?
6. Describe a time in your life when you experienced stage fright. How did you deal with it? What did you learn from the experience?

Web Search

How can you develop your learning skills by using the Internet? Internet surfing is often called a time waster, but even idle surfing, e-mailing friends, and conversing in chat rooms can help develop useful skills, like rapid keyboarding, critical thinking, problem solving, and written communication. In the exercises in Part II you will be using the Internet for an even more valuable purpose—as a treasure trove of easily accessible information.

Knowing how to find information in a hurry is a skill that will pay huge dividends—in college and throughout your career. On-line databases like InfoTrac College Edition© and sophisticated search tools like Yahoo, AltaVista, Infoseek, Hotbot, and Excite make it easy to find information on the Internet. "Metasearch" tools such as Metafind (http://www.metafind.com) will run your search through several search tools at once. But sometimes the sources of information they identify are so varied and numerous that it's difficult to know where to look next. So it's helpful to learn a few search techniques.

If you're just beginning to develop your Internet search skills, here is an excellent Web site:

> Selected Internet Subject Directories
> http://infopeople.berkeley.edu:8000/src/hart.html

Visit this site, which provides a nifty "cheat sheet" for various search tools (Yahoo, Magellan, WebCrawler, HotBot, and others). Then choose any *three* of the listed search tools by clicking once on the name. Now, suppose you're giving a speech on scuba diving in the Miami Beach area. First, type *scuba* and write down the number of locations that were identified. Next, type *Miami Beach* and write down the number of locations. Finally, type *scuba and Miami Beach* and write down the number of locations. Which keyword combinations were the most helpful in finding sources for your paper? Which of the three search tools was the most helpful?

6

How to Study (and Still Have a Life)

Self-*Assessment*

Check the statements that apply to you.

☐ **1.** I study in the same places, at the same times of day.

☐ **2.** I can successfully minimize distractions when I study or read.

☐ **3.** I do most of my studying in a place designed for that purpose.

☐ **4.** My job seldom gets in the way of my studying.

☐ **5.** I spend more time studying than I do attending class.

☐ **6.** When I read a textbook, I am able to stay focused.

☐ **7.** I rarely have to reread an assignment because I can't remember what I read.

☐ **8.** It's easy for me to get motivated to study, even if I don't have an exam coming up.

☐ **9.** When a job becomes too difficult, I break it into more manageable tasks.

☐ **10.** I have a terrific memory.

If you checked fewer than half, this chapter will be especially valuable to you.

Write **Before** *You Read*

A. Spend about a minute surveying this chapter. Then write three questions you expect to find answers to in this chapter.

1. ______________________________

2. ______________________________

3. ______________________________

B. Spend another minute writing down any thoughts that come to mind about the topics below. Write freely and rapidly.

1. My study headquarters: ______________________________

2. My reading and study habits: ______________________________

3. Balancing work and play: ______________________________

PREVIEW

Real learning comes from long hours of effort, a systematic approach, and steady application. This chapter contains many helpful tips for using your study time efficiently; setting up a friendly workplace; getting more out of your textbook; getting motivated to read, study, and keep at it; and remembering what you read and what you need to recall for quizzes and tests. The suggestions in this chapter are based on ample research and the experience of generations of successful learners. They really work—and will create more time for recreation—but only if you do.

HOW MUCH TO STUDY, WHERE, AND WHEN?

Two to three hours of study time for every hour you spend in class is what your instructors will expect of you. This is an average: some classes will require more study time, some less. If you're a full-time student, taking a full course load, this works out to considerably more than a 40-hour week, the equivalent of a professional job. If you're also working 10 to 20 hours a week at a part-time job, you will have to manage your time very carefully.

There are some techniques to managing your study time effectively, but this is the heart of it: **Make a schedule and stick to it.** Lay out all your syllabi side by side on your desk; then set a goal for each class. For each class, develop a written plan. Make lists of "things to do" and do them in priority order. Anticipate major tasks and break them up into smaller, more manageable ones.

Do the work as assigned, with no shortcuts or end-runs. Alternate business with pleasure.

Everybody needs a study headquarters.

Where to Study

You'll be studying in various temporary locations—in the library, under a spreading chestnut tree, at the kitchen table, in a lounge, in your car.

Remember to carry work or reading with you for those unplanned "empty" times—when you're waiting between classes or at the laundromat, for instance. But **you should also have a personal headquarters** where the tools of your trade—your computer and personal reference library, office supplies, calculator, dictionary, a clock or timer, a good light—are close at hand. Use your headquarters only for studying; do your eating and sleeping in other places more suited to those purposes. If you think of this exclusively as a place for study, that's what you'll do when you go there.

Concentration, for some people, requires utter silence. Others need the aural stimulation of rap, reggae, or rock. Some people need a window with a view; others prefer a blank wall for minimum distraction. The prolific French novelist Honoré de Balzac needed lots of thick Turkish coffee (not recommended—he drank 50 cups a day and died of caffeine poisoning).

Owning Your Own Computer

Computers are an indispensable work tool, at home, at the office, and in college. The sooner you become accustomed to working with them, the better.

If computing facilities on your campus are inadequate or inconvenient, consider owning your own computer.

Check the classified ads in your local paper for used computing equipment. With computer technology changing so rapidly, earlier-generation equipment and software can often be purchased at unbelievably low prices. Frequently, the seller will throw in software for nothing. (Because computers have few moving parts, they don't suffer from wear and tear like other used goods.)

Or consider buying a new system through your college, which is likely to have a purchase arrangement with major computer suppliers at attractive discounts.

If you can afford it, a modem (phone link) is a valuable peripheral item because it will enable you to tap into the Internet and software now provided by most colleges.

Computer notebooks are more expensive (though they're fast becoming cheaper and more powerful), but they're an appealing option because they are mobile and save space. Keep an extra battery in your book bag.

American novelist Ernest Hemingway began a writing session by sharpening 30 pencils; then he wrote standing up and didn't quit until the last pencil was dull. He liked a "clean, well-lighted place," whereas Edgar Allan Poe preferred dark tapestries, a guttering candle, and the smell of incense.

When you read or study, keep the heat at a comfortable level—too much heat will make you drowsy. Work in an area with ordinary room light but with a strong light directed on your work. If possible, use a desk with plenty of surface area so you can spread out. (A banquet table or an unfinished door set on two two-drawer filing cabinets or sawhorses makes an adequate, inexpensive desk.) Sit on a chair with armrests; it should be comfortable but force you to sit upright. Your bed is a good place for sleeping but a bad place for studying.

When to Study

Use a trial-and-error method for finding a study time that works well for you. Some people are most alert in the morning; others function best at night. Many people feel sluggish in the early afternoon, which is siesta time all over the world. **Do your most demanding tasks at times when you feel most alert**; save those easy, low-pressure, routine tasks for your less productive periods. Pay attention to the demands of mind and body; when you're really fatigued and have reached a point of diminishing returns, sleep.

Take advantage, too, of brief opportunities to study or read; not every study session has to be a marathon.

What's best is what works for you. Experiment until you find it.

GETTING MOTIVATED TO STUDY

Having a clearly defined goal—not what you *ought* to do but what you *choose* to do—is the best motivator in the world.

No one will force you to study in college. And it's a rare student who "feels like studying." You have to **find the motivation in yourself**. If your reasons for going to college are negative or based on other people's goals—"It was either college or find a job. It was what my parents wanted. My friends were going. The party scene sounded fun."—you are less likely to succeed. If your reasons are positive and based on your goals—"I want to prepare myself for a successful career. I want to become educated."—you will succeed if you keep those reasons in the forefront of your mind. When you find yourself procrastinating or partying when you should be studying, remind yourself why you are here. Poorly defined goals are costly in college, in more ways than one.

> I must endure the presence of two or three caterpillars if I wish to become acquainted with the butterflies.
>
> The Flower in Antoine de Saint-Exupéry's *The Little Prince*

A clear set of goals is the key to motivation. Goals may be short-range, mid-range, and long-range.

- Short-range goals are what you intend to accomplish in one study session, or what you plan to do tomorrow, or in the year ahead.
- Mid-range goals are what you hope to accomplish in one to three years: decide on a major, have a career plan, be admitted to the College of Engineering, and so on.
- Long-range goals are life goals: your chosen career, the salary you hope to earn, the lifestyle you'd like to achieve.

Try to visualize what it would be like to achieve your goals. Break large goals down into smaller, more immediately achievable tasks. Write your goals where you will see them frequently (tape them to your lamp or tack them on your bulletin board, at eye level).

On **Your** *Own*

Motivation and Goals

List your current goals below. Restrict yourself to three in each category and list them in order of importance—most important first. Be as specific as you can.

A. Long-range goals (for my life)
1. ______________________
2. ______________________
3. ______________________

B. Mid-range goals (for my college career)
1. ______________________
2. ______________________
3. ______________________

C. Short-range goals (for this year)
1. ______________________
2. ______________________
3. ______________________

Are your goals consistent—that is, will your short-range goals help you to achieve your mid- and long-range goals?

Here's a way to find out. Examine your short-range goals one by one. Which of them will help you achieve a particular mid-range goal? If C. 1, for example, will help you achieve B. 3, write C. 1 in the column next to B. 3. Continue this process—short-range to mid-range, and mid-range to long-range.

If you find very few connections, make three new lists, starting with long-range goals and working down, making sure that your shorter-range goals are ones that will help you achieve your longer-range goals.

MAINTAINING CONCENTRATION

To maintain concentration when you study and to remember more, **study actively**. Always read with a pencil in hand and mark up your books or notes. The SQ3R study method described in the following pages is a good way to study actively.

If you are a competitive, superactive person who has a hard time sitting still for long, think of studying as energetic—"hitting the books." The American novelist Thomas Wolfe, a six-foot-six-inch bundle of manic energy, sometimes wrote standing on a refrigerator, flinging pages down to his typist as he finished them. A restless insomniac, he walked the streets at night, singing his prose aloud. Keep your pencil active. Organize and arrange your notes. Get up and walk around when you feel the need, or **read and recite aloud as you pace the floor**.

Plan 50-minute study periods followed by a 10-minute reward break—a phone call, a snack, a computer game. If you have trouble concentrating for 50 minutes at a stretch, try 30. Some study experts recommend making a check mark on a blank sheet of paper each time you find your mind wandering. If you catch yourself staring out the window or looking away from your work when someone walks past, make a check mark; eventually you'll find the check marks becoming fewer.

Another way to avoid fatigue and to motivate yourself is to break up a long reading assignment into segments of, say, ten pages at a time. Your survey of chapter subheadings will give you a feeling for where the natural idea breaks will occur. Keep going until you've completed the segment. If you're on a roll, forget the break and push on. Limit your break to a specified time; then immediately begin the next unit. Set your own goals—either in minutes to read or number of pages to be read—meet them, and reward yourself for meeting them.

> If you want a place in the sun, you've got to put up with a few blisters.
>
> Abigail Van Buren
> *Advice columnist*

If you're studying somewhere other than your headquarters, make sure you've got everything you'll need to take with you. Keep your book bag or briefcase stocked with essential study supplies. Sharpen pencils and get everything laid out before you begin. Plan to study, and be ready.

It's normal for concentration to be interrupted by physical needs. Take care of these needs—thirst, hunger, fatigue—before your study session begins. If they assert themselves while you're studying, take care of them immediately and return to work. It's impossible to concentrate if your stomach is growling.

ACTIVE READING: SQ3R

As with the listening and note-taking skills discussed in Chapter 5, you must **read actively** if your reading-as-test-prep is to be effective. Most first-year college students are able to focus on a text for only a few minutes before their attention wanes. **SQ3R is an active reading process designed to offset the tendency of the human brain to wander**. As you make SQ3R a habit, you'll find you can concentrate longer each time you sit down to read a textbook assignment or study your notes.

Before reading, skim the text and write down several questions you believe you'll be able to answer as you read.

SQ3R is a five-step approach to studying and retaining what you read. It has been tested on several generations of college students since it was devised by Ohio State University professor Francis P. Robinson in 1941. And it really works—especially in content courses like history, sociology, psychology, or political science.

The abbreviation SQ3R stands for

Survey
Question
Read
Recite
Review

Virtually all study systems are a variation on these five basic steps. Some reading experts have added a fourth R (Reflect), a fifth (Record or [w]Rite), and even a sixth (Reconnoiter). But the basic principles remain the same.

Step 1: Survey (or Skim)

To survey before you read is like looking at a map before going on a trip or going through a stretching routine before you exercise: it warms up your brain.

Before plunging into a reading assignment, take sixty seconds to **look at the big picture**. Survey the book's Introduction, which may give an overview of how the book is organized. Look over the Table of Contents—chapter headings and subtopics. Does the book contain any supplementary sections (glossary, index, appendix, charts, diagrams, tables) that will be helpful to you?

When reading a chapter, start with the title. Ask: why this title? Do I understand all the words in the title? Take a guess at the meaning, write it next to the word in pencil, and look it up later if you haven't discovered its meaning by the end of the chapter. What do I already know about this subject? Some textbook authors begin chapters with a schematic overview of the topic and conclude with a summary and review questions. Skim these before getting into the body of the text. How has the author organized the information? What will this chapter be about? Where are we headed here? Underline anything that looks like a main idea. Skim the headings and subheadings, which are usually set in larger or bolder display type.

As you survey, train yourself to look for sections that can be skimmed rapidly or passed over altogether: highly detailed supporting material, transitional wordiness in moving from one idea to the next, unnecessary summaries, surplus examples and illustrations, departures from the point. Some of this material can be fascinating and valuable if you have plenty of time. If not, learn to set priorities in your reading and skim the nonessentials.

Step 2: Question

Your assignment is to read a chapter entitled "Depression" in your psychology text. After you've skimmed the chapter as outlined in Step 1, take a moment to think about the topic and ask some questions: What is depression exactly? Is it an illness with a physiological basis? Can it be treated or cured? How? How widespread is the problem? I get depressed sometimes; am I sick? Ask questions like, What will this be about? What's the point? Why is this likely to be important? How does it affect my life? If you put questions to the text before you read, you will be on the lookout for answers. Your concentration will improve if you have a mission in mind. And without knowing it, you are probably formulating questions that will appear later on a test.

Before you begin to read, write your questions down, each on one side of a 3″ x 5″ card or sticky note. Then, as you read and find answers, write each answer on the other side. You can use these as flashcards to study for a test. If you have trouble generating questions, turn headings and subheadings into questions. "Effects of Depression," for instance, becomes "What are the effects of depression?"

Just as we check road signs for distances to the next city, exits, junctions, and mile markers, check in your reading for directional signals, called transitions. A transitional phrase lets us know where we've been and where we're going next. It tells how a part fits into the whole. For example:

"We will begin by looking at . . . " (introduction of topic)
"Finally . . . " (last of a series of points)
"As we have seen . . . " (recap)
"To illustrate this phenomenon . . . " (an example)
"There are five basic types of . . . " (a list to remember)
"Furthermore . . . " (another important point)
"On the other hand . . . " (an opposing idea)

Spotting transitions helps us, as readers, keep a sense of the big picture.

Step 3: Read

While you read, look for answers to the questions you asked. On your first pass through a reading assignment, move along at a fairly deliberate speed. Aim for a general understanding without getting bogged down in particulars.

Notice when your attention wanders. Does it wander after one minute? Five? Fifteen? Break up your reading into time periods that coincide with your ability to concentrate.

Stop whenever your attention wavers and do a quick body check: Am I alert? Am I getting tired? Has my mind been wandering? Am I getting too relaxed? Fatigue and boredom are reasons to take a break, not to quit. Take a brief time-out to psych yourself up for the next reading stint.

During your break, reject all negative thoughts: I'm bored. My mind is a sieve. This is dull stuff. I'm tired. This is too difficult. I don't understand. I wish I were doing something else. Replace them with positive thoughts: I'm on a roll! My mind is a steel trap! I won't stop until I know this stuff cold!

I took a course in speed reading and was able to read *War and Peace* in twenty minutes. It's about Russia.

Woody Allen
Writer/filmmaker

Always read with a pencil in hand and stay active as you read by marking up your text. This will personalize it for you and help you remember the information.

Avoid buying used books that have been "personalized" with someone else's underlining and marginal comments. You'll want to make your own judgments about what's important. Tests show that yellow highlighters are a less effective means of reinforcing and retaining information than underlining passages in pencil, numbering lists of related items, circling words and dates, putting transitional phrases in a box, jotting down brief summaries of the main ideas in the margins, and bracketing your own ideas.

Marking up a text makes reviewing easier.

- Underline key passages that seem to express the main idea.
- For especially important points, put an asterisk(*) or exclamation point (!) in the margin.
- Circle key words and definitions, names and dates, causes and effects—anything you think may be important later.
- Draw a box around transitional phrases such as "as we have seen," "on the other hand," and "three reasons why."
- Jot a brief word or phrase in the margin that expresses the main idea.
- Using a dictionary or the glossary, define unfamiliar terms.
- Write your own ideas, questions, and examples in the margins and enclose them in [brackets] to distinguish them as your own.
- Put a question mark in the margin if you don't understand a passage.
- Use sticky notes as page markers and to expand space available for note making.

On a separate sheet of paper or in your notebook, group related ideas together in lists. Keep a running list of new terms and names that you may be asked to identify or define. If you encounter a section that explains two or more abstract concepts by comparing and contrasting them, make a simplified grid listing similarities and differences in abbreviated form.

In other words, anticipate test questions and begin formulating your answers.

Tips

Studying

1. Take a ceremonial approach to studying. Develop a preparation ritual (clearing your desk, putting on special music, arranging your notes, preparing a certain brand of tea, sharpening pencils, putting on a "study cap"). Balzac put on a monk's robe when he sat down to write. Think of your study time as "sacred"—a time alone to clarify your values, sharpen your intellect, equip yourself with the tools for living.
2. Make a commitment to someone you care about—roommate, professor, spouse, friend—that you will complete a task or have an assigned project finished by a certain time. Sometimes we are more likely to keep commitments made to others than to ourselves.

Stamp your own identity on the text and don't worry about the resale value of a marked-up text. The grades you get from being an active reader will be worth far more to you than the price of a used textbook.

Step 4: Recite

Reciting is an essential step in retaining what you read. To understand the importance of this step, consider an analogy between a computer and a human brain.

When you enter data on a computer, it is stored electronically on a chip. If you experience a power failure or turn off the computer before you have saved your data (stored it permanently on a disk), your data will be lost for-

I am part of all that I have read.

John Kieran
American journalist

On Your Own

Mark up Your Text

Survey the textbook passage in Figure 6.1. Then follow the directions below.

1. Find a short phrase that succinctly expresses the *main idea* of the passage. Draw a box around it in the text and write *Main Idea* in the column next to it.
2. Find brief definitions of the terms *nature* and *nurture.* Circle the terms, underline the definitions, and write *Def* in the column next to the definition. Can you find any other definitions in the passage? If so, do the same with them.
3. Write *Ex* in the column next to any examples or illustrations.
4. Put a *(?)* in the column next to anything you don't understand.
5. Put a *(!)* in the column next to anything you think is especially interesting or important.
6. Relate the passage to your own life or to something you already know (for example, an identity you possess by nature and a characteristic you acquired by nurture) by writing a brief note in the column. Draw a happy face or write *me* next to it to identify it as your own idea.
7. Double-underline major ideas and definitions.
8. Single-underline secondary ideas and definitions.

continued on next page

On Your Own *continued from previous page*

Now imagine yourself being tested on this passage. Write three test questions based on the passage.

1. ____

____

2. ____

____

3. ____

____

If the following question appeared on a test, how would you answer it?

> Is human behavior primarily influenced by an individual's inherited genetic makeup or by the individual's life experiences and environment? Explain and give examples.

On a clean sheet of lined paper, write your response. Take no more than ten minutes to answer the question.

Collaborate

Exercise Swap

Finally, swap this completed exercise—the annotated passage and your written questions and response—with a classmate. Comparing and contrasting your varied choices, discuss these choices with your partner.

ever. Similarly, when you read, you are imprinting information on your short-term memory, where it will remain only briefly. When you recite what you read, you are storing information in your long-term memory, where it is far more likely to remain.

Reciting does not necessarily mean *reading aloud* or quoting from the text verbatim. It *is* memorization, but with the goal of comprehending what's read rather than word-for-word repetition. You will recite best by paraphrasing or summarizing; a key component of this step, however, is that you **say it out loud**.

Pause after each paragraph or section or every ten minutes, cover what you've read with your hand or a note card, and ask yourself, What did I just read? What were the major ideas and key points in that section? Say the answers out loud. If it's fuzzy, look back over what you read and reconstruct the argument. Say it out loud again. Continue the process until you no longer need to refer to the text to prompt your memory.

Learning theorists have established a direct, measurable connection between reciting and remembering. According to researchers, the more you recite, the more you remember. For passages that are loaded with facts, figures, dates, names, and new terms, this is especially true. To achieve full recall may require as much as an hour of recitation for every fifteen minutes of reading.

Reciting is an especially effective means of building your vocabulary (Review the Tips box on page 103 for more ways to add to your vocabulary.)

Nature and Nurture

No discussion of socialization can ignore the importance of nature and nurture to physical, intellectual, social, and personality development **Nature** is the term for human genetic makeup or biological inheritance. **Nurture** refers to the environment or the interaction experiences that make up every individual's life. Some scientists debate the relative importance of genes and environment, arguing that one is substantially more important than the other to all phases of human development. But most consider such a debate futile; it is impossible to separate the influence of the two factors or to say that one is more important. Both are essential to socialization. Trying to distinguish the separate contributions of nature and nurture is analogous to examining a tape player and a cassette tape separately to determine what is recorded on the tape rather than studying how the two work together to produce the sound (Ornstein and Thompson 1984).

The development of the human brain illustrates rather dramatically the inseparable qualities of genes and environment. By our human genetic makeup, we possess a cerebral cortex—the thinking part of the brain—which allows us to organize, remember, communicate, understand, and create. The cortex is made up of at least 100 billion neurons or nerve cells. The number of interconnections is nearly infinite: it would take 32 million years, counting one synapse per second, to establish the number (Hellerstein 1988; Montgomery 1989).

Perhaps the most outstanding feature of the human brain is its flexibility. Scientists believe that the brain may be "set up" to learn any of the more than 5,000 known human languages. In the first months of life, babies are able to babble the sounds needed to speak all of these languages, but this enormous potential is reduced by the language (or languages) that the baby hears and eventually learns. Evidence suggests that the brain's language flexibility begins to diminish when the child reaches one year of age (Ornstein and Thompson 1984; Restak 1988). The large implication is that genetic makeup provides essential raw materials but that these materials can be shaped by the environment in many different ways.

The human genetic makeup is flexible enough to enable a person to learn the values, beliefs, norms, behavior, and language of any culture. A multitude of experiences must combine with genetic makeup, however, to create a Palestinian who desires a homeland, believes that he or she should not "pay" for the Holocaust, and protests actively against the occupation. Likewise, nature and nurture combine to create an Israeli who values a homeland, and believes the Jews have a legitimate right to land they were forced to leave 2,000 years ago.

FIGURE 6.1 Sample Textbook Passage

From Joan Ferrante, *Sociology: A Global Perspective*, 2nd Edition (Belmont, CA: Wadsworth 1995), p. 153. Reprinted with permission.

The "recite" step works well with a study partner: You can tell each other what you read or remember, sharpen each other's memories, and ask each other review questions.

Reciting material out loud in your own words helps you personalize and internalize it. If you own it, you're more likely to remember it. It also gets you actively involved—a key to remembering. And when you recite cor-

On Your Own

Underlining

Compare the four identical passages below and then answer these questions:

Which one is underlined too much? ______

Which one is underlined too little? ______

Which one is about right? ______

Which one is underlined in a meaningless way so that it doesn't fairly represent the text? ______

A. Be selective when highlighting items in your textbook or class notes. Too much underlining or highlighting is just as bad as none at all. Nothing stands out. If you highlight everything, you are not making thoughtful judgments about what's important. Make sure your underlining accurately represents the major point of the passage.

B. Be selective when highlighting items in your textbook or class notes. Too much underlining or highlighting is just as bad as none at all. Nothing stands out. If you highlight everything, you are not making thoughtful judgments about what's important. Make sure your underlining accurately represents the major point of the passage.

C. Be selective when highlighting items in your textbook or class notes. Too much underlining or highlighting is just as bad as none at all. Nothing stands out. If you highlight everything, you are not making thoughtful judgments about what's important. Make sure your underlining accurately represents the major point of the passage.

D. Be selective when highlighting items in your textbook or class notes. Too much underlining or highlighting is just as bad as none at all. Nothing stands out. If you highlight everything, you are not making thoughtful judgments about what's important. Make sure your underlining accurately represents the major point of the passage.

(Answers: The underlining in **A** is about right. In **B** it is meaningless. In **C** it is inadequate. In **D** it is too much.)

rectly, you'll know you're making progress. This feeling of success will motivate you to keep reading and learning.

Step 5: Review

Research shows that *immediately* reviewing material you've written, heard, or read triples the amount of information you retain and reduces study time by up to 90 percent. Remember these rules of review:

- Before a lecture, *review* the last lecture.
- Before previewing a chapter, *review* the previous chapter.

Review twice—once immediately after a lecture or a reading session (that's when we forget most of what we learn—unless we review) and once more a week or so later. Five or ten minutes should suffice for reviewing a lecture or a chapter. Go back over your notes or reading assignment and notice key points, your own marginal notes and underlinings, and any review or quiz questions provided. Rewrite or add connecting phrases to lecture notes that are unclear or were hastily scrawled. Review the answers to questions you have generated and written down.

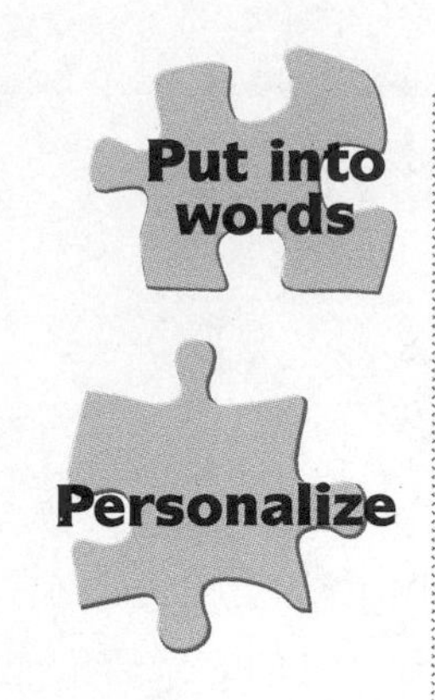

The trick is to be an active learner, to contribute something of yourself to someone else's material, and to have a dialog with the author or speaker. Ask, "How does this reading assignment fit in with what we've been learning in class?" Integrate notes on your reading with your lecture notes by adding key words and ideas in the left column.

Above all, try to see connections between what you're reading and what you already know. When you can find a connection between the new and the known, the new material will be more meaningful, and you are more likely to remember it.

MEMORY TECHNIQUES

Forgetting is not a fault as much as an annoyance. It's a nuisance to forget car keys, people's names, a grocery list, an appointment, a good joke.

Why do we forget? For lots of reasons. Sometimes we don't get the facts straight in the first place—as, for example, when we're introduced to someone with an unusual name. Sometimes we "forget to remember" distasteful obligations, such as getting the car serviced. Sometimes new information replaces old: we know our current phone number, but we forget our old one as soon as we no longer need it. And, of course, there are some things that are just as well forgotten, like an ancient grudge.

> The man who does not read good books has no advantage over the man who can't read them.
>
> Mark Twain
> *Author and humorist*

> I never forget a face but in your case I'll make an exception.
>
> Groucho Marx
> *Comedian*

On **Your** *Own*

Applying SQ3R

Apply the principles of SQ3R to your next textbook reading assignment in one of your other courses. Then bring your text to class to show your instructor how you marked it up. Bring also eight to ten 3" x 5" cards, inscribed with questions developed for—and answers derived from—your reading.

On Reading Well

Strong, capable readers are made, not born. They grow up in language-rich environments, immersed in words. They learn to read and write as a logical progression of the earlier language acts of speaking and listening. Yet reading is an act we never completely master. We learn to read—and read to learn—simultaneously, throughout our lives. As our language evolves, so does the way we read. New words come into being; old words fall out of favor. The "things" we read evolve, from label to billboard, newsprint to split-screen TV. Increasingly, our reading is icon-driven rather than alphabetic, as we move toward a more global, universal language.

To grow as readers, we must be flexible, adaptable, and always ask: What is my *purpose* for reading this? Purpose will dictate whether to read slowly or hastily, once or three times, with a dictionary or without. Next, read what *interests* you as much or more than just what's assigned; in this way, you will develop both the habit and the skill of reading. To have the knowledge of particular written works is another reason to read, to enrich our lives by conversing across the miles and years with people we might never otherwise meet.

Reading expands our experience immeasurably. It rewards our investment many times over. If you read less joyfully than you hope to one day, make that day this day. Pick up something you've been wanting to read and read it—right now.

Lots of Learning Styles

We learn through all our senses: sight, sound, taste, touch, smell. Each sense enables us to receive raw data and process it, thus making "sense" of the world around us. Whenever two or more senses are engaged simultaneously, one reinforces the other, and we're better able to recall what we've seen, heard, or felt.

In the world of school, sight and sound—the visual and the aural—have long been the emphasized modes of perception and instruction. More of what we are expected to understand and remember comes to us through our eyes and ears than by any other means. Yet we human beings are infinitely various in our perceptual preferences and forms of expression. It is natural, then, to expect that our learning styles will vary. Neurologists and psychologists consistently confirm this.

For example, let's say you want directions to a party. Do you prefer verbal directions or a map? Your task is to set the clock in your new car: Do you read the owner's manual or push buttons at random until you hit it right? Many claim they learn most thoroughly what they must "do"; that hands-on, physical manipulation is the best teacher. That may well be, but think again about what such "total engagement" engages. That's right: all the senses, simultaneously.

To recognize factors that influence how (and how well) you learn, consider your preferences with respect to:

CONDITIONS
peer affiliation
instructor affiliation
competition
organization
autonomy

CONTENT
numbers
visual images
qualitative
animate
inanimate

MODE
talking
listening
reading
writing
direct experience

RESOURCES
observation
conversation
imagination
memory

How much "affiliation," for instance, do you need? Can you tolerate moderate disorganization, or are structure and order important to you? Your preferences help shape your learning style. Once you are able to describe that style, there are two ways to improve: address difficulties with the intent to improve, and capitalize on obvious strengths.

Our personal learning styles shape our preferred forms of expression. Isadora Duncan, a dancer in the 1930s, once said "If I could *tell* you what I mean, there would be no point in dancing."

On **Your** *Own*

Your Learning Style

Describe your learning style, in writing, as fully as possible. Include the conditions, content, modes, and resources with which you believe you learn best, and why. If any term listed above is unfamiliar to you, ask your instructor to clarify it before you begin this assignment.

Collaborate

Share What You Read

In turns of one to two minutes each, with a timekeeper and without interruption, *share* something interesting (aloud, and with four to six group members) that you have recently read. Too often, we have no one to talk with about what we read; telling somebody facilitates comprehension and recall. If group members take turns recording, on paper, others' oral reports, note-taking and listening skills are strengthened along with reading and speaking facility.

On Your Own

Making Memories

Write down everything you ate yesterday, first to last. On a scale of 1–10, how accurate do you believe this list to be?

Write down all the names you can of the people in this class. Expressed as a percentage of the whole, how well did you do?

Collaborate

Comparing Memories

Take a few moments to recall the first session of this class: how you found the room, who spoke to you first, your first impressions of the instructor, class activities, your first assignment, and so on. Take turns sharing with the class one thing you remember about the first class period. Were your memories vivid or hazy? Did you remember a lot or almost nothing? Did other people remember things you had forgotten? How do you explain the fact that there were some things everyone remembered and others that only one person remembered?

Just as there are good reasons for forgetting, there are good reasons for remembering. We remember what we want to—how much people owe us, for example. We remember what we need to, like the April 15 filing date for federal income tax. As we gain more experience with the consequences of absentmindedness, we learn the importance of **intending to remember** and reminding ourselves with helpful devices: a note on the refrigerator ("Pay bills") or a rubber band around our wrist or saying "Don't let me forget" to a friend. **Remembering is largely a matter of intention**. We forget by accident, but we remember on purpose.

Most people have no problem remembering what's genuinely important to them. It's much harder to remember something that has no personal significance or immediate importance. Unfortunately, much of what we learn in college, especially in required courses unrelated to our major interest, seems of this latter type at the time. Students get higher grades in their majors because they want, need, and intend to remember what they learn. The more you know about a subject, the more you want to know. But you've got to start someplace.

This is where memory techniques (the technical term is *mnemonics*) come in handy. Mnemonics is a skill that can be learned. People who are good at it (former NBA star Jerry Lucas is an example) can study a page in the phone book for ten minutes, then recite the entire page without looking.

Mnemonic tricks have limited value. For most of us, the things we really need to recall but can't are so few that spending hundreds of hours mastering the skill, as Jerry Lucas and other memory experts have done, is hardly worth the effort. Critics of mnemonics say it's just a crutch—that rote learning is not learning at all, that memorizing a book word for word has nothing to do with learning. Mnemonic tricks *are* a crutch, but crutches can be useful when you're having trouble walking.

Mnemonics for Majors

Art majors are familiar with ROY G. BIV, whose name represents the colors of the spectrum in their proper order. Can you name them?

Red

O ____________________

Y ____________________

G ____________________

B ____________________

I ____________________

V ____________________

English majors recall the I before E spelling rule by an old rhyme:

I before E
Except after C
Or when sounding like A
As in *neighbor* and *weigh*.

(The exceptions to this rule are expressed in this sentence: Neither weird foreign scientist at leisure seized the height of either species.)

For a history major, No Plan Like Yours To Study History Wisely spells out the royal houses of England:

Norman

P ____________________

L ____________________

Y ____________________

T ____________________

S ____________________

H ____________________

W ____________________

What do the following mnemonic devices mean to music majors?

FACE
Every Good Boy Does Fine
All Cows Eat Grass
Good Boys Do Fine Always

Men Very Easily Make Jugs Serve Useful and Numerous Purposes helps astronomy majors remember the planets in the order of their distance from the sun.

Can you name them?

Mercury

V ____________________

E ____________________

M ____________________

J ____________________

S ____________________

U ____________________

N ____________________

P ____________________

In biology, Kings Play Cards On Fairly Good Soft Velvet stands for the taxonomy of nature. Can you name these categories in order from large to small?

Kingdom

P ____________________

C ____________________

O ____________________

F ____________________

G ____________________

S ____________________

V ____________________

Premed students need to know the difference between cyanates, which are harmless, and cyanides, which are deadly. Here's how:

I ate cyanate
I died from cyanide.

Geography majors can remember the Great Lakes (from west to east) by Super Man Heaved Earth Out, or:

Superior

M ____________________

H ____________________

E ____________________

O ____________________

Here's a code for math majors to figure out. (Hint: It's a way of remembering the value of pi—the ratio of the circumference of a circle to its diameter.)

How I wish I could determine of circle round
The exact relation Archimedes found.

When you really need to remember something for the limited purpose of a test, here are some basic mnemonic principles to guide you. They are adapted from Walter Pauk's valuable book *How to Study in College* (6th ed., Houghton Mifflin, 1997, pp. 93–116).

1. **Get motivated.** If you don't feel motivated, concentrate on how good you'll feel when you ace the test, on proving to the professor that you really are smart, on calling home and telling mom the good news. Or make a wager with a classmate on who will get the highest grade. Make up a motivation. As you accumulate knowledge in this way, you'll find yourself wanting to know more. Your motivation, which started out as artificial, will become genuine.

2. **Be selective.** If you try to memorize everything, you'll only be frustrated. Focus on one or two important major ideas that you know will be on the test.

3. **Intend to remember.** Tell somebody your intentions. Write a statement of your intention, sign it, and tape it to your lamp or door. Be specific: say exactly what it is you plan to remember.

4. **Organize the material.** Make a scratch outline. Reduce the material to a skeleton that will fit on a 4″ x 6″ card. Pick out key words from a list that together form a sentence, or whose first letters form a word (called an acronym). For example, the three stages of conflict resolution are negotiation, mediation, arbitration—NMA—No More Arguments.

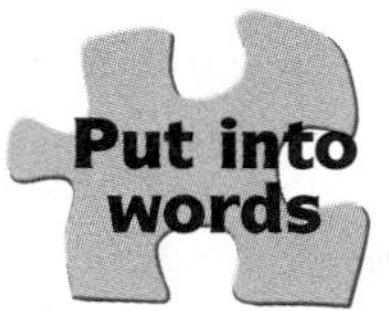

5. **Recite.** This is an essential study skill. Say it out loud. Sing it, if you want to. Make it a rap! After you recite, go back to your textbook or notes and check yourself for accuracy. If you didn't get it right, recite again until you do. Ten minutes later, check your memory to see if it's still there. If it is, chances are it'll be there for a long time.

6. **Visualize.** Turn abstract concepts into something concrete, a mental picture. For example, think of visual symbols for the five causes of World War I:

   the alliance system = a leash
   murder of Archduke Ferdinand = Ferdinand the bull
   militarism = a pistol
   imperialism = the globe
   social Darwinism = an ape

   Draw a picture (mental or actual) of Ferdinand the bull holding a pistol in one hand and holding an ape on a leash in the other, astride a globe. If you're a visual learner, you'll remember the silly picture, as well as the abstract causes of the war.

Mnemonic devices are especially useful for remembering lists and sequences. Many adults remember the days of the months by the nursery rhyme they learned as children:

Thirty days hath September,
April, June, and November.
All the rest have thirty-one,
Except February alone.

You can develop your own mnemonic devices for remembering lists. For example, consider the five basic components of strategic planning:

Situation analysis
Goals and objectives
Timelines
Accountability
Indicators

To remember them for a test, make a sentence out of the first letters (S, G, T, A, I), for example: **S**et **G**oals **T**o **A**ccomplish **I**tem.

Mnemonic devices are worth employing—judiciously. Bear in mind their limitations, and they can be useful to you.

SUMMARY

Successful students, like successful professionals, keep long and regular hours in an office designed for work. They begin each study session by surveying the job and devising a study plan. Then they stick to it. They take an active approach to studying, asking questions and answering them out loud and in writing, revising their notes, marking up their texts as they read. When attention wanes, they take short breaks and then go back to work. They remember what they learn primarily by frequent review and recitation and by connecting what they learn to what they already know. When these students have difficulty remembering something they need to know, they devise mnemonic techniques that work for them. When they complete a work session, they reward themselves. Successful students aren't geniuses, just hard workers.

Strategic *Plan*

Look over your Self-Assessment at the beginning of the chapter and identify an area in which you'd like to make a change. Then develop a Strategic Plan, using the format below.

I. Situation analysis

A. One problem I'm having with studying is ______________________________

____

B. One change I think I could make is ______________________________

____

continued on next page

Strategic *Plan* *continued from previous page*

C. The benefits of making the change are ______________________________

____

D. The consequences of not changing are ______________________________

____

E. Some obstacles I'll have to overcome are ______________________________

____

F. Some resources I'll need are ______________________________

____

II. Goals, objectives, deadlines, and indicators

A. My goal is to ______________________________

____

Deadline: ______________________________

Indicators of success: ______________________________

____

B. Here's what I'm going to do to achieve my goal, along with a reasonable deadline for each task:

	Objective	Deadline
1.	______________________	____________
2.	______________________	____________
3.	______________________	____________
4.	______________________	____________
5.	______________________	____________

III. Self-test

YES	NO	
☐	☐	**A.** Are my goals and objectives stated simply and clearly?
☐	☐	**B.** Does each one have a single focus?
☐	☐	**C.** Are they stated in a positive way?
☐	☐	**D.** Are they realistic?
☐	☐	**E.** Can I achieve them by the deadline?
☐	☐	**F.** Will I know if I've achieved them?

Journal **Ideas**

1. Describe, in detail, the place where you study most often. Does it work for you? What would you like to change about the times and location of your study sessions?
2. Have you had a difficult time concentrating on your work? If yes, why? What might you do to minimize distraction and improve concentration?
3. What is your chief motivation in life? What makes you most excited and happy? Describe an ideal day in your life, ten years from now.
4. Have you tried the SQ3R study method? What do you think of it? What methods do you use most often, when reading or studying, to recall the material? What methods might you try that you haven't tried?
5. Do you ever use memory aids when you study? Can you think of any examples?

Web **Search**

Visit this Web site:

> Finding Information on the Internet: A Tutorial
> http://www.lib.berkeley.edu/TeachingLib/Guides/Internet/FindInfo.html

This site contains the basics of Internet workshops offered year-round for the faculty, staff, and students at the University of California at Berkeley.

First, click on "Glossary of Internet and Netscape Jargon" and read the descriptions of the terms. Second, click on "Things to Know Before You Begin Searching the WWW" and read the entire contents. As time permits, return to this site and read any section that interests you. By the time you finish, you should be an accomplished WWW researcher.

The Library and Beyond: Tapping Resources

Self-*Assessment*

Check the statements that apply to you.

☐ **1.** I'm familiar with the resources of our college library and know how to find what I'm looking for.

☐ **2.** I feel at home in most libraries.

☐ **3.** I spend most of my time on campus.

☐ **4.** I've already chosen my major and have a clear sense of my career goals.

☐ **5.** I understand the formal procedure for dropping a course.

☐ **6.** I know where to get help on campus for any academic or personal problems I might encounter.

☐ **7.** I see myself as a full-time student and do not plan to be employed while enrolled in school.

☐ **8.** I am involved in more than one campus organization.

☐ **9.** I'm familiar with the student organizations on campus and know which ones I plan to join.

☐ **10.** I know most of the buildings on campus and have been inside them.

If you checked fewer than half, this chapter will be especially valuable to you.

Write **Before** *You Read*

A. Spend about a minute surveying this chapter. Then write three questions you expect to find answers to in this chapter.

1. ______________________________

2. ______________________________

3. ______________________________

B. Spend another minute writing down any thoughts that come to mind about the topics below. Write freely and rapidly.

1. My experience with libraries: ______________________________

____

____

____

____

2. Initial impressions of campus: ______________________________

____

____

____

____

3. Rumors I've heard about the college: ______________________________

____

____

____

____

PREVIEW

This chapter is a brief overview of the academic and personal support services available on most college campuses today. Some (academic advising, for example) are discussed in greater detail elsewhere in *Right from the Start*. Some may have a different name on your campus. If your college is small, these services may be part of a larger operation or may not be available at all. (Your instructor can explain this for you.) The important thing is to get to know your campus as early as possible so you'll know where to go when you need help. Because the library is the most important single resource on any college campus, we'll start there, then take a less detailed look at some others, in alphabetical order.

THE LIBRARY

Your college library may be called something else, like the Learning Resources, Media, or Information Center. Most college libraries nowadays are electronic "nerve centers" containing much more than books.

Here you'll find a confusingly large number and variety of periodicals and journals; old newspapers and magazines dating back to the last century on microfilm, microfiche, and CD-ROM; films, videos, listening rooms, braille rooms, computer workstations, government documents, rare book rooms, photo archives, tutoring centers, electronic classrooms, reference works, copy and duplication facilities, darkrooms; and much, much more.

Librarians are professional educators—and a great resource.

If your library doesn't have what you want, chances are it can get it for you through its online computer links and loan agreements with other libraries. Many college libraries have online catalogs and databases that are easily accessible by remote terminals. Articles from thousands of journals are available on CD-ROM or over the Internet and may be downloaded and printed out. If your residence hall room has a computer port, or if you own a personal computer with a modem at home, you can do library research without ever leaving your room.

Far from the cartoon image of the village librarian—an intimidating grouch whose main function is shushing people—college librarians tend to be helpful, highly trained, well-educated, interesting people. Many of them hold faculty rank and terminal degrees in library science or a specialized field. They'll be pleased if you ask them to share their knowledge with you. Walk right up to the reference or information desk (usually the first thing you see as you enter) and say hello. Pick up a brochure describing the layout of the building, holdings, collections, services, and open hours. Then take a tour or just wander around and explore. Becoming familiar with the library early in your first year of college will pay tremendous dividends.

> If truth is beauty how come no one has their hair done in a library?
>
> Lily Tomlin
> *American humorist*

MANAGING INFORMATION: USING THE INTERNET

Learning is not so much a matter of memorizing information as learning where to *find* information and how to *use* it. Because the sum of the world's knowledge is now doubling every two years, no one can hope to learn more than a small portion of it. And even that knowledge rapidly becomes obsolete.

A better alternative is to **become an *information manager***—a person who knows how to locate relevant information and to organize, synthesize, generalize, and utilize it.

Until recently, the world's information was largely contained in printed materials that were stored in libraries. Now, more and more information consists not only of words, but also of pictures and sound, all stored on computers linked together by fiber-optic cable in a system known as the Internet. This global network already contains more information than many libraries combined.

Begun in 1969 by the U.S. Department of Defense as a way of linking the federal government with its industrial suppliers and with scientists at a handful of research universities, "the Net" has grown rapidly, swallowing up smaller networks, and now links thousands of separate computer networks all over the world.

The easiest available map for navigating the information highway is called the World Wide Web (WWW). Developed in 1989 at the European Center for Particle Physics in Switzerland, "the Web" has been called the "Swiss Army Knife of the Internet." Some go further, calling it the most important advance in publishing since the printing press. Software to help you navigate the Web—Netscape and Microsoft's Internet Explorer are the best-known browsers—will soon be built into all new computers and eventually into TVs and hand-held computers as well. The Web is accessible by most college students (any many high school students) either through direct access from ports in the library, student union, or your residence hall, or by modem from your home.

You can use the Internet not only to access information but also to participate in discussions with people all over the world on every conceivable subject. Participating in computer discussion groups can become addictive. Set time limits for your session and stick to them.

The electronic superhighway is still under construction, and drivers must expect construction delays and potholes. As on any other highway, you'll want to avoid rush hour. Noon to 2 P.M., for example, is a period of heavy usage, and you can expect long delays in retrieving files.

Still, it is possible to travel faster than the speed of sound and not quite as fast as the speed of light. In the time it takes to read this paragraph you could travel to Paris, locate and scan a document in the Bibliothèque Nationale, and send copies to students in Hong Kong and New Delhi.

As the tools for using the Internet become more user-friendly over the next two or three years, the information revolution will affect us all. Take advantage of whatever resources your college provides to learn more about this revolutionary new way to communicate and learn.

Tips

Using the Library

1. You don't need a library card, but you will need your student ID to check out books.
2. "Circulating" books are ones you can check out (usually for two or three weeks). Other materials—such as reference works, periodicals, special collections, and rare books—have to be used inside the library.
3. The library's online catalog will tell you the status of the book or article you're looking for—whether it's part of the library's holdings, if it has been checked out, and when it is due back. (An item may also have been withdrawn for repair or be available only on reserve.) Otherwise, check the stacks. If the book or journal you want is supposed to be there but isn't, first check the adjacent area (someone may have reshelved it in the wrong place). Then ask an employee at the front desk for help. If it has been checked out and you really need it, fill out a request form. At most colleges, instructors and graduate students can keep books out almost indefinitely. If the book you need has been checked out and you fill out a request form, the library will call it in.
4. You can generally renew books (sometimes with a phone call) unless someone has requested them.
5. At most colleges, checked-out materials must be returned by the end of the term. Your grades may be held up if you haven't returned a book.
6. If the library doesn't have what you need, it may be obtainable from another library through a system called Interlibrary Loan. Ask.
7. Materials placed "on reserve" are for students in a particular class. Sometimes they can be checked out overnight or for longer periods; some must be kept in the library and used for a limited time so that other students can have fair access.
8. Books and articles are searchable by author (last name), title, subject, keyword, and call number. If you're doing a general search by subject or keyword, you may have to experiment. Start with your specific topic, then attach one or two additional keywords ("limiters") in a series connected with "and" or "or." For example, if you're testing a hypothesis that diabetes is caused by poor nutrition, enter "diabetes and (nutrition or diet)." Tie paired keywords together with parentheses to avoid getting many irrelevant references. Your online catalog will offer several alternative keyword headings, and you can select those that look most promising.
9. Magazines and journals are often a better place to start your research than books: They may contain more current information in a more compact, readable format.
10. Because magazines and journals are expensive and take up a lot of space, many have been transferred to a microform room, where they are compactly stored on rolls of microfilm or microfiche cards. Microfilm reading machines are easy to use.
11. To find what else is available, start with an electronic periodicals index. Because there are many specialized indexes, ask a librarian to recommend which to begin with for the topic you are investigating. If your subject is the start-up phase of a small business, for example, the ERIC (Educational Resources Information Center) database won't be useful to you, because it contains only articles related to education.
12. Some libraries subscribe to services that deliver the full text of articles over the Internet. The library pays real money for these electronic subscriptions, but the material is made available to students, faculty, and staff at no charge. After you graduate, this service will no longer be available to you. (We are moving closer to the dream of every researcher—to sit at a terminal and search the contents of hundreds or thousands of titles and then retrieve the full text with the click of a mouse button.) Databases like InfoTrac College Edition® or Electronic Collections Online® are useful because they contain a wide variety of articles on many topics and provide the full text of articles, which most indexes do not. So when you see a promising title whose text is not available online, you need to answer two questions: (1) Does my library own the desired issue of the periodical? and if so, (2) Where is the issue located?

On **Your** Own

Getting Acquainted with the Library

Complete the following:

1. What are the library's hours?

   Weekdays ________ Saturday ________ Sunday ________

2. Who is director of the library? ________
3. List three materials available in the library other than books and periodicals.
   - a. ________
   - b. ________
   - c. ________
4. List three services the library provides other than checking out books.
   - a. ________
   - b. ________
   - c. ________
5. Look up a book entitled *The Feminine Mystique* on the online terminal and provide the following information:
   - a. Author ________
   - b. Subject(s) listed under ________
   - c. Number of pages ________
   - d. Call number ________
   - e. Publisher ________
   - f. Date of publication ________
6. How many books are listed under the subject heading "Swahili"? ________
7. In a periodical index, find an article published in 1998 on the subject of "fitness" and give the following information:
   - a. Author ________
   - b. Title of article ________
   - c. Title of periodical ________
   - d. Volume and issue number ________
   - e. Issue date ________
   - f. Number of pages ________
8. What is the earliest year for which copies of *The New Yorker* are available in the library?

   ____

9. How much does it cost per copy to use a copy machine? ________
10. Where is the *Congressional Record* found? ________

continued on next page

On Your Own *continued from previous page*

11. Find a newspaper article on the subject of "abortion" and give the following information:

a. Title ______

b. Published by ______

c. Where found ______

d. Date of publication ______

12. List three types of audiovisual materials available in the library.

a. ______

b. ______

c. ______

13. For how long can you check out books? ______

For how long can you renew a book? ______

Explain the renewal procedure: ______

______

______

______

______

14. Does your library have an electronic periodicals index? ______

If so, where are the terminals located? ______

Can you print out an on-screen reference? ______

Will your librarian do a database search for you? ______

If so, what is the fee, if any, for this service? ______

On Your Own

Using Microfilm

Go to the library microform room and look up a newspaper published on the day you were born. Write a few of the headlines in your journal. Your library may have either microfilm (a roll of celluloid) or microfiche (a celluloid card) or both. Both technologies involve photographic reduction of a printed page to microscopic size, which is then enlarged on the machine. They enable libraries to store and protect enormous quantities of old documents.

OTHER ACADEMIC SUPPORT SERVICES

Academic Advising

Most students depend on Academic Advising primarily for scheduling assistance, but there are other good reasons to see an adviser. If you're planning to transfer from a two-year to a four-year college, your adviser can tell you about "articulation" (how the course credits you earned at one college apply to the requirements of another). If you're undecided about a major or a career, an adviser can help you match your aptitudes and interests with an appropriate field. Your adviser can tell you what you need to do to qualify for a professional program like physical therapy or business, or whether you need to take developmental coursework.

Maintaining state-of-the-art computing equipment is a major challenge for most colleges.

The Advising Office is also a good place to go for advice if you're thinking of withdrawing from a class or dropping out of college altogether. They won't try to talk you out of it, but will let you know your options and the consequences of various courses of action. When you're ready to declare a major, they have the forms. This office may also handle "credit by examination" (College Level Examination Program, or CLEP, tests), which is a way of earning credit for a course by demonstrating mastery of the subject. Academic advisers don't usually do counseling of a personal nature, but they can refer you to professionals who can help. On smaller campuses, academic advising may be handled by specially trained faculty members. See Chapter 12 for more information about academic advising.

Tips

Password Security

Whenever you log on to a computer network, you must provide a password. A password is a secret identity that proves you are who you say you are. If someone else learns your password, that person could masquerade as you and have complete access to your files, e-mail, money, and personal information. He or she could modify or destroy your files, send electronic threats that appear to be coming from you, or purchase goods and services for which you will be obliged to pay.

Here are some ways to protect yourself:[1]

- Change your password often.
- Use passwords that contain at least seven characters, and the more the better (as long as you can remember them).
- Choose a password that's easy for you to remember, but difficult for another person to figure out (for example, your uncle's nickname).
- Intersperse punctuation marks or symbols such as #, *, @.
- Mix UpPer- and loWER-case characters.
- Never write down a password or tell someone else your password—even a friend.

[1] Adapted from "Password Security," Office of Policy Development and Education, Information Technology Division, University of Michigan, 1998.

Tips

E-Mail Etiquette

E-mail is a communication medium that offers many advantages over memos and voice mail: it's fast, it's easy, and it doesn't require that both parties be available at the same time. But it does have limitations and pitfalls. Those who understand the risks of e-mail will be in a better position to avoid them. Here's how:

- Because e-mail messages are written rapidly and sent instantaneously and irretrievably, and because the nonverbal signals of spoken conversation (eye contact, tone of voice, body language, gestures) are missing, the *tone* of an e-mail message can be easily misunderstood. Typing words in ALL CAPS appears like shouting to the reader (it's better to surround a word with *asterisks* or _underscores_ to emphasize a word or point). Some people use "emoticons"(see below) as graphic equivalents of facial expressions or hand gestures.
- E-mail messages leave a permanent record that may easily be forwarded and copied to others again and again. If you want your message to be kept confidential, explain this to the recipient. Think overnight before sending an angry or defamatory message. Before sending, review all messages for punctuation and grammar and make sure they really say what you want them to say. If you receive a message that seems hostile or offensive, don't rush to judgment. Be patient with inexperienced users.
- Keep the line length of your e-mail messages short enough to be read on any monitor (under 70 characters), so that it can be read with ease.
- When responding to a discussion group message, keep in mind that you are "talking" to everyone on the list. To address someone privately, use that person's own e-mail address.
- When responding to a message, quote a few lines of the message so others will know which message you are responding to.
- Include your name and e-mail address at the end of your message, but remember that any information you reveal about yourself (name, address, phone, fax) will become public and could be used inappropriately by others.

Tips

E-Mail Emoticons and Acronyms

Emoticon[2]	Meaning
:-)	smiling, happy
:-(	frowning, sad
:-o	surprised, shocked
;-)	winking, teasing
:-D	very happy, laughing
:-|	indifferent smile

Acronym	Meaning
BTW	by the way
FWIW	for what it's worth
IMHO	in my humble opinion
OTOH	on the other hand
LOL	laughing out loud
ROTFL	rolling on the floor laughing
HHOK	ha ha, only kidding
BBL	be back later

[2] View with your head tipped slightly to the left.

Tips

Computer Conferencing

Computer conferences and discussion groups are important means of academic discourse. They cost nothing to attend, and people can participate at their leisure by asking or answering questions and sending public messages to the list or private messages to list participants. Computer conferences (CAUCUS is the best-known software) are designed around a particular topic and may be open to anyone or restricted to a select list of participants. Internet discussion groups ("listservs") are usually managed by volunteers and may be open to all or restricted to members of an organization. Your instructor or the conference organizer will explain how to log on, or you can check the HELP menu for instructions.

Because some conferences and discussion groups continue for many years, it is likely that a wide variety of topics of common interest have already been discussed before you logged on. If you are new to an established list (a "newbie"), it is wise to "lurk" in the background for a while and read the FAQs (Frequently Asked Questions section, if there is one) before joining the discussion.

On **Your** *Own*

Campus Tour

A. If your Admissions Office provides campus tours, take one. (Rather than posing as a prospective student, identify yourself and your purpose and ask permission first.)

Afterward, write a brief account of the experience. Did you learn anything new about the campus? How would you evaluate the tour guide's performance? Was the information accurate? Helpful? Too hurried? What campus attractions received the most emphasis? If you had been the tour guide, what would you have said or done differently?

B. An alternative is to examine an Admissions Office video or viewbook. Does it accurately portray your college? Are there distortions or omissions? How would you revise it to be more accurate or effective?

Computing

Computers are essential tools for today's college students. The ideal is owning your own state-of-the-art, networked computer, but if you don't, ask your academic adviser or resource librarian what computing facilities are available on your campus. Your campus may have one major computing center with PC workstations wired to a large mainframe. On some campuses, every dorm room is connected to a server by underground fiber-optic cable. More likely, you'll find satellite centers all over campus. Some of these may be officially accessible only by department majors and faculty, but sometimes others can use the equipment when usage is light. If you find you have to wait a long time for a terminal, ask the person in charge when the best times are.

Continuing Education

This community outreach program has many names. Sometimes it's called Lifelong or Extended Learning because its services—classes at convenient

Distance Education: The Virtual Classroom

Continuing Education once consisted primarily of courses taught by correspondence or at satellite campuses. Today, new communication technologies—satellite, microwave, fax, compressed two-way video, and fiber-optic cable networks—are rapidly changing the way people learn. People who live long distances from a college campus or who work or care for children when college classes are available now have access to a new form of learning: the virtual classroom.

In virtual classrooms, communication occurs over a two-way interactive video and the Internet. An instructor in a studio can see students on a monitor and respond to their questions by speakerphone or voice-activated cameras. Quizzes and exams can be faxed to a distant site and monitored by local proctors. Instead of holding office hours, instructors advise their students and provide tutorial support over the Internet. Many courses and textbooks are available on the Internet.

Distance learning offers exciting advantages, notably reducing the cost of higher education and reducing the barriers to learning of time and space. At the same time, it has raised serious questions. Some critics of distance learning express concern about the need for personal interaction between students and instructors. And if a college course can be taught electronically to thousands of students at once, many instructors worry about their jobs. As one college administrator put it, "Any instructor who can be replaced by a computer deserves to be replaced."

times and locations plus life-enriching, noncredit learning opportunities—are attractive to adults who want to take a class for self-enrichment, work full-time, or live some distance from campus. This office may also handle Study Abroad.

Honors Program

An honors program offers great benefits for the academic top 10 percent—namely, small, challenging classes with excellent instructors and other advantages. Honors students aren't geniuses, just people who take academics seriously and achieve good grades. Many students avoid honors, thinking it will have an adverse impact on their grades, but in fact the reverse is true. Honors usually requires a GPA in the 3.30 to 3.50 range. Many two-year colleges are now offering honors courses, and most four-year schools can accommodate transfers, nontraditional students, and "late bloomers." For those who qualify, honors is a great opportunity to get an Ivy League-quality education without paying Ivy League tuition.

International Studies

Sometimes called Foreign Study or Study Abroad and often a subsidiary of Continuing Education, this is the place to go if you're considering a summer, quarter, semester, or year abroad. Some offices even provide the usual services of a travel agency, but deal mainly with programs earning academic credit. Here you'll find brochures describing academic programs abroad, many sponsored by other colleges and universities. You'll find that many are not only surprisingly affordable but also fully accredited, allowing you to transfer credits back to your home institution. Study abroad is a valuable, life-changing opportunity. In some cases tuition is less than you're paying now. Staff can also answer questions foreign students may have about English proficiency requirements and visa status.

Registrar (Records)

If a college were a bank, the Registrar's Office (sometimes called Academic Records) would be the vault. This is where your academic records are kept. Here are some reasons for visiting the Registrar's Office:

- to declare a major
- to change your name, address, or major
- to find out if you're eligible for varsity sports
- to ascertain your class standing and rank
- to learn how to qualify for residency status
- to verify your enrollment
- to get a copy of your transcript
- to learn which of your transfer credits were accepted
- to correct a grade error
- to find out whether you've completed requirements for graduation (senior checkout)

In smaller colleges, the functions of this office may be combined with Admissions, Academic Advising, and/or Registration.

Registration

If you don't have phone-in registration, this is where you go to register for classes, get permission to audit a course, arrange a pass/fail, drop or add a course, cancel your registration, or withdraw from school. See Chapter 12 for more information about scheduling your classes.

Tutoring

To seek tutoring in a tough subject is a sign of strength, not of weakness. On any day of the week, you'll find math geniuses in the writing clinic and straight-A English majors in the math clinic.

At the first hint of trouble, get help. Most colleges have an Academic Support or Study Skills Center (it might be called something else, but the service is the same.) Here you'll find trained tutors both for general problems (test anxiety, reading disabilities, organization and study skills, speed reading, using a computer) and problems specific to an academic discipline. International students can get help with English as a second language.

Also, check with the department in which you're having difficulty. You'll find writing clinics, literature centers, math labs, and so on. These often operate in the evening in an empty classroom and are staffed by upperclass or graduate students majoring in that discipline. The help they give is almost always one-on-one—the best kind—and it's usually free.

If you find these options unsatisfactory, it's possible to hire a tutor. Place an ad in your campus paper or put a note on the bulletin board of the honors dorm. You don't have to put your name in the ad. State the subject you need help in, your phone number, and what you're willing to pay (offer

$5.75/hour negotiable" for starters). It isn't free but it's not a bad deal either: two hours of personalized help per week for the price of a movie.

PERSONAL SUPPORT SERVICES

Admissions

This is the office that sent you all that recruitment literature. If you think you'd enjoy assisting in the recruitment process, your Admissions Office may employ a number of student volunteers who function in an ambassadorial role for the college by hosting special events, giving tours, doing phone recruitment. This is a great way to make friends and give something back to your school. At smaller colleges, admissions offices sometimes also perform the functions of Records and Registration (see p. 144).

Bookstore

Often located in the student union, college bookstores of course sell books. But books have almost become a sideline compared to the customary outpouring of college identity items: Cardinal sweatshirts, Bobcat tea mugs, Terrapin diapers, Wolverine toilet seats, and the like.

Check around. There may be competing bookstores off campus where you can buy the same things for less money. **When buying textbooks, always keep your receipt**, especially if you buy your books before the semester starts: instructors may change their minds, or the assigned instructor may have been replaced by another who wants to use a different text.

Campus Life

Sometimes called the Student Activities Center, this office coordinates extracurricular activities (concerts, speakers, special events, orientation). It

If College Were a Business

Colleges and universities, whose costs have been escalating faster than the inflation rate for over a decade, have been the target of scathing criticism for their inefficiencies and unbusinesslike practices. But Robert L. Woodbury, chancellor of the University of Maine System, reminds us that colleges and universities do many things well.* Among them:

- Higher education is one of the few American industries universally recognized as the best in the world.
- Unlike U.S. industry, American colleges have a favorable balance of trade: nearly 470,000 students from abroad enroll at American universities, compared with only 80,000 American students studying abroad.
- Higher education has been a growth industry for the past twenty years, despite a shrinking pool of high school graduates.
- Cases of college bankruptcy, defaults, or high-level criminal behavior are all but unknown.
- No other industry has assembled so much talent at so little cost. The average professor has six years of education beyond the bachelor's degree and earns an average of $54,000.
- Colleges supply housing, food, art centers, athletic events, entertainment, libraries, and all the amenities of a small city—to say nothing of an education—at an average cost of $12,000 a year, compared with the $25,000 annual cost of incarcerating a prisoner.

* Robert L. Woodbury, "Why Not Run a Business Like a Good University?" *The Christian Science Monitor* (Mar. 23, 1993), 7.

Collaborate

Getting to Know the Campus

Campus Pursuit

Bring to your next class session three Trivial Pursuit–type questions about support services available on your campus. Also, bring with you three small prizes (sugar-free candy, notepad, gum, refrigerator magnet, and so on). Picking up a few brochures around campus should give you a ready supply of questions, for example:

Name the vice president for Student Affairs.
In what building is the Office of Multicultural Affairs?
Describe the athletic team logo.

In class, sit in a circle (small group or large) and take turns asking the person on your left one of your questions. If the person knows the answer, give him or her a prize. If the person doesn't know the answer, he or she must give you a prize.

Get acquainted with your campus as early as possible.

may also house student government, legal aid for students, landlord/tenant assistance, and the offices of student organizations, including Greek life (sororities and fraternities). See Chapter 9 for more information about getting involved in campus organizations.

Career Services

Usually combined with the Employment or Placement Office, this office will become more important to you as your college career goes on. But first-year students will find it valuable for career counseling, aptitude and interest testing, and finding a part-time job on or off campus. If you later decide to pursue an internship or co-op placement, this is the place to start. Career Services also offers free workshops on useful job-hunting skills (Dress for Success, Business Etiquette, How to Prepare a Winning Resume, Interviewing Skills). See Chapter 12 for more information about career planning.

Cashier

You can cash a personal check here with a student ID, but the principal function of the Cashier's Office (also called Student Accounting or Bursar) is to send you bills and process your payments. Pay close attention to the due date on your bill. If you're mailing a check on the due date, take it to the Post Office and insist on a date stamp. If you anticipate a payment problem, make an appointment well in advance to work out a mutually acceptable payment schedule.

Tips

Chronic Health Problems

On the first day of class, let each of your instructors know if you have a health problem or disability that might affect your performance in the classroom or require routine or emergency assistance. Most instructors have a rudimentary knowledge of what to do in cases of epileptic seizures or insulin attacks. Let them know your symptoms and needs before an emergency occurs.

Child Care

Child care is a wonderful service, but it's often available only on large campuses that have a significant population of older students. Campus day care will probably cost a bit more, but the care is almost always first rate. The professional staff are specialists in early childhood development and are assisted by student apprentices majoring in the same field. And you can always check on your child between classes.

Commuter Lounge

These are becoming more common on today's college campus. Some have adopted the space-age name "Adult Re-Entry Center" and come fully equipped with lockers, study carrels, conversation pits, and counselors who can provide financial, academic, and personal assistance for nontraditional students. See Chapter 9 for some commuting tips.

Disability Services

If you are a person with a disability, contact this office for advice on available equipment and services. If no special office exists, there will be someone on campus qualified and designated to assist students with disabilities; call Student Affairs or Student Services for a referral. The Americans with Disabilities Act, passed by Congress in 1992, has forced colleges to expand considerably the services they provide to students with disabilities. If you have impaired vision or dyslexia, for example, it's possible your college will hire readers for you.

Financial Aid

Call for walk-in hours or, if possible, make an appointment, especially if you run into a financial bind. It will save time for everybody if you ask for the same staff member each time you visit, because that person will be familiar with your case. Financial aid advisers say no a lot (there's always more need than there is money) and have to put up with a lot of unfair hostility from students. On the other hand, sometimes financial aid counselors can make your serious problem disappear with a single computer keystroke. This is more likely to occur if you treat them like human beings. If you're in a tight spot, you may be able to obtain a small grant or short-term loan of a few hundred dollars at low interest. See Chapter 4 for more information about financial aid.

Make healthy choices in the cafeteria.

Health Care

The Health Center (or Infirmary) can be anything from a major hospital to a part-time doctor/nurse team working out of the gym. (Community and commuter colleges usually don't have a health center.) It's a good idea to write your health center's phone number and hours of operation next to your phone and find out whether they offer 24-hour emergency service.

High-quality, low-cost health care is one of the great benefits of being enrolled in college. Laboratory and X-ray services may be available on larger campuses. Staffed by licensed medical doctors and registered nurses, your health center may also have a pharmacy for prescriptions, over-the-counter medication, and health aids. Condoms are often distributed free of charge. Spouses and dependents of registered students may also qualify for campus health care. Many health centers provide alcohol and substance abuse treatment and smoking cessation programs. Pick up a brochure and find out what's available; it could literally be a matter of life or death. See Chapter 11 for an extended discussion of personal health issues.

Housing and Food Services

Some housing offices provide listings and referrals for off-campus housing, but mostly they deal with on-campus housing only. You probably won't have to go there unless you need to change your housing assignment in midyear, want to get out of your housing or meal contract, or want to take a complaint up the chain of command. See Chapter 9 for an extended discussion of living options.

Students who stay fit experience less stress.

International Student Services

Most large institutions have an office to assist students from other countries. This office helps students cut through bureaucratic red tape involving visas, TOEFL tests, scholarships, academic transcripts, and housing. It may also provide host families on holidays, host mixers and multicultural events, and generally ease the transplant shock international students experience when they arrive in the United States for the first time.

Intramurals/Recreation

Even if you're a couch potato, you'll find something fun to do in the recreation area. These range in quality from small gyms to large fitness centers featuring Olympic-size pools, free-weight and Nautilus equipment, aerobics and martial arts rooms, billiard parlors, batting cages, racquetball courts, banked indoor tracks, trampolines, indoor tennis courts, outdoor swimming pools and skating ponds, band shells, barbecue pits, and a rental service for skis, carabiners, canoes, and camping equipment. See Chapter 11 for more information about recreation and physical fitness.

Multicultural Center

Large campuses with a diverse student population sometimes have an office or lounge for underrepresented minority student groups (African American, Hispanic American, Native American, and others). Here you can find a network of friends and mentors, get connected with a student organization that promotes awareness of your culture, hear speakers, view displays, study, or just relax. See Chapter 10 for a discussion of cultural diversity issues.

Ombudsperson

An ombudsperson plays the roles of secular chaplain, red-tape cutter, conflict mediator, and Supreme Court justice. (If your college doesn't have one, the Dean of Students may perform the same function.) Skilled in mediation and conflict resolution, an ombudsperson is the court of last appeal for people with unresolvable academic or interpersonal problems and can help students accept the reality of their situation even if the problem is insoluble.

Collaborate

Getting to Know the Campus Even Better

Scavenger Hunt

Bring something good to eat to class. Form groups of five. Agree as a class on a time to return to the room before you go around campus trying to obtain as many of the listed items as you can. The first group to return with all the items, or the group with the most items by the time you agree to return, is the winner. The winning group gets the goodies.

THINGS TO FIND

1. A book checked out from the library.
2. A current list of courses available through Continuing Education.
3. An Honors Program brochure.
4. The signature of the person in charge of any of the offices listed above.
5. A tongue depressor.
6. A housing brochure.
7. A financial aid form.
8. A button, sticker, or pin advertising a campus office.
9. The statement OUR GROUP IS NUMBER 1 printed from a word processor.
10. A change-of-address form.
11. The title, date, time, and location of a scheduled, upcoming study skills workshop.
12. A blank intramurals sign-up sheet.
13. A list of services available at the Health Center or Counseling Center.
14. A Student Employment Request form.
15. A list of approved campus fraternities and sororities.
16. A napkin from the student union coffee shop.

(**17–20**: optional items to be added by your instructor)

17. ______________________________
18. ______________________________
19. ______________________________
20. ______________________________

Parking

Parking is usually handled by the Campus Police or Security Office. You may need to buy a parking permit for your car. If you get a parking ticket, this office may also be where you pay your fine (do so promptly; failing to pay will result in increased fines and could prevent you from registering for classes and even graduating). The parking office may also coordinate ride boards and carpooling for commuters.

Personal Counseling

On small campuses, personal counseling is sometimes provided by the Academic Advising Office. At larger institutions the Counseling Center is part of the Health Center and is staffed by certified psychologists who can make psychiatric referrals. If your problem is not urgent, make an appointment. If it's an emergency, you'll get immediate care. The counseling center is a good place to go for problems with relationships, stress, or adjusting to college because—unlike with a roommate—the help is objective and strictly confidential.

Special Student Services

These usually operate under the Dean of Students, who also handles cases of student misconduct. Special services may include Students with Disabilities, Foreign Student Affairs, Greek Life, Minority Affairs, Student Government, Veterans Affairs, Volunteer/Community Service, Student Media, and others.

Student Union

A place to go between classes, your Student Union may have a coffee shop, cafeteria, vending machines, and other amenities such as a pool hall, art gallery, barber shop, post office, ticket office, travel agency, meeting room, ballroom, bookstore, as well as various offices. This is often where you'll find "ride boards"—bulletin boards with notices by students who need or can provide a ride home on weekends and holidays or students who want to form a carpool.

Women's Center

The Women's Center offers support services for women, especially (but not only) for older adults juggling the roles of wife, mother, student, and future professional. It is a good place to go for academic advising, career counseling, and financial aid assistance, as well as knowledgeable advice about birth control, sexual harassment or assault, and gender discrimination. See Chapter 10 for a discussion of gender issues.

SUMMARY

Every student should make it a point to become familiar with the library and all available learning technologies—both are crucial to your success in college. There are many other support services and resources on your campus, and all have a single purpose: to help you succeed, both academically and personally. They will reach out to you through brochures, posters, radio and TV announcements, ads in the campus paper, or speakers in classes and residence halls. But they can't help you if you don't respond to their offers. Even if you don't need help right now, knowing what's available and where it's located will enable you to get help when you do need it or to advise a bewildered friend.

Strategic *Plan*

Look over your Self-Assessment at the beginning of the chapter and identify an area in which you'd like to make a change. Then develop a Strategic Plan, using the format below.

I. Situation Analysis

A. One problem I'm having in making full use of campus resources is ______________________

____

B. One change I think I could make is ______________________

____

C. The benefits of making the change are ______________________

____

D. The consequences of not changing are ______________________

____

E. Some obstacles I'll have to overcome are ______________________

____

F. Some resources I'll need are ______________________

____

II. Goals, objectives, deadlines, and indicators

A. My goal is to ______________________

____

Deadline: ______________________

Indicators of success: ______________________

____

B. Here's what I'm going to do to achieve my goal, along with a reasonable deadline for each task:

	OBJECTIVE	DEADLINE
1.	______________________	__________
2.	______________________	__________
3.	______________________	__________
4.	______________________	__________
5.	______________________	__________

continued on next page

Strategic *Plan* *continued from previous page*

III. Self-Test

YES	NO	
☐	☐	**A.** Are my goals and objectives stated simply and clearly?
☐	☐	**B.** Does each one have a single focus?
☐	☐	**C.** Are they stated in a positive way?
☐	☐	**D.** Are they realistic?
☐	☐	**E.** Can I achieve them by the deadline?
☐	☐	**F.** Will I know if I've achieved them?

Journal **Ideas**

1. What feeling do you get when you enter a library? Describe it. Think back on past experiences you've had with libraries. How have these experiences influenced your present attitude? Discuss.
2. What was your initial impression of your college campus? Was it easy to find your way around? Were you able to find your classes on the first day? Explain.
3. Describe an experience you have had since arriving on campus that was scary, satisfying, embarrassing, exciting, or funny.
4. What academic support service do you expect to use most often? Why?
5. Do you pay an activity fee or general fee at your college? How much is it? What do you get for it? Do you feel the fee is justified? Why or why not?

Web **Search**

Visit this site:

University of Albany Libraries—Searching the Internet: Recommended Sites and Search Techniques
http://www.albany/edu/library/internet/search.html

This is another tutorial designed to increase your skill in conducting Internet searches. Click on "Evaluating Internet Resources" and read the section carefully. Then click on and review the section called "General Search Strategies."

Test Management

Self-*Assessment*

Check the statements that apply to you.

☐ **1.** I typically test well.

☐ **2.** I prepare for tests well in advance.

☐ **3.** I always read test directions carefully before I begin a test.

☐ **4.** I answer all objective test questions, even if I'm not sure of the answer.

☐ **5.** I generally feel well prepared for exams.

☐ **6.** I seldom leave an exam early.

☐ **7.** I have very little test anxiety.

☐ **8.** For essay exams, I predict the questions and outline practice answers.

☐ **9.** I excel at essay exams.

☐ **10.** When I get a test back, I review it carefully.

If you checked fewer than half, this chapter will be especially valuable to you.

Write **Before** *You Read*

A. Spend about a minute surveying this chapter. Then write three questions you expect to find answers to in this chapter.

1. ______________________________

2. ______________________________

3. ______________________________

B. Spend another minute writing down any thoughts that come to mind about the topics below. Write freely and rapidly.

1. The grading system: ______________________________

____

____

____

____

2. Preparing for tests: ______________________________

____

____

____

____

3. Taking tests: ______________________________

____

____

____

____

PREVIEW

If you're using the SQ3R method, you're preparing for tests every day, day by day. If you attend class regularly, listen actively, use an effective note-taking system, review and recite your notes after each class, and practice the SQ3R principles, you'll need very little additional time to study for exams. Spend what time you do have condensing your notes and text material into capsule form. Once you begin the test, the key words you've committed to memory will trigger an entire chain of facts and ideas.

STUDYING FOR TESTS

Tests are the most frequent means of measuring, or assessing, what you've learned in a college class. Although rarely anyone's favorite thing, test taking need not cause undue anxiety. You can be a better test taker with systematic attention to the process—the preparation, completion, and review of every exam.

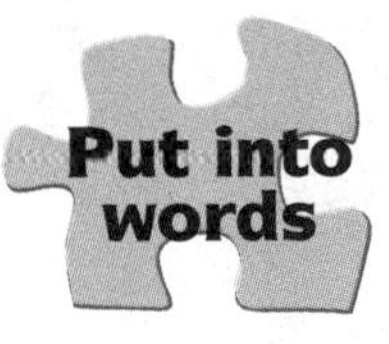

Whatever note-taking system you use, it should be designed to help you study for tests. If you've been using the Cornell Method, for example, take your notes out of your binder, lay them in a pile, and spread them out so only the left-hand columns are exposed. Look at the key words and main ideas in the column and try to **recite out loud** as much of the covered-up material as you can. (The column notes function much like flashcards.)

If time permits, **make up study sheets** geared to helping you answer specific types of exam questions. For "identify" or "define" sections, for example, you might list terms, dates, and names, with brief descriptions for each. Gather these from your reading and lecture notes, and circle items as you read. Write each important item on one side of a 3″ x 5″ card, then write a one-paragraph description on the back. Use them like flashcards. For "compare and contrast" questions, you could make lists of characteristics of related items. Or you could use a question-and-answer format in which a question you asked as you were studying is answered. For a math test, you might have one sheet for formulas, another for problem-solving strategies, and so on.

To study for essay tests, predict likely questions and outline your answers in writing. Remember that every essay response must be complete, clear, factually accurate, and well supported.

Crib Sheets

See if you can reduce all your study sheets to one side of a single 4″ x 6″ card that contains all the main ideas in shorthand form. Carry the card in your purse or pocket and review it from time to time. Before long, each single word or symbol will automatically trigger a long chain of ideas and information. You will "know it cold"—a certain cure for test anxiety.

Study Groups

Research shows that students who study in groups perform better on tests than students who study alone. You may be invited to join a study partner or

Tips

Math and Science Aversion

Many people dislike math and science, and for good reason: numbers and formulas are abstractions, and people don't think in abstractions. Picture $E = mc^2$. What do you see? Now picture a cherry red Corvette. Which was easier to visualize?

Scientists and mathematicians don't think abstractly, either. Chemists form mental pictures of invisible chemical systems and reactions. Physicists, reflecting on the theory of relativity, may form an image of a dynamic cosmos shrinking and expanding simultaneously. Some mathematicians come to think of certain numbers as personalities, animated creatures with distinctive lives and identities all their own.

When solving problems, scientists and mathematicians fumble around and make mistakes just as you and I do. They know there are many ways to solve a problem, some more efficient than others. They imagine possible solutions, make false starts, draw diagrams, discard scraps of paper filled with dead-end doodles, and press on. They learn from their mistakes.

You don't have to become a rocket scientist. You will have accomplished a lot if, by taking required math and science courses, you learn something about the scientific method, the natural universe, and the beauty of numerical systems; if you learn to think systematically and to withhold judgment until all the facts are in; or if you acquire some workable strategies for solving problems.

Here are some tips that may make math and science a bit more palatable:

1. **Turn an abstraction into something concrete.** Compare the molecular structure of a compound with the shape of a praying mantis or a baseball diamond. Write out symbolic equations as English sentences; translate a symbolic problem into a word problem ("Four boys had five apples . . . "). Study the glare of your lamp as you think about light waves and particles.

2. **Be patient.** Math and science disciplines evolved one discovery at a time, each building on the last. Take your time and make sure you understand an axiom or formula or theory and how to apply it before moving on.

3. **Practice a lot.** Work through all the assigned problems with pencil and paper. If you have time, do a few more or make up some of your own. Skill in math and science requires practice and exercise, just like skill in sports. Some students stop as soon as they understand the principle involved. That's like thinking you're ready for Comedy Central after telling one joke. After you read a new concept in your text, start practicing it immediately.

4. **Experiment.** Solving problems is like putting a jigsaw puzzle together. You start with total chaos, find something that fits, and gradually work outward. You realize it's going to take time and a lot of trial and error. (So did the history of math and science.) Enjoy the process and don't worry about the outcome: patient effort will always be rewarded.

5. **Be systematic.** Have a strategy in mind when solving problems. Write out the steps. Strategic planning works well in math and science. Your goal, for example, might be to "solve for *x*." Your objectives are the steps of an experiment or the calculations you will need to perform. The resources at your disposal are your lab materials or, in math or physics, the givens and formulas (and a calculator). And the correct answer or desired outcome is your indicator of success.

6. **Get organized.** Reorganize your notes after each class. Write unfamiliar terms, symbols, formulas, theorems, proofs, procedures, and scientific laws on the front of a 3" x 5" card, with definitions, examples, and illustrations on the back.

7. **Study your errors.** Make sure you understand the kinds of errors you make most frequently and note patterns that emerge. Did you fail to understand a concept? Did you understand the concept but apply it incorrectly? Are you making careless calculation errors? Once you see a pattern of error, devise a strategy to change it.

8. **Get help.** If you're having trouble, get help immediately. Make an appointment with your instructor to go over your homework and tests, visit the math clinic, find a study partner, enlist a tutor, or all of the above.

Tips

Preparing for Tests

1. Anticipate the testing format of a class before you enroll. Check class capacity: the larger the class, the more likely the tests will consist of objective questions, because these are easier to grade than essays. If you prefer essay exams over objective, for instance, enroll in a small class instead of one with more than 100 people.

2. Most instructors keep old tests in files in their offices and may offer the class a chance to look them over. Some student organizations, especially fraternities and sororities, keep similar files. Some professors who pride themselves on never using the same test twice keep old tests on file in the library. Some hand out exam study guides or offer test review sessions. Always ask.

3. If you've been given no hint on the format of the first exam, think about the format of the course so far. Have the lectures consisted mostly of information (objective test) or the instructor's interpretation of that information (essay test)? If you've spent more class time in *discussion* than in *lecture*, essay questions are more likely than are objective questions. On a well-constructed test, the number of questions about a topic will be proportional to the class time spent on that topic.

4. If you have no idea what the instructor is likely to ask, make up your own test. Go over your reading and notes and make up a set of reasonable questions, as if you were testing someone else on the material. Ask a classmate to do the same; then see if you can answer each other's questions. If time permits, outline sample essay answers. If the lectures have been largely anecdotes, digressions, and tangents, you may want to spend more time studying your textbook than your notes. Show your sample test to your instructor and ask for a critique and suggestions.

5. A week to ten days before the test, ask your instructor what to expect: What is the test format? What will it cover? How long will it take? How much does it count toward the final grade? Ask also what you may bring to class on test day (calculator, bluebook, dictionary) and what materials—pen versus pencil, paper versus bluebook—your instructor prefers. Will the instructor be handing out a study guide?

6. One week before the test, make a study schedule. Write in your exam dates and then work backward, filling in specific hours with specific study tasks. Dig out supplies for the test: bluebook (an inexpensive booklet filled with lined pages, available at the bookstore), scratch paper, dictionary, calculator (with extra battery), extra pen or pencil, wristwatch.

7. Study your first test in a class to prepare for the second, and so on. "Unit" exams, in any given class, tend to be similar in language and format. A thorough review of your first exam may, in fact, be your best preparation for the second.

a small study group, or you may wish to arrange a group study session yourself. Group study is a good opportunity to recite ideas and facts out loud, which will help you remember. Other students may have heard or read something you missed or may possess a particular skill that you lack.

Cramming

Cramming won't be necessary if you have been following the study suggestions in this book. If not, you may be reduced to a cram session. Cramming is probably better than not studying at all, but not by much. The old saying "Easy come, easy go" applies to cramming: five minutes after the exam, everything you've memorized will fly out of your mind. You'll be utterly wasted the next day and probably won't remember much. Cramming increases test anxiety too. If you've been keeping up, it's better to get an extra hour of sleep before a big test than an extra hour of studying. If you haven't been keeping up, it won't matter anyway.

Tips

Forming an Effective Study Group

- Keep the group small (three to five people).
- Choose people you respect, who are serious about learning, and who will make a positive contribution to the group.
- Meet in a location that promises minimal distractions.
- Divide up the workload in advance, so that each person comes prepared to serve as "expert commentator" on some aspect of the material.
- Agree in advance on an objective and a time limit.
- Elect or assign one group member to be your "task director." If group work gets sidetracked, this person has vested authority to steer the group back to task.
- Allow some time after the group disbands to review the material on your own.
- Make your own private, independent judgment about what is important. Your classmates can help you learn, but you are ultimately responsible for your learning.

Cramming for a test can leave you feeling wasted on test day.

If you have to cram, be smart about it. Skim your textbook assignments and whatever notes you've taken. Then **prioritize the material** into categories of importance and study the most important first. Make study sheets as you go. Get into a rhythm of "write and recite." As you commit material to memory, gradually cover up more and more of your notes until all have been transferred to your long-term memory. If time permits, move on to the second category of importance and do the same. Read from your study sheets aloud into a tape recorder; then listen to the recording as you rest your eyes.

Get as much sleep as you can. Leave yourself at least an hour before the exam to check your memory against your study sheets.

TAKING TESTS

Tests have much the same importance to a student that scheduled competitions have to an athlete. The primary goal of an athlete is the perfection of his or her athletic talent. A golf tournament, tennis match, or football game is a periodic means of measuring just how much progress the athlete has made. It's the same with tests and grades. Their importance is secondary to learning, which is the real reason for going to college. But they are important nevertheless. **Tests and grades give us feedback.** They let us know how far we've come and how far we still need to go.

There is so much to remember when taking a test that some students forget the two most important things:

1. Put your name on your test.
2. Read the directions.

Listen carefully at the beginning of the exam session to spoken instructions as well. Sometimes these are different from the printed instructions on the test.

The third important rule is to **look over the entire test before you begin**. Note choices available to you (for example, "choose either A or B" or "answer 5 out of 8 questions"). Estimate the amount of time you have in relation to the number of questions and the point value assigned to each. (This is where the wristwatch suggested on page 159 will come in handy.) Avoid the major error of spending half your time on an essay question worth only 10 points out of a possible 100. Then **budget your time** accordingly. Take all the time allowed. If there's still time left when you've finished, proofread your test carefully using the dictionary you brought with you (see page 159) for this purpose.

Objective Test Skills

Many students prefer objective tests because they think they are easier and less susceptible to the subjective bias of the grader. But a well-constructed objective question can be difficult. To do well on an objective test, you need to read all questions and alternative answers carefully, proceed with deliberate speed, and use logic.

On objective tests, read all the questions and **answer the ones you know the answers to first**. This helps you roll up points and builds confidence. Make a small check mark next to the questions you must come back to. This will serve as a warmup and also as a review, because one test question may help you answer another.

As you review your test, make sure you have a strong rationale for changing an answer. Studies conflict about the advisability of changing test answers. In other words, proceed with caution, and don't assume the instructor is asking a "trick question." Most test questions are straightforward, and it is unwise to overinterpret them.

Remember: Instructors want you to do well. If a question seems "too easy," that probably just means you know the answer.

Multiple Choice On a multiple choice section, make sure you understand whether only one or more than one correct answer is possible. If you're using computer-graded answer sheets, there will be only one correct (or best) answer. A good multiple-choice question usually has four or five alternatives: one is correct, two or three are tempting decoys but still incorrect, and one is obviously incorrect.

Before reading the alternatives, look away from the test and **think of the answer**. Then try to find it among the alternatives. If you don't, use the process of elimination. Cross out the obviously wrong answers and see what's left. When more than one of those seem correct, pick the one that best answers the question or completes the sentence. It sometimes helps to read the question with each answer separately and treat each statement as a true/false question. If all seem correct or none seem correct, look for d (All of the above), or e (None of the above).

Be wary with "None of the above" as an option, however. From the test writer's point of view, it is difficult to create *one* plausible wrong response, let alone several. The easiest test question and response to write is one the

On Your Own

Erase to Remember

One way to memorize something for a test is to write it out completely in pencil and then progressively erase words as you commit them to memory. The illustration below shows four stages of erasures in the process of memorizing the Preamble to the Constitution of the United States. Find a short passage from the text or a detailed section of your notes from a lecture class and try this technique yourself.

We, the people of the United States, in
order
to form a more perfect union, establish
justice, insure domestic tranquillity, provide
for the common defense, promote the
general welfare, and secure the blessings of
liberty
to ourselves and our posterity, do ordain
and establish this Constitution for the United
States of America.

1

We, the people of the , in
order
to form a more perfect union, establish
justice, insure domestic tranquillity, provide
for the common defense, promote the
general welfare, and secure the blessings of
liberty
to ourselves and our posterity, do ordain
and establish this for the
of

2

We, the of the , in
order
to form a more perfect , establish
, insure domestic tranquillity, provide
for the common , promote the
general , and secure the blessings of

to ourselves and our , do ordain
and establish this for the
of

3

We, the , in
order
, est
ins prov
prom
and sec
do ord
estab

4

writer believes to be true. Ditto with true/false questions: it is easier to write a *true* statement than a *plausible false* one. Moreover, the correct test response option is often the longest or most inclusive. For this reason, "All of the above" is more frequently correct than "None of the above."

On Your Own

Following Directions

Before you begin to write, read all ten of the directions below slowly and carefully.

1. Write your name here. ____________________
2. Add 2 and 3 and write the answer here. ________
3. Draw a circle around your answer.
4. Multiply that answer by 2; write the product here. ________
5. Subtract 2 from the last answer and write it here. ________
6. Divide the last answer by 4; write the answer here. ________
7. Add 10 and write it here. ________
8. Multiply by 3 and write it here. ________
9. Subtract 10 and write the answer here. ________
10. Subtract 1 from 2, place it in the first blank, and do not complete any of the other nine items above.

Now follow the instructions in number 10.

Finished? If you followed directions, the number 1—not your name—should appear in the first blank.

On Your Own

Budgeting Your Time on Tests

You have 50 minutes to complete the following test. How much time should you spend on each part?

		Minutes
I.	True/false (10 pts)	________
II.	Multiple choice (15 pts)	________
III.	Fill in the blank (5 pts)	________
IV.	Matching (20 pts)	________
V.	Essay (50 pts)	________

Did you leave yourself any time to go over your test and correct mistakes?

Logic is a useful skill on multiple-choice questions. Consider this example:

Which of the following cities are located in Iraq?

a. Basra
b. Nasireyeh
c. Baghdad
d. All of these
e. None of these

The word "are" tips you off that there may be more than one correct answer. But logic can also help you if you are sure, for example, that Basra and Baghdad are in Iraq, but are unsure about Nasireyeh. Logic tells you that if there are two correct answers, the third is also correct; therefore, you should select d (All of these).

Unless you're being penalized for wrong answers, answer all multiple-choice questions, because you then have at least a 20 percent chance of guessing correctly.

True/False On true/false questions, remember: if a statement is not completely true, it is false. If a statement is not completely false, it is still false.

T/F

____ The Treaty of Versailles was signed by Woodrow Wilson and David Letterman, the King of France.

Read test questions carefully before choosing your answer.

If guessing is not penalized, be sure to answer all true/false questions, because you then have a 50–50 chance of guessing correctly. Those would be favorable odds, except that instructors are smart. One way of complicating a statement is to devise compound and complex sentences, parts of which are false and other parts true. Another way to make a true/false question difficult is to include qualifiers like *all, most, some, no, always, usually, sometimes,* and *never.*

How do the qualifiers *all, most, some,* and *no* affect the truth value of these statements?

T/F

____ a. All trees are deciduous.

____ b. Most trees are deciduous.

____ c. Some trees are deciduous.

____ d. No trees are deciduous.

Even if you don't know what *deciduous* means, which statements are most likely to be false? Can b and c both be true?

Is it logically possible that all four statements are true? The first three statements?

Watch out for double negatives, which cancel each other out:

T/F

____ It is not the case that Rasputin never influenced the decisions of the Tsar.

Cheating

Integrity is important in all walks of life. Academic integrity means taking responsibility for your own work. Academic dishonesty generally takes the form of cheating or plagiarism (copying someone else's original work). Those who cheat or plagiarize are intentionally and falsely representing someone else's work as their own.

Although students who cheat usually think of it as a misdemeanor, most students and faculty consider it a felony. The penalty for cheating on a test lies entirely in the hands of the instructor and may range from being asked to take a new (usually more difficult) test, to receiving a failing grade for the quiz or exam or course, to probation or suspension from college. Cheating in the public sector can have equally or more serious consequences—lawsuits, heavy fines, and even imprisonment. Theft of intellectual property is a crime.

Cheating on a test often involves referring to concealed notes or copying from a neighbor's test. But it's also important to avoid the *appearance* of cheating on a test. If you seem to be cheating, it may come down to your instructor's word against yours. Always keep your eyes on your own test and keep it concealed from prying eyes. Leave your study notes and books in your book bag, out of sight. If you leave to go to the bathroom, avoid chatting with people en route. As suggested on page 159, wear a watch and bring an extra pencil so you won't have to ask the person next to you. If someone talks to you during a test, don't feel obligated to respond.

Eliminating the two negatives (not . . . never) leaves you with

T/F

____ Rasputin [sometimes] influenced the decisions of the Tsar.

Here's an even tougher one, which you'll never be asked except by a diabolical philosophy instructor:

T/F

____ All generalizations are false including this one.

If you get confused, or if you simply don't know the answer, remember that sweeping generalizations containing words like *all, always, never,* and *none* are almost always false; if they are true, they are likely to be trivial and obvious. For the same reason, statements containing qualifiers such as *sometimes, generally, in most cases, probably,* and *seldom* tend to be true.

Q. What's the fastest way to make a true statement false?

A. Add the word *not.*

Read true/false questions carefully—and watch for *not*s!

Analogies Although true/false and multiple-choice are the most common types of objective test questions, there are others. Analogies, for example, test your ability to see relationships, like this:

A penny is to a nickel what a:
a. nickel is to a quarter.
b. dock is to a lake.
c. child is to an adult.
d. tee is to a golfer.
e. dime is to a nickel.

What is the relationship between a penny and a nickel? Think about the similarities and differences between the two. Then do the same with the possible answers. First, a penny and a nickel are both coins (two of the answers have to do with coins). One is smaller than the other (but that's true of all the answers and "all of these" is not one of the choices). No meaningful similarities come to mind between a penny and a dock, child, or golf tee, or between a nickel and a lake, adult, or golfer. So a and e are the most likely to be correct. Which is better? Why?

Essay question: What is the most serious problem facing today's youth—ignorance or apathy?

Classic response: I don't know and I don't care.

Matching, Fill-In, Define/Identify/Describe, Listing These are useful formats when the instructor wants you to remember lots of terms, names, places, and dates. In a *matching* section, check to see if each column has the same number of items. Then scan both columns quickly. Begin with item number 1 in the left column and look through all the options in the right column to find a match. At first, match only those items you're sure of and cross off the matching item in the right column. Continue this process of elimination. Guessing is dangerous, because one wrong answer at the beginning can trigger a long chain of wrong answers.

Fill-in-the-blank and *define/identify/describe* questions are often considered more difficult than true/false or multiple-choice questions because guessing is not a profitable option.

With *fill-in-the-blank* sections, read the entire passage first; often it will contain clues that will help you recall an answer. Sometimes the length of the blank will betray the length of the desired answer. The article *a* or *an* may signal a word beginning with a consonant or a vowel; a verb form may tell you whether the word you're looking for is singular or plural.

When you *define* or *identify* an item, say just enough to distinguish it from all other items in the same category. For example, identify Zola as "the author of *Nana*," not simply as "a French writer." If you're asked to *describe* something, your instructor may be looking for as much information as you can muster. To describe, say everything that comes to mind and that time permits.

If you are asked to *list* things, your instructor probably prefers very brief answers. Unless you are asked to explain or discuss the items, the following should suffice:

What Instructors Look For

Objective tests are not foolproof. There may be flaws in their construction, although time spent looking for flaws would be better spent in careful consideration of the content. Nonetheless, when you are truly stumped, remember what follows. On a poorly constructed test, the correct answer will generally

- be longer than the incorrect options.
- be qualified to give it precision.
- not be the first or the last option.
- not be one of the extremes in a set of options.
- be one of two similar—or opposing—options.
- be in a sentence bearing familiar phrasing.
- not contain language or technical terms that you have not heard.
- not be a joke or an insult.

Never resort to these clues when you have better reason to select an answer.

List five movements in the history of art between 1870–1920:

1. impressionism
2. futurism
3. surrealism
4. dada
5. northern expressionism

Say just enough to show you know the material.

Essay Test Skills

On objective tests, you either get it right or you don't. Evaluating essay answers is more subjective—good, better, best. Before grading an essay test, instructors usually read several essay answers to get a feeling for the range of quality. Contesting a grade on an essay test is usually futile, because the grade represents the instructor's honest opinion of your work. Another instructor might have graded it higher or lower.

Bring plenty of paper (or an extra bluebook) for essay exams, use large margins, write on one side of the page only, and leave a blank page at the end so the instructor has room to write comments. Bring an extra pen or pencil. If the clock is in the back of the room or nonexistent, bring a watch. Finally, if permitted, bring a dictionary. Here are some things most instructors look for when grading essay tests:

- `Did the student understand the question and answer it completely?
- Is the answer well organized, coherent, logical?
- Are generalizations adequately supported by facts?
- Is this student obviously knowledgeable?
- Is the writing legible and understandable?
- Is the writing mechanically, grammatically, and stylistically correct?

Although neatness is not a stated criterion, studies show that **essays written neatly and legibly earn higher grades**. Similarly, although students are often urged by instructors to disagree with their view, remember that their view is the result of many years of study. If you do disagree with the instructor, plan to provide plenty of convincing factual support for your stance.

Before . . . Read essay questions carefully, underlining key words (the ones that tell you what to do). Make sure you **do exactly what you are asked to do**. Look for direction words like *summarize, list, evaluate, exemplify*, or *trace*.

As suggested on page 159, ask if your instructor prefers you to use pen or pencil, double- or single-spaced written responses, or a bluebook. Adhere to the presentational guidelines given at all times.

Define/Identify. To define or identify requires that you say just enough about an item to distinguish it from all others in its class. To define a chicken as a biped, for example, would fail to distinguish it from a human being. To identify Marie Curie as a Nobel Prize–winning scientist would not distinguish her from her husband, Pierre.

Compare and Contrast. To compare and contrast means to show both similarities and differences between two items. If you only show differences,

Station	Format	Status	On the Air	Special Features
KXOL	Rock and Rap	Commercial	24 hours	Top 40 Countdown
WOMU	Jazz	Listener supported	6 to 11	Talk Net, Jazz Beat

FIGURE 8.1 Compare-and-contrast grid. This grid displays some basic differences between two local radio stations.

On **Your** *Own*

Matching Quiz

Match the essay-direction verb in the left column with the best definition for it in the right column.

_____ analyze	a.	show order of events or progress
_____ trace	b.	support with facts
_____ prove	c.	break into separate ideas
_____ enumerate	d.	explain precisely
_____ state	e.	list ideas, aspects, events, qualities, or reasons

On **Your** *Own*

Write Your Own Midterm

Write what you think would be a fair yet challenging midterm examination for this course. Include at least some objective and some essay questions. When you finish, ask yourself:

- Can the test be completed in the available time?
- Have I included point values for each section?
- Does the test cover all aspects, or at least the most important aspects, of the course?
- How would I grade the test?
- How would I do on it?
- Are any questions too easy or too difficult? Why?

Collaborate

Test Each Other

Write ten true/false questions about testing to quiz comprehension of this chapter. Exchange quizzes with a classmate; then discuss your responses. Place a 1, 2, and 3 next to your three best questions. Submit completed quizzes, with both names affixed, to your instructor.

Collaborate

Test Each Other Again

Make five copies of the sample midterm you created, bring them to class, and share them with your group. Each person should receive copies of everyone else's test.

Discuss the basic similarities and differences among the five tests. Try to agree on which areas of the course have been most important (and are therefore most likely to appear on your real midterm, if one has been scheduled). Whose test is the most difficult? Whose is easiest? Which do you think are the best questions? Discuss how you would answer them.

your answer will only be half right. Because professors are fond of compare-and-contrast questions (which require both knowledge and judgment), make a grid as you study related terms. If, for example, you are asked in a broadcasting class to compare and contrast two local radio stations, your grid might look like the one in Figure 8.1.

During . . . As with the objective portion, skip ahead if you encounter a difficult question. Start with an easy question—the one for which you're best prepared—and save the tough ones for later after you're warmed up.

After you read and understand an essay question, **plan your answer**. This will save you time later and improve the organization of your answer. Make a brief outline on scratch paper (use the extra paper you brought for this purpose). Rapidly empty your brain of all you know about the topic by jotting down facts, names, dates; in other words, transcribe as much of your study sheets as you can remember. If time is short, write down the facts you think you might forget.

Keep introductions and conclusions brief. A good essay answer usually opens with a terse, fairly general topic sentence that answers the question, followed by an orderly array of supporting factual detail. Move quickly from the general to the specific and provide as much of the latter as possible. Instructors dislike padding. The key to a good essay is concrete, specific detail arranged in a logical fashion. Use your "good stuff" first. Provide clear transitions and conclude with a brief summary statement.

For essay exams, your instructor may ask you to write your test in a *bluebook*—a blank test booklet of lined white paper bound in a blue paper cover, cheaply available at the bookstore.

On essay answers it's OK to cross things out, correct spelling, and make last-minute additions. Erasing or whiting out mistakes and false starts is likely a waste of time, however. Just draw a line through any false starts and insert what you intended. Double-space what you write in case you need room later to insert an idea or to enable reader response. Instructors appreciate neat, legible writing (preferably in ink), but you won't have time to completely recopy messy work.

After . . . When you get your test back, go over it carefully to check for grading errors and to see where you did well, and not so well. Try to **figure out where you went wrong and how you might have corrected the problem** by following directions, reading questions more carefully, being

Use your grades—good, bad, or indifferent—as a source of motivation. When you get a good grade, figure out what you did right.

more attentive in class, taking better notes, or studying differently. On essay exams, note any comments the instructor made. Do you understand the comments? Were you marked down because of content or style? Did you say enough to answer the question? Did you misunderstand the question? Was your answer too vague?

Look also at the essay answers your instructor seemed to like and your correct objective answers. Try to recall how you were able to remember the objective answers and how you prepared for the essays. As you prepare for the next test, avoid repeating your mistakes, but also repeat and strengthen the study and testing techniques that proved successful.

Appealing a Grade

If you don't agree with your grade or don't understand why you received it, make an appointment with the instructor as soon as possible. (Be sure to bring the exam with you to the appointment.) Keep in mind that your test grade reflects only what you wrote on the test; it is not a reflection on how hard you worked, your study habits, your comprehension of the material, or your character. Be polite. Arguing, complaining, and criticizing will only antagonize your instructor. Unless an obvious grading error has occurred, **go in with the purpose of finding ways to improve your performance** on the next test, not getting the instructor to change the grade. Instructors are quite willing to correct an inadvertent error, but most resent vague or unsupported accusations of "unfairness."

Keep all quizzes, exams, and papers returned to you in a file. (Final exams and term papers are not usually returned unless you make a special arrangement with the instructor.) If there's a problem with your final grade, you'll have evidence to back you up.

MANAGING TEST ANXIETY

Nothing in life is to be feared; it is only to be understood.

Marie Curie
French chemist

Even the best students get nervous before and during a test. It's normal. If you can keep your jitters under control, they can even help you by keeping you alert and giving you an extra burst of energy.

Test anxiety, however, is nervousness that has gotten out of control. You hyperventilate, your hands get cold and clammy, you break into a cold

Irrational Progression

Some people spend their test preparation time worrying about the consequences of not studying rather than actually studying. They indulge in a self-destructive pattern of thinking known as "irrational progression," which is based on either/or thinking. For every desired outcome there is a "dreadful alternative"—and nothing in between.

Irrational progression goes like this:

If I can't remember the bones in the foot, I'll lose a lot of points on my anatomy midterm.

If I lose a lot of points, I'll probably fail the test.

If I fail the test, I'll fail the course.

If I fail the course, I'll never get into med school.

If I don't get into med school, my father will kill me.

Therefore, if I can't remember the bones in the foot, I will die.

It's hard to study when you've got a noose around your neck.

The cure for irrational progression is common sense and positive thinking:

If I can recall the major bones in the foot, I should do pretty well on the midterm.

If I do well on the midterm, I'll get at least a B for the course.

If I get at least a B for the course, I should do well in the premed program.

If I do well in the program, I'll be qualified for lots of satisfying careers.

Therefore, I will now turn my attention to the bones of the foot.

If you have to eat a toad, don't stare at it for too long.

African proverb

sweat. When you first look at the test, everything looks foreign to you. You blank out.

Test anxiety is a serious problem. For very severe test anxiety, or phobia, seek a professional ear. Many colleges have staff psychologists and counselors whose services are available to you, often at no cost (or already paid for in your student fees).

Those who experience test anxiety often have poor study skills, resulting in a long personal history of failure on tests. You can't change your personal history, but you can change your study habits. The past is gone. **Start a new history** today—a history of success. As you pile up one success after another, your test anxiety will decrease to a manageable level. With time, you may find yourself actually looking forward to tests because they offer the chance for yet another success.

Tips

Curbing Test Anxiety

Next time you're worried about a test, review these tips:

- Candidly identify each of your negative thoughts and repudiate them, one by one.
- Replace each negative thought with a positive one: "I have the feeling I'm going to do really well on this test. I've been practicing good study skills. I've attended class regularly. I've stayed alert, taken good notes, and reviewed after each class. I'm well prepared. I feel rested and confident."
- Arrive for the test early. Use the extra time for review.
- Get a good seat up front, where you won't be distracted by others.
- Don't sit next to a friend.
- Avoid talking to classmates before a test. Somebody might throw you for a loop by mentioning some "major" idea you thought was quite minor and didn't spend much time on.
- Scan the entire test. Carefully read all instructions and time limits and decide how much time you'll need to complete each section.
- When you start feeling anxious during the test, stop everything. Put your pencil down, cover your eyes, breathe slowly and deeply, move around a bit in your chair, and get in touch with your body. When you are calm and focused, pick up the pencil again.
- If you run into a mysterious question, skip it and move to something more familiar.
- If you're still stumped later by the same question, ask the instructor what it means. Most instructors are happy to help you "prime the pump" to get you going. They want you to do well.
- Mark up the test questions with your pencil. Circle key words. Make brief notes in the margin about things you remember.
- Use the entire time allotted—don't leave early!
- Get active! Get moving!

SUMMARY

Test anxiety, as well as the time you spend preparing for tests, will be substantially reduced by active listening and note taking in class, followed by a brief review within 24 hours. Prepare for tests by condensing the material into a portable, manageable format and by predicting and answering likely test questions. Review periodically. During the test, read directions carefully, noting time limits and point values. Begin with the questions for which you feel most prepared. Relax.

As you get into the test, you will remember more and more and can go back and answer questions you left blank. Take time to organize your thoughts before you answer an essay question. If you need clarification (of vocabulary, or directions), ask your instructor. If time permits, go over your test to correct wrong answers, improve your writing, and review presentation.

Strategic *Plan*

Look over your Self-Assessment at the beginning of the chapter and identify an area in which you'd like to make a change. Then develop a Strategic Plan, using the format below.

I. Situation analysis

A. One problem I'm having with tests is ______________________________

____

B. One change I think I could make is ______________________________

____

C. The benefits of making the change are ______________________________

____

D. The consequences of not changing are ______________________________

____

E. Some obstacles I'll have to overcome are ______________________________

____

F. Some resources I'll need are ______________________________

____

II. Goals, objectives, deadlines, and indicators

A. My goal is to ______________________________

____

Deadline: ______________________________

Indicators of success: ______________________________

B. Here's what I'm going to do to achieve my goal, along with a reasonable deadline for each task:

	Objective	Deadline
1.	______________________	____________
2.	______________________	____________
3.	______________________	____________
4.	______________________	____________
5.	______________________	____________

III. Self-test

YES	NO	
☐	☐	**A.** Are my goals and objectives stated simply and clearly?
☐	☐	**B.** Does each one have a single focus?
☐	☐	**C.** Are they stated in a positive way?
☐	☐	**D.** Are they realistic?
☐	☐	**E.** Can I achieve them by the deadline?
☐	☐	**F.** Will I know if I've achieved them?

Journal **Ideas**

1. Have you had a history of success or failure on tests? How do you account for this pattern?
2. Describe your usual method of preparing for tests. Do you think it's a good one? Has it worked for you? What would you like to change about it? How might you make these changes?
3. Do you prefer essay or objective tests? Why?
4. What kinds of mistakes do you make most often on tests? What could you do differently to eliminate these mistakes?
5. Do you suffer from "test anxiety"? What techniques to combat test stress have you tried, or might you try?
6. Discuss your attitudes about tests and grades. Are they necessary? For whom, and why or why not? What do tests and grades do for us? Describe your favorite—and least favorite—method of being tested.

Web **Search**

To be admitted to college, you may have taken the SAT (Scholastic Aptitude Test), which is sponsored by the College Board. Check out College Board's "Test Taking Tips for the SAT" at

www.collegeboard.org/sat/html/students/prep002.html

Which tips are specific to the SAT? Which are helpful for other tests as well? Next, check out the Kaplan Educational Center's "Top 10 Test-Day Tips" at

www.kaplan.com/precoll/SAT_ACT_tips.html

Which of these tips could you use on your next major test?

Think of three more test-taking tips you might offer to your fellow students based on your own test-taking experience.

College After Class

Self-Assessment

Check the statements that apply to you.

☐ **1.** I'm getting along well with my roommate/housemates.

☐ **2.** I share my concerns with my roommate/housemates openly and freely.

☐ **3.** I have adequate privacy.

☐ **4.** My interpersonal skills are strong.

☐ **5.** I'm thinking about pledging a fraternity/sorority.

☐ **6.** I'm thinking about renting my own apartment.

☐ **7.** Commuting causes few problems for me that I am unable to resolve.

☐ **8.** I get adequate support from home.

☐ **9.** I'm getting involved in campus life and keeping up in class.

☐ **10.** I am able to occupy my time purposefully.

If you checked fewer than half, this chapter will be especially valuable to you.

Write **Before** *You Read*

A. Spend about a minute surveying this chapter. Then write three questions you expect to find answers to in this chapter.

1. ____________________

2. ____________________

3. ____________________

B. Spend another minute writing down any thoughts that come to mind about the topics below. Write freely and rapidly.

1. My living arrangements: ____________________

2. Dealing with conflict: ____________________

3. Getting involved in campus life: ____________________

PREVIEW

Most college students don't have much choice about where they live while in school; it's a matter of economic or personal necessity. If more than one option is available to you—an apartment on or off campus, a rooming house, a fraternity or sorority, commuting from home—you will need to make an informed choice. Many college students live in close quarters with at least one other person in a more or less constant state of tension. Although this can lead to conflict, it can also be an opportunity to develop strong, lasting friendships and valuable interpersonal skills. Involvement in cocurricular activities on campus will make you a better student because you'll learn a sense of ownership and responsibility. And the busier you are, the better. You'll need to use every free minute to its best advantage.

COMMUTING

Almost all college students in the world commute except in the United States, where the residential pattern was established during the colonial period after certain European universities that catered to male aristocrats. Until the twentieth century, most American college students grew up on farms far from the city and had to travel long distances to attend college; commuting was rarely an option.

That pattern has changed today. With over 3,500 colleges and universities in the United States, nearly everyone lives within commuting distance of one of them. A majority of American college students spend a good portion of their day traveling to and from campus by car, bus, subway, motorcycle, or bicycle.

Some are commuters by choice. They enjoy the company of family and friends and consider home a safe and comfortable harbor where they can drop anchor after a hard day at school. They have as much freedom and privacy as they want. The food is great, the price is right. Some even enjoy the daily commute itself and see it as a chance to meditate, mentally review assignments, or think through an assigned paper topic.

More often, students who commute do so because of financial necessity or family commitments. They just don't have much choice. The major drawbacks for commuters are transportation problems, academic barriers, and family pressures.

Table 9.1 shows the most common challenges faced by commuters and some strategies for dealing with them.

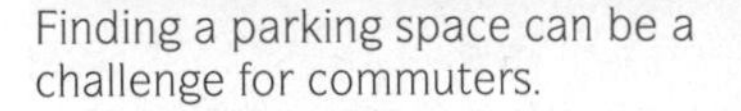
Finding a parking space can be a challenge for commuters.

RESIDENCE HALL LIVING

Residential colleges usually require first-year students to live in residence halls. Because **a residence hall provides a fairly structured existence while offering a good deal of personal freedom**, it's a nice transition from the stifling rules of adolescence to the dizzying freedom of adulthood. There are rules (quiet hours, no drinking if you're not legal age and then only in your room)—but there is freedom, too. You can have visitors in your

> Everything in life is somewhere else, and you get there in a car.
>
> E. B. White
> *Author*

> Ya got ta *go* there ta *know* there.
>
> Zora Neale Hurston
> *Author/anthropologist*

room with the door locked. There are no "lights out" rules or bed checks. You can decorate your room more or less as you please and be as messy as your roommate will allow.

A residence hall is also a good place to make new friends through study groups, games, contests, dances, talent shows, and special programs in the lounge. There are trained staff down the hall who can help you with a problem, work with you to plan programs and parties, invite faculty over, and make you aware of useful information. Most residence halls are within walking distance of classes, cafeterias, and student services, so you feel part of what's going on. And despite the distractions of institutional living, studies show that residential students not only have higher GPAs than those who live in apartments, but also a much lower dropout rate.

Not all residential students are teenagers. I knew a woman in her late 30s who lived in the residence hall for four years. Happily married, the mother of four teenage daughters, she spent four days a week on campus and the other

Challenge	Strategies
Transportation. Some commuting students spend as much as two hours a day on the road, fighting bad weather, subway strikes, and rush-hour traffic. When they do arrive on campus, there is the daily struggle to find parking space, which is usually inadequate and expensive.	Carpooling is a way of sharing costs and driving burdens and alleviating the pressure on limited parking space. You can study en route or converse with other commuting students. On the other hand, you lose your freedom to come and go as you like. In urban areas, public transportation is another solution, but it may be crowded and the schedules inconvenient.
Academic barriers. It's often difficult to create a schedule that avoids large gaps between classes. Many campuses lack commuter lounges and other convenient places to study. Commuters often miss important announcements that are communicated routinely in the residence halls. They feel cut off from what's happening and have a hard time following class discussions of campus issues. They miss the parties, bull sessions, and study groups that allow the free exchange of ideas so important to learning. Returning to campus for evening and weekend events is nearly impossible.	Buy a meal pass and get to know some residential students at lunch. Keep abreast of campus issues by reading the student newspaper. Adopt a residence hall (most offer free access in the daytime). You can use the lounge for studying and meeting people. Take advantage of campus events scheduled during the daytime (usually late afternoon) and leave early if you must. Find out if your campus has a commuter lounge where you can meet people with similar concerns. Join a club or organization that meets in the late afternoon. If you drive, resist getting locked into a habitual arrival and departure time. If you can manage it, reserve one evening a week to have supper on campus and attend an evening event.
Family pressures. Depending on the support system at home, the commuter's family may be a lodestone or a millstone—a comforting buffer or just another source of stress. At home there is pressure to do chores, be home by a certain time, fulfill traditional roles.	Hold regular family meetings in which all get a chance to express needs and expectations. Help your family understand what your life is like when you're away at school. Tell them exactly what you can and cannot do. Accept the fact that you can't be all things to all people. Accept the fact that your decision to remain at home while attending college requires a commitment to the people you live with, just as you would have certain responsibilities to a roommate.

TABLE 9.1 Commuter Challenges and Strategies

three at her home (four miles away). She joined clubs, held office in several organizations, participated in all-nighters—in short, did all the things traditional-age residential college students do. After graduation from high school, she had married and then worked to support her husband's education. Now that her children were older, she felt her turn had come to get a total college experience—and she wasn't going to miss a thing.

Friendships sometimes collapse under the pressure of close quarters.

Getting Along with a Roommate

Housing experts don't recommend rooming with your best friend from high school. Such friendships often collapse under the pressure of living in close quarters. As the old saying goes, "Familiarity breeds contempt." Ironically, some of the more successful roommate relationships result from carefully constructed and mutually respected barriers.

Roommates don't have to become friends. They don't have to go everywhere together or bare their souls to each other. They do have to be tolerant of each other and respect each other's rights.

If you and your roommate have a problem, **talk it over right away** (it won't go away and could get worse). In fact, why wait for a problem to come up? Go out for ice cream and have a candid discussion of your

Tips

For Car Commuters Only

1. If you lock yourself out of your car or your car won't start, call the campus police instead of a locksmith or a towing service. They have jumper cables and other equipment to get you back on the road, free.
2. Searching for the ideal parking spot or waiting at the gate for someone to leave wastes time and fuel. Take the spot on the outskirts of campus that you know is available and accept the ten-minute walk, or shuttle wait that comes with it.
3. Anticipate bad weather, traffic problems, and breakdowns by stocking your car with an umbrella, extra clothing, jumper cables, flares, sand, scraper, washer fluid, flashlight, de-icer, extra key (in a magnetized case attached to the exterior of your car), and a granola bar.

A Roommate's Bill of Rights

- Reasonable undisturbed study time.
- Reasonable undisturbed sleep time.
- Respect for personal possessions.
- A reasonably clean, healthful environment.
- Free access at all times to the building and room.
- Personal privacy.
- Guests who respect a roommate's rights.
- Reasonable use of shared equipment, such as the phone, mirror, lights, and windows.
- Freedom from physical and emotional assault.
- Self-expression free from guilt or intimidation.

Collaborate

Negotiating Roommate Issues

Figure 9.1 is a questionnaire you and your roommate can take turns reading to one another, to see how you stand on issues that could become sources of conflict. Have your roommate number 1–25 on a blank sheet of paper, then respond to each question on a scale of one to ten as you read it. Score 1 as "strongly agree," 5 "neither agree nor disagree," and 10 "strongly disagree." Compare and discuss your responses after you have both completed the questionnaire. Identify areas of significant agreement and disagreement. Discuss your feelings and negotiate some rules. If you like, write out a set of rules you both sign and date (you can always change them later).

My husband and I have figured out a really good system about the housework. Neither one of us does it.

Dottie Archibald
Writer

preferences, habits, and mutual expectations. Use Figure 9.1 as a guideline for your discussion as described in the "Collaborate" box above.

If you disagree on a lot of things, arrange another meeting a day or two later to negotiate a set of rules you can both live with.

Here are some potential trouble spots to anticipate and negotiate in advance:

1. ***Guests in the room.*** Some roommates have an arrangement that works something like this: a shoelace hanging on the outside doorknob means knock three times and then disappear for at least fifteen minutes, by which time the door is to be unlocked and the shoelace removed. You can come to some similar agreement.

2. ***Respect for personal property.*** Let your roommate know what you are willing to share (your refrigerator, your dictionary, the care and feeding of your boa constrictor) and what you're not willing to

1. Cleanliness and personal hygiene are very important.
2. I have strong feelings about furniture arrangement and decoration.
3. I like to get up early.
4. I go to bed late.
5. I need lots of privacy.
6. I study a lot.
7. I party a lot.
8. Radio/TV noise bothers me.
9. I'd like to have overnight guests sometimes.
10. I'd like to entertain visitors in the room.
11. You are welcome to borrow anything of mine.
12. You have some things I'd like to borrow.
13. There are some things I'd like to buy for the room if you're willing to share costs.
14. I'm good about leaving messages.
15. A smoke-free atmosphere is important to me.
16. An alcohol-free atmosphere is important to me.
17. I don't like profanity.
18. There are some issues I'm not willing to negotiate.
19. I think we have very similar values.
20. I'm depressed a lot.
21. It's hard for me to share my feelings.
22. I worry about having enough time to do all I need to do.
23. I worry about money.
24. I miss my family.
25. I think you'll be easy to get along with.

FIGURE 9.1 Roommate Questionnaire

share (drugstore supplies, the food in your fridge, your term paper). If you find your property is being borrowed without your knowledge and not returned, share your concerns with a resident adviser. Pay shared bills (such as telephone bills) and pass along all messages promptly.

3. ***Personal habits.*** Most couples are odd couples: a morning person and a night person, a grade grind and a party animal, a neat freak and a slob. The problem is what happens next. Couples begin to label each other ("You're such a slob!" "You're a neat freak!"), which makes the problem worse. The neat person begins to illustrate neatness at every opportunity, as if to teach a moral lesson. The slob demonstrates independence of spirit by becoming even sloppier. It's a vicious circle. Best to practice the Golden Rule: be tolerant, tactful, and considerate, and you're likely to get the same treatment.

If the rules don't work, **renegotiate**. (People change a lot during their first year of college. You may feel differently later on.) **Compromise** on things like furniture arrangements and purchases for the room. The clichés about marriage ("It's give and take" and "The first year is the hardest") apply to roommates, too.

CONFLICT RESOLUTION

The best time to cope with conflict is immediately. Most people put off dealing with a problem until it snowballs into a major crisis. **Serious conflicts start out as small incidents that are easy to ignore.** Your roommate borrows a pair of socks. Later they turn up in her sock drawer. You ignore it. Why get upset about a pair of moldy old sweat socks? Days later, some change is missing from your desk drawer. The next week you can't find your new compact disc. You ask your roommate about it, but you can't even hear her answer because she's wearing your turquoise necklace.

You explode, "You thief! You're robbing me blind! Why can't you respect my stuff?"

Then your roommate, who is harboring a few grudges herself, says "Oh yeah? Who are you to talk about respect, the way you party in the room all night when I'm trying to study!" What started out as shadow boxing ends in a mutual declaration of war.

A verbal argreement isn't worth the paper it's printed on.

Samuel Goldwyn
Film producer

Collaborate

Resolving Conflicts

Get together in a small group and take turns sharing an actual incident involving interpersonal conflict (pseudonyms may be necessary). Briefly describe the incident, the parties involved, and how it was resolved, if at all. How was the solution arrived at? To what extent was each party satisfied with the outcome? If the conflict is still unresolved, what advice would other group members give the two parties in conflict? Record responses.

Collaborate

Negotiate a Solution

With a partner from your small group, choose one of the "potential" roommate conflicts listed in Figure 9.1; then suppose it has achieved its potential. Role playing the parties in dispute, negotiate a solution to this conflict that is acceptable to both, following the guidelines for negotiation given in this chapter. If you generate more than one acceptable solution, select the best and explain why it is better than the others.

On **Your** *Own*

Conflict Can Be Beneficial

Conflict is not always undesirable. Without it, our world would be a dull and dreary place. Conflict is essential to athletic competition, free enterprise, good government, and scientific discovery. In writing, identify, explain, and discuss at least three ways in which conflict can be beneficial.

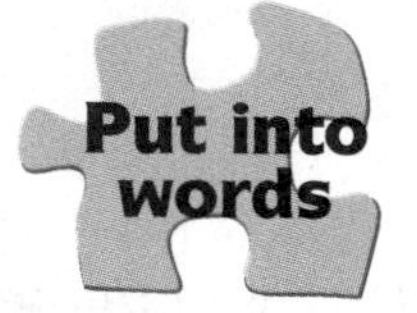

If a problem comes up, address it immediately before it gets worse. You don't have to make a federal case of it. Express yourself in a friendly way and with a sense of humor. Avoid heated accusations by using "I" language rather than "you" language (this is described below). Remember: the person most bothered by a problem has primary responsibility for seeing it resolved. If you don't express yourself, it's your problem. If you do express yourself, it's somebody else's problem. And if you both express yourselves, you're on your way to resolving the conflict.

Whether it's a roommate conflict, a labor dispute, or a feud between countries, the process of conflict resolution has two basic stages: informal attempts at negotiation and a more formal stage of mediation.

Negotiation

Informal negotiation is possible during the early stages of a conflict, when both parties are talking to each other. Here are some guidelines for effective negotiation:

- **Set aside a time** and neutral place where you won't be disturbed.
- **Take turns talking.** Do not interrupt when it isn't your turn.
- **Express your concerns frankly.** Look the other person in the eye. Address specific behaviors rather than attitudes; focus on what the other person *does* rather than on who he or she *is*. Telling the other person how to behave ("You should always return the things you borrow") won't get the results you want; instead, focus on your own feelings by using "I" statements (for example, "I get upset when my things are borrowed and not returned"). Avoid sweeping judgments: "You're always borrowing my things. You never return anything." Try to understand your feelings and explain why you feel strongly about an issue ("I'm paying my own way through college, so the few things

I own are important to me"). It's not necessary to apologize for your feelings—feelings are never right or wrong. You have a right to your feelings as well as a responsibility for them.

- **Listen to the other party.** Resist the impulse to explain or justify your behavior. Your job is to listen and understand, not to agree or disagree. Show by your body language (nodding, leaning forward, making eye contact) that you are making a sincere effort to understand. Repeat back to the person what you think you heard ("So you're saying you don't like my girlfriend?") and give the person a chance to clarify what was said until you understand each other clearly. Remember: you don't have to agree with the other person's opinions or share the same feelings, but you do need to understand and respect them. The best way to do that is to imagine what it's like to be the other person. Put yourself in his or her place.
- **Be willing to compromise.** When one party in a negotiation is passive and the other is assertive or aggressive, there's danger of a "win/lose" solution, which is no solution at all. People don't keep promises made under duress. Only when both parties are satisfied is a solution likely to work. Good solutions require imagination and hard work. Negotiations break down when parties think they have to choose between two solutions, mine or yours. Avoid either/or thinking. There are always lots of alternatives, some better than others. You can take the lead by making an offer ("How about no guests after 11 P.M.?"). If the other party makes an offer you consider unacceptable ("You can use my makeup if I can borrow your clothes"), make a counter offer ("OK, but you have to ask first and I want them returned immediately and in good condition").
- **Keep your agreement.** Make sure the agreement you arrive at is clear and unequivocal. A vague commitment ("I'll try to keep the noise down") is no commitment at all. Good commitments need to be verifiable (that is, you can tell if they've been kept or broken, for example, "I won't play my music after 10 p.m. on weekdays"). If your agreement is so long or complex that parts of it may be forgotten, write it out with dated signatures and a copy for both parties.

Negotiation requires good communication skills on both sides. It is preferable to mediation. When it works, both parties give a little and come out winners.

Mediation

Mediation is necessary when negotiation fails: the parties in the conflict are no longer on speaking terms and emotions are running high. Mediation involves bringing in an objective, outside party with special skills to referee the conflict. The mediator makes the rules. When you agree to mediation, you agree to the rules. Mediation still involves negotiation, but the mediator makes sure both parties have a chance to express themselves; don't fight; listen to each other; and, if possible, reach an acceptable compromise.

Only through successful negotiation can both parties in a conflict come out winners. **You always give up something in the negotiation process,**

Take some time to resolve differences with your roommate.

but you get something too: a good working relationship with the other party, improved communication skills, the satisfaction of having taken responsibility for resolving your own problems. Successful mediation and arbitration leave you with a working agreement of sorts, but you might not be as happy with it. Your communication skills will be no better than they were before, and you have to live with the knowledge that your destiny was taken out of our hands. Tolerating the intolerable takes a toll, too: eventually, you crack. When it is critical to take a stand and defend that stand, do so without apology.

A roommate relationship is not a marriage. If you can't work things out (your roomie's into Satanism, let's say), make an appointment with your residence hall director and request a room change. If you are contemplating such a move, it will help your case to document your roommate's unacceptable behavior in writing as fully and fairly as you can (with dates and specific behaviors) and bring these with you to the meeting.

Good conflict resolution skills are worth cultivating. They will serve you well throughout your life in all interpersonal interactions.

Frats Can Be Fatal

Although it has been seventeen years since 63 national fraternities adopted a resolution outlawing hazing, the practice has not stopped—it has simply gone underground. Between 1983 and 1993, 23 people died as a result of hazing rituals and fraternity-related activities, often euphemized as "pledge training" during "Hell Week."

Causes of death are various and familiar: binge drinking (sometimes forced), induced vomiting, sleep deprivation, abandonment and exposure to the elements on "road trips," paddling, branding, and other forms of physical abuse.

An Indiana University student was struck over 100 times. Another student at Paine College was paralyzed after being struck in the head. Michael Davis, a journalism student at Southeast Missouri State, died of internal bleeding after being kicked, punched, and body slammed by fraternity brothers.

Some students are fighting back. In October 1994, six members of Kappa Alpha Psi at Tennessee State violated an unwritten code by filing suit against their own national fraternity for failing to act against a pattern of violence. And some enlightened fraternity chapters have found more salutary methods of indoctrinating members, through academic competitions, community service projects, and workshops on Greek history and culture.

Greeks sometimes develop strong bonds that last a lifetime.

FRATERNITIES AND SORORITIES

The popularity of Greek life seems to be a barometer of social and political change. Greek life was immensely popular in the Roaring Twenties, dormant during the Depression years, back in vogue in the postwar Eisenhower period, and out of fashion again in the Kennedy era. During the Vietnam War it was cool to crash in pads, not frat houses. The end of the war, a shift to the right with Reagan (an old fraternity brother himself, Tau Kappa Epsilon), and the movie *Animal House* changed all that. Despite (or maybe because of) the outrageous behavior of star John Belushi, *Animal House* made fraternities look like an awful lot of fun. By the end of the 1980s, 62 percent of all first-year students were pledging, an all-time high.

A rash of well-publicized hazing deaths and fraternity-party gang rapes in the early 1980s led universities to crack down on the Greek system. Some campuses banned all fraternal organizations on campus; others created university-owned "Greek rows"—uniform housing units on campus that were leased and more easily supervised. Fraternities responded to this danger by trying to change their image. "Hazing," the practice of harassing and even torturing pledges, has been outlawed. Some frats are trying to educate members about acquaintance rape and substance abuse. They're doing more community service, rewarding academic achievement, and hosting alcohol-free parties and public dialogues on the dangers of alcohol abuse. In 1993, the Sigma Chi chapter at the University of Maine made history by declaring its fraternity house an alcohol-free zone.

Much remains to be done, however. A 1997 nationwide study published by Rutgers University reports that fraternity leaders are among the heaviest drinkers and most out-of-control partygoers. This casts doubt on the utility of working with fraternity leaders to effect meaningful, systemic reform.

For many students, living in a fraternity or sorority house remains an attractive compromise between residence hall and apartment living, a happy combination of privacy and sociability. Members often develop strong bonds, some continuing to meet and interact long after graduation. Many feel **one of the most valuable aspects of Greek life is the support system** of fraternity brothers and sorority sisters nationwide, a network that provides social and business contacts in adult life.

Pledging a fraternity or sorority represents a major time commitment. The pledging process is time-consuming, emotionally taxing, financially draining, and physically exhausting. Your instructors will view your pledge responsibilities as social amusements at best and never as a legitimate excuse for being unprepared or for missing class.

APARTMENTS

Apartments are the home of preference for many college students of traditional age. Students who have moved from a residence hall to their first apartment testify that, for perhaps the first time in their lives, **they feel truly free and truly adult**. You'll be paying your own bills, buying and prepar-

Tips

Buying a Place to Live

Depending on the economy, the real-estate market, your living standards, and your family finances, you may be better off buying a place to live than renting.

Buying makes sense if:

- Your parents have more than one child at the same school who will need a place to live for five years or more (at least five years are necessary to recoup closing costs and sales commissions).
- Student enrollments at the college are stable or rising (this affects whether the unit can be sold at a profit when it is no longer needed).
- The site is within walking distance of campus.
- Monthly carrying costs are comparable to average rental costs.

You can structure the purchase either as a second home or as rental property. The second-home option makes mortgage interest and real estate taxes deductible, although any loss on resale will not be deductible. (No rental income is permitted under this option.)

If you structure the purchase as a rental property, income or loss is treated as passive under the tax code and is therefore deductible for most people. Depreciation and limited travel (for example, visits by parents to campus) are also deductible. The rental property option may be attractive if there are paying roommates.

Under the right set of circumstances, buying can be an appealing option because more pleasant, larger quarters may be had for the same price as a rental unit. Of course, either you or (more likely) a loved one must have enough cash for the down payment and the mortgage and the financial security to accept the risk of resale loss.

Before you and your family take the plunge, review all options carefully with a trusted realtor and your tax accountant.

ing your own food, parking in your own space, sleeping in a room somewhat larger than a closet (with a lock on the door). And you'll be liberated at long last from the germ-ridden air of your residence hall. If you've chosen a roommate to share the cost of food and utilities, you'll perhaps save a few dollars too (but not much more than that, according to studies) over the fixed costs of dining and residence hall contracts.

There's also a downside to apartment living. When you do have a problem, there will be no resident adviser or hall director to help. You'll probably be farther from campus and the services and opportunities it provides. You may not enjoy spending your free time on such routine chores as paying bills and rent, shopping, and fixing meals. You may feel (and be) less safe in an off-campus urban neighborhood than on a well-lit, police-patrolled campus. (Experienced apartment dwellers recommend avoiding ground-floor apartments for security reasons.) When your sewage system backs up for the first time, you may be shocked to learn that your landlord lives in Aruba. At year's end, you may also discover how difficult it can be to recover your damage deposit.

CAMPUS INVOLVEMENT

During the first few weeks of classes, you may feel pressure to join campus organizations. Bulletin boards grow shaggy with announcements of organizational meetings, rush parties, petitions, intramural signups, and membership drives. You'll discover interest groups in amazing variety—for rock climbers, skiers, religious groups, chess players, sci-fi fans, and bands. You'll be introduced to social action groups that will want your help in eliminating toxic waste, planting trees, saving dolphins and rain forests, and bringing about world peace.

Students who get involved on campus do better academically.

Check the temptation to overcommit, especially during your first semester. Make sure you are on solid ground academically before you get overly involved in activities. The first semester of the first year of college is the most difficult semester you are likely to have. Once you feel confident about achieving your academic goals, you can look for meaningful ways to spend your free time.

When you are ready to make some cocurricular commitments, **choose carefully**. It's impossible to maintain in college all the interests you had time for in high school. Something has to give. Choose organizations that might teach you new skills that will be helpful later on: leadership; speaking in front of a group; organizing a meeting; writing plans, proposals, and minutes. If your life has been largely self-interested and you'd like to change that, find a service organization that allows you to make a civic contribution. If you are confident about your major, consider a club or honorary society specific to that discipline—History Club, Physics Club, Accounting Club. This will enable you to learn more, meet others with similar interests, and meet guest speakers and leaders in your field.

Campus involvement is also a way to discover new talents and alternative career directions. If you're a music major but like to write, join the campus newspaper staff to see if you're cut out for journalism. If you're majoring in social work but are interested in politics, run for student government.

Students who become involved in cocurricular activities earn higher grades and are more likely to graduate than those who restrict their

On **Your** *Own*

Interview

Spend about ten minutes interviewing a student who lives in a manner different from your own. For example, if you live on campus, interview someone who commutes. What does he or she like about that lifestyle? What does he or she dislike? Summarize the student's comments in writing. Then share your findings with your group.

On **Your** *Own*

Campus Organizations

Get a list of campus organizations from the Student Affairs or Activities Office. Choose one organization that interests you and find out more about it. Try to answer these questions:

Name of organization ______________________________

1. What is the purpose of the organization? ______________________________

____

2. How long has it existed? ______________________________
3. Who are the officers and faculty advisers? ______________________________

____

4. How many members are there? ______________________________
5. Where and when do they meet? ______________________________
6. Why would someone want to join this organization? ______________________________

____

Share what you learn with your class or small group.

commitment to the classroom. Students who get involved feel a part of their institution. They develop loyalty, ownership, and responsibility for it. They learn more about how it works and meet staff people who can be helpful to them. Above all, involved students are forced to manage their time and use every free minute wisely. As a result, their study periods are usually briefer but far more concentrated and intense. They have an easier time applying what they learn in the classroom to what they encounter in their busy lives. It is, of course, possible to be too busy, but moderately busy people get more done and feel better about their lives than do people who claim to have too much time.

Be genuinely interested

If you do decide to make a commitment to a cocurricular activity, do your best to keep it for a reasonable time. Get involved to learn and grow, not to pad a resume. Job recruiters are not taken in by lists alone. They are likely to say, "I see you were a member of Golden Key Honorary Society. What was the nature of your involvement? Did you hold an office? Did you participate in service activities? Take charge of a fundraiser? What did you learn as a result of that involvement? How did it change you as a person? Always make your commitments to cocurricular activities genuine and sincere.

SUMMARY

The circumstances of your life outside the classroom can have a profound effect on your academic success. Among the options available to college students—each with its own advantages and drawbacks—are living at home, in a residence hall, in an on- or off-campus apartment, or in a fraternity or sorority. Any living situation is a potential source of emotional growth and support and of conflict that can be minimized with effective negotiation. Involvement in campus organizations, though challenging for commuting students, can also greatly enrich your college learning experience.

Strategic *Plan*

Look over your Self-Assessment at the beginning of the chapter and identify an area in which you'd like to make a change. Then develop a Strategic Plan, using the format below.

I. Situation Analysis

A. One problem I'm having with my life outside class is ______________________________

____

B. One change I think I could make is ______________________________

____

C. The benefits of making the change are ______________________________

____

D. The consequences of not changing are ______________________________

____

continued on next page

Strategic *Plan* *continued from previous page*

E. Some obstacles I'll have to overcome are ______________________________

____

F. Some resources I'll need are ______________________________

____

II. Goals, objectives, deadlines, and indicators

A. My goal is to ______________________________

____

Deadline: ______________________________

Indicators of success: ______________________________

____

B. Here's what I'm going to do to achieve my goal, along with a reasonable deadline for each task:

	OBJECTIVE	DEADLINE
1.	______________________	____________
2.	______________________	____________
3.	______________________	____________
4.	______________________	____________
5.	______________________	____________

III. Self-test

YES	NO	
☐	☐	**A.** Are my goals and objectives stated simply and clearly?
☐	☐	**B.** Does each one have a single focus?
☐	☐	**C.** Are they stated in a positive way?
☐	☐	**D.** Are they realistic?
☐	☐	**E.** Can I achieve them by the deadline?
☐	☐	**F.** Will I know if I've achieved them?

Journal **Ideas**

1. Describe your living situation. What do you like about it? What would you change about it if you could?
2. Describe a conflict you recently faced—and resolved—with one other person. How was it resolved? Were both parties satisfied? Explain.
3. Describe your ideal place to live while attending college.
4. If you commute, what kinds of problems has this presented for you? What do you plan to do about them? What advantages to commuting have you found?
5. If you work part-time or are involved with a campus organization, describe your involvement. To what extent does it interfere with your academic success? How has it helped you so far?

Web **Search**

Go to the following site and take the assertiveness test:

www.psychtests.com/cgi-bin/assert.pl

When you finish, hit "send" and you'll receive an evaluation of your assertiveness.

Then click on "continue" to check out the other self-tests at this site.

10

Values, Culture, and Relationships

Self-Assessment

Check the statements that apply to you.

☐ **1.** I expect my values to change while I am in college.

☐ **2.** I usually act in accordance with my beliefs.

☐ **3.** I respect and listen to people with values and beliefs different from my own.

☐ **4.** I have made many new friends since I started college.

☐ **5.** I have friends who come from backgrounds very different from my own.

☐ **6.** I've traveled outside the U.S. and/or studied a second language.

☐ **7.** I believe stereotypes can be dangerous.

☐ **8.** I speak up when I feel that I, or others, have been treated unfairly.

☐ **9.** I practice safe sex and know what to do to protect myself.

☐ **10.** I believe that when someone says "No," he or she really means "No."

If you checked fewer than half, this chapter will be especially valuable for you.

Write **Before** *You Read*

A. Spend about a minute surveying this chapter. Then write three questions you expect to find answers to in this chapter.

1. ____________________

2. ____________________

3. ____________________

B. Spend another minute writing down any thoughts that come to mind about the topics below. Write freely and rapidly.

1. Rules I live by: ____________________

2. How I interact with others: ____________________

3. Male and female roles: ____________________

PREVIEW

Refining values—our view of what is good/evil, true/false, ugly/beautiful—intensifies in college, because the values we acquired in childhood now face the test: Were we told the truth? Will our youthful beliefs sustain us in adulthood? Our answers to these questions depend, in large part, on the relationships we form in college.

College offers us many opportunities for making new friends and extending the boundaries of our world. Most colleges make an effort to simulate the world we will inhabit after graduation by actively recruiting students from varied cultural backgrounds. If you have come from an ethnocentric community (where "my culture is the majority culture"), you may find this adjustment bewildering, even frightening. But to resist it—preferring to hang with students who speak, look, and act like you—could cause you to miss out on an exciting passage to a larger world and worldview.

Developing strong values becomes increasingly important as we make new friends and face complex issues involving sex, morality, and autonomy.

DEVELOPING STRONG VALUES

All students begin their first year of college with well-established values already in place. Many fail to realize **those values will be challenged** more during their college years than at any other time in their lives. Your encounter with different cultures and new ideas—in the classroom, in moments of study and reflection, and as you interact socially—will challenge you to reassess everything you have learned.

Role models can have a powerful influence on our values.

Our attitudes about right and wrong, acceptable and unacceptable social behavior, as well as our relationships with other people and the natural environment, are primarily derived from two sources: authorities (parents, books, religious instruction, teachers, coaches, government, the media) and our own personal experience. If your values are already strong, they may undergo relatively little change. Encounters with new ideas and people will help you fine-tune your value system without having to overhaul it. If your value system is weak, you may feel a need to make radical changes.

What do we mean by "strong" or "weak" values? Values are strong when consistent with everything we have experienced and are likely to experience. They are reliable reference points that let us feel oriented and secure and give us courage in situations full of risk. Weak values, on the other hand, are unreliable: they don't work in all situations, especially in a crisis. Even if they protect us, they don't inspire us.

> If a man hasn't discovered something that he will die for, he isn't fit to live.
>
> Dr. Martin Luther King, Jr.
> *Civil rights leader*

Sidney Simon and other ethics philosophers have studied the way value systems are formed, and have identified some fundamental **conditions for a strong set of values.**

1. Strong values are chosen freely and deliberately from among several thoughtfully considered alternatives.
   - A strong value must result from free choice. We may learn values from authorities, but only if we do so of our own free will. A value imposed or coerced is a weak value. Real values guide our lives even when no one is watching.
   - A strong value has been chosen from among other carefully considered alternatives. Authorities sometimes coerce us into thinking our choices are limited to two: good or evil, hell or heaven, kill or be killed, love it or leave it. In reality, the array of ethical choices available to us is vast. In those rare cases when we face a situation that offers only one acceptable alternative (for example, drink water or die from dehydration), we are not making a value judgment, just obeying a survival instinct.

Collaborate

Where Do Our Values Come From?

Look over the list of issues in the left-hand column and the list of influences on the right. Which of the items on the right most strongly influenced your present attitude toward the issues on the left? (Put the corresponding letter in the blank. If you have no opinion, leave it blank.)

Issues	Influences
1. _____ the U.S. economy	**A.** books
2. _____ abortion	**B.** TV
3. _____ ecology issues	**C.** movies
4. _____ self-expression through personal appearance	**D.** magazines
5. _____ alcohol and drugs	**E.** newspapers
6. _____ sex	**F.** friends
7. _____ personal hygiene/grooming	**G.** family
8. _____ religion	**H.** my own thinking
9. _____ education	**I.** teachers
10. _____ capital punishment	**J.** religious teachings
	K. my own experience

Which influence appeared most frequently? ________________________________

On which issues are you most open to reevaluation or change? List three.

On which do you think you are least likely to change your opinion? List three.

When you have completed this exercise, discuss your responses in small groups.

- Strong values result from careful consideration of the consequences of action available to us. It is not a value adopted impulsively, on the spur of the moment.

2. A strong value is positive, a position we're proud of, one that gives us satisfaction. There is comfort and motivation in having a strong sense of values. When we make a difficult decision on the basis of a strong value, we feel good about it. A strong value can be affirmed and recommended to others without embarrassment. If we keep a value to ourselves because it may be unpopular, it's a weak value.

3. A strong value repeatedly affects our lives. We don't just talk about it; we act on it. We budget our time and our money in accordance with our values. They influence our lives daily. It is hypocritical (a weak value) to say we care about protecting the environment if we don't recycle or contribute to organizations with environmental goals.

I don't know the key to success, but the key to failure is trying to please everybody.

Bill Cosby
Actor/comedian

PASSIVE, ASSERTIVE, AGGRESSIVE

Having a strong set of values—of right and wrong, justice and fair play, individual liberty and respect for others—doesn't necessarily mean a person is able to communicate these values successfully. **Some people adopt passive or aggressive behaviors in order to manipulate or manage the responses of others.**

Learning to assert yourself effectively takes lots of practice.

Aggressive people tend to get what they want, but usually at someone else's expense. Aggressive behavior can include speaking loudly, interrupting, accusing, or invading another person's physical or emotional space. Aggressive behavior is highly manipulative.

Passive people, on the other hand, want to be liked and will do almost anything to please others. Although they often manage to avoid interpersonal conflict, their prolonged habit of giving in to others can create a deep reservoir of anger and resentment.

Assertive behavior falls somewhere in between. Assertive people respect themselves and others equally. They express their feelings without judging or blaming others. When there is conflict, they are more interested in finding solutions than in finding fault.

Collaborate

Comparing Our Value Systems

A. **Comparing Values.** Take a few minutes to indicate how you feel about the statements below.
When you've finished, take turns explaining how you came to hold your view and how strongly you feel about it. Which would you consider very strong values, based on the criteria described on pages 196–197. Which are weak values? Tell why.

		Agree	Unsure	Disagree
1.	There is no such thing as a holy or just war.	☐	☐	☐
2.	It's a dog-eat-dog world; everybody's out for themselves.	☐	☐	☐
3.	My country, right or wrong!	☐	☐	☐
4.	Abortion is murder.	☐	☐	☐
5.	Homosexuality is immoral.	☐	☐	☐
6.	Desire is the root of all evil.	☐	☐	☐
7.	Eat, drink, and be merry, for tomorrow we die.	☐	☐	☐
8.	Do unto others as you would have them do unto you.	☐	☐	☐
9.	Do unto others before they do it to you.	☐	☐	☐
10.	The meek shall inherit the earth.	☐	☐	☐

B. **Rules for Living.** List five values you were taught by authorities (parents, teachers, government, religious teaching), for example, wash your hands before you eat, don't work on the Sabbath, be kind to strangers.

1. ______________________________
2. ______________________________
3. ______________________________
4. ______________________________
5. ______________________________

Read your list to your group. Then say which, if any, you still practice and why.

Learning to assert yourself will help you surmount many problems you may face in college: roommate or spouse conflicts, bureaucratic mixups, unfair treatment by instructors, or threatening ideas and pressures from peers and family members. Assertiveness takes practice, but it can be learned and does work.

There are strong pressures in our society to keep our ideas to ourselves, swallow our pride, yield to people who are stronger than we are, go along with the crowd, avoid conflict, and be liked. Women, in particular, are often raised to believe these passive approaches are somehow expected of them, that true happiness is achieved by winning approval and affection from others. Men are often taught the opposite—to stand up for their rights, fight back, gain the upper hand, achieve dominance—that it's a jungle out there.

Over the last few decades, research has uncovered the prejudice in gender determinism. It has exposed the folly of passive and aggressive modes of behavior and given rise to "assertiveness training"—**a way of firmly expressing our values, needs, and rights without bullying the weak or giving in to the strong**. Assertiveness training has helped both men and women confront anger, anxiety, depression, resentment, and bitterness. These emotions can lead to what is sometimes called "passive-aggressive" behavior: giving someone the "silent treatment" or withholding affection.

The problem with both passive and aggressive behavior is that, in the long run, **they don't work**. Passive behavior tends to win contempt, not approval. Aggressive behavior wins an occasional battle but always loses the war by provoking fear, loathing, and avoidance.

Being assertive simply means expressing your feelings and ideas openly without an attempt to evoke a certain response. Assertive people understand that they, and they alone, are responsible for their own happiness and no one else's. They feel good about themselves. They say no without feeling guilty, make mistakes without undue embarrassment, ask questions without feeling stupid, are turned down without feeling rejected. Instead of accusing others, they describe how they feel about another's behavior (not "You make me angry" but "I feel angry"). Assertive people express themselves and listen to others. Their self-possession is evident: they stand tall and look you in the eye. Assertive people are in control of their lives.

RELATIONSHIPS

The friends you make in college could influence your life both professionally and personally for a long time. They need to be chosen and nurtured with great care.

Having good friends is one of life's greatest gifts. Friends have seen you at your worst and still like you. They listen to your problems without judg-

"I" Messages and "You" Messages

Passive and aggressive people tend to use "you" messages when they don't like someone's behavior, for example:

Why don't you take out the garbage once in a while?
I wish you'd quit interrupting.
If you really loved me, you'd take me out more often.

Assertive people express their needs and desires by using "I" messages, for example:

I can't carry this alone. Can I get some help?
I'd like a chance to express myself without being interrupted.
I'd really enjoy going out dancing this Friday night.

"I" messages focus on one's own feelings, needs, and reactions to another's behavior. "You" messages focus on the other person's behavior. They assign responsibility for a problem to the other person. They attempt to make the other person feel blamed, put down, guilty, rejected, defensive, unworthy. They usually make the other person want to retaliate and escalate the argument or clam up, resent the accusation, and resist change.

"You" messages are misguided attempts to change another's behavior. They almost never accomplish the desired result.

"I" messages don't always work, either. The other person may not care how you feel or may not want to change. But they work better than "you" messages, and you will know that you made an honest effort to express yourself without hurting somebody else.

ing you. They offer advice only when asked. When you need them, friends are there. They will do just about anything for you. Friends may be members of the opposite sex, but often aren't: friendship and romance are a rare mixture. Friends are both different from and similar to each other. The differences challenge us to grow and see life from a fresh perspective. The similarities comfort and enable us to see ourselves more clearly.

On **Your** *Own*

How Do I Relate to Others?

Circle one phrase from each horizontal row below that best describes you. Be honest.

A	B	C
I avoid problems.	I attack problems.	I attack people.
I relinquish my rights.	I claim my rights.	I impose my rights.
I feel inferior.	I feel equal.	I feel superior.
I fear others.	I respect others.	I dominate others.
I let people guess how I feel.	I let people know how I feel.	I make people feel how I feel.
I seek to please.	I seek solutions.	I seek satisfaction.
I store anger.	I express anger.	I act out anger.
I respect others.	I show mutual respect.	I respect myself.
I lack confidence.	I am confident.	I act superior.
I hope for a response.	I ask for response.	I demand a response.
I give in.	I negotiate.	I dictate.
I feel guilty.	I take responsibility.	I blame others.
I am abused.	I am respected.	I am feared.

Where are most of your circles? Column A (passive)? Column B (assertive)? Column C (aggressive)? Do you think the results of this exercise accurately reflect how you relate to others? How might you put this information to use? Write your response on one or more separate sheets of paper. Write as much as you wish about this topic.

Having friends is essential to learning and personal growth. Friends and classmates give feedback and let you know how you're doing. They know things you don't, and vice versa. All people have a responsibility to help each other learn and grow.

Friendships don't just happen; you make them happen by reaching out to others and taking emotional risks. It's no fun feeling alone and cut off, worrying about whether people will like you or reject you, waiting for someone else to make an approach. If you find yourself in this situation and want to change, consider adopting some **active strategies for making friends:**

1. ***Let people know you're available.*** Hiding in your room studying or staring at your feet as you walk across campus is a message to others that you want to be left alone. Making eye contact, smiling, saying hello, asking someone a question, paying a compliment, or even making a comment about the weather are ways of letting others know you're open and available. Reach out to people. If they respond, personalize the conversation by sharing your own thoughts and feelings and asking them how they feel.

Collaborate

Role Playing

A. Six volunteers are needed to improvise a skit—three men and three women, in pairs. Each pair will improvise a five-minute scene in which the man tries to get the woman to go with him to a keg party at a local fraternity. The man's role is simply to get the woman to agree to go to the party. The woman really doesn't want to go. She has heard rumors about these parties degenerating into drunken violence. Her role, then, is to resist the peer pressure she is feeling from him.

Characterizations are assigned as follows: Actress 1 acts out passive refusal strategies. Actress 2 is assertive. Actress 3 uses the aggressive approach. (The audience should not know in advance which is which.)

After all skits have concluded, discuss as a class which woman was most effective in getting her point across, and why.

B. Three scripts follow that can be read or presented in front of the class. After each, discuss whether the behaviors were passive, assertive, or aggressive, and in what ways. How could the characters have altered their behavior to communicate more successfully?

Scene 1

A: OK, who left their inline skates on the stairs?
B: I'm sorry. I'll move them right away.
A: I mean, what are you trying to do, kill me?
B: I said I'd take care of it.
A: You're always leaving your stuff where somebody can trip over it. How many times do I have to tell you?
B: Come on, give me a break! I've had a rough day.
A: No way. We're going to have this out, right now.
B: Please, I'm sorry. It won't happen again, I promise. What can I do to make it up to you?
A: Nothing. You're hopeless!

Scene 2

A: Did you go to econ today?
B: Of course I went to econ today! I *never* miss class, unlike some people I know.
A: And I'm not a geek, like some people I know.
B: You don't have to call me names.
A: So let me borrow your notes, OK?
B: The last time you borrowed my notes, you spilled beer all over them.
A: It was an accident, so sue me! They were legible. What's the problem?
B: Promise you'll give them back?
A: I'll give it some serious thought.

Scene 3

A: Hey, give me a hand with this ceiling joist!
B: No can do, pardner. I've got to finish wiring this circuit.
A: You're doing a great job with that, by the way. Hey, I'm all alone here and I really need help. This'll take all of ten minutes.
B: Tell you what. I'll help you toe in the joist and you can strip a few wires for me. This has to be done by quitting time.
A: You got a deal.

Friendship should be more than biting Time can sever.

T.S. Eliot,
American poet,
in The Naming of Cats

On Your Own

The Qualities of a Friend

Spend five minutes making a list of the qualities you look for in friends (for example, loyalty, honesty, generosity).

Now go back and put check marks next to the three qualities you consider most important.

Finally, consider your current network of friends. Put their initials to the right of the quality each possesses. Do these qualities describe your best friends? Do some of your friends possess few of the qualities you listed? Are you choosing your friends wisely? Do you possess these qualities yourself? If so, does your behavior toward your friends reflect it?

Three things in human life are important. The first is to be kind. The second is to be kind. And the third is to be kind.

Henry James
Author

2. ***Be a good listener.*** Listening is the highest form of compliment. Make a conscious decision to forget about yourself and get interested in others. Ask open-ended questions ("How do you feel about . . . ?") that let people reveal themselves to you. Look them in the eyes and let them know by your body language that you are taking their answers in.

3. ***Take risks.*** Assume from the beginning that some people you approach will not return the gesture. If some lack the grace to respond to your overture, pity them and look elsewhere. Some relationships will be deep and lasting; others will be brief or superficial. X may become a racquetball partner; Y someone you commute with; Z may be the one you turn to for advice about love.

4. ***Be worth knowing.*** People will like you and accept you in direct proportion to how much you like and accept yourself. If you want to have friends, you must believe you are a person who deserves friends. Once you establish a relationship, maintaining it means being a faithful friend: keeping commitments, returning phone calls and favors, listening without judgment, being honest without causing pain, offering support.

Lasting friendships are one of the best things about college.

To have a friend, be one.

Anonymous

WHAT IS A CULTURE?

A culture is a group of people bound together by traditions and values. Cultures define themselves in many ways—by clothing, diet, language, religion, music, rituals.

As cultures become larger and more complex, they overlap with other cultures, forming subcultures. These may be based on any of the factors listed above as well as age, sex, ethnicity, disability, geography, and interests. We become part of a culture according to values important to us. Less important aspects of our lives define our attachments to subcultures.

Shyness

Shyness can have adverse effects on academic performance in class, on learning outside of class, and, of course, on social life.

With great courage and often painful effort, shy people can overcome the appearance of shyness, but they seldom overcome the condition itself. If you are not shy, be sensitive to it in others. If a person responds to your friendly gesture by mumbling or turning away, it's probably not his or her intention to be hostile or rude. In a social situation, shy people freeze with irrational fear. Once you get to know them, most are quite fun in private and often very interesting. Although the extrovert may talk, the shy person listens and observes.

If you suffer from shyness, keep working to overcome fears and acquire the social behaviors needed to function in society. Meanwhile, know that you have some special talents that result from your shyness: powers of observation, discretion, tact, and insight into human nature. Try not to resent misinterpretations and unjust assumptions people make about your reticence.

Remember that people aren't mind readers. If you're not wearing your "Shy Person" button, some may misinterpret your behavior. If others reach out to you as friends, let them know that shyness is a problem for you. Give cues about how you like to be treated. Do the same thing with your instructors. If you're afraid to approach them directly, write a note.

Collaborate

How Others Perceive Me

Get together in your small group. Take turns asking the other members of your group the following questions:

What specific behaviors of mine have you observed so far in this class that have had a positive impact on my interaction with other members of this group?

What behaviors could I work on that would improve my interaction with the group?

In this exercise, each member has the right to expect constructive feedback and candor. Comments should focus on specific behavior—not attributes or character traits. Before you begin, discuss the differences between these three.

A culture is a group of people who share common traditions and values.

The desire to be part of a recognizable culture is a natural, wholesome human instinct. We do it to feel the joy of connectedness with others, and for a family and a home where we can feel relaxed, accepted, and secure. The American poet Robert Frost defined home as the place where "when you go there, they have to take you in."

Just as the decision to attend college implies a recognition of much to be learned, the decision to embrace difference implies a recognition of prejudice. **No human being, no matter how saintly, is entirely free of prejudice.** To admit our prejudice openly is the first step toward greater acceptance of cultural difference. We can say, "I am a prejudiced person but I repudiate that prejudice. I want to become a person who accepts others as they are."

No nation is more culturally diverse than the United States.

A NATION OF IMMIGRANTS

Although no nation in the world is culturally uniform, no nation is more culturally diverse than the United States. Unfortunately, our ignorance of the rest of the world became painfully clear in a recent survey conducted by the National Geographic Society in which most Americans were unable to locate Great Britain, France, or Japan on a map of the world. In another Gallup study, two out of three couldn't find France. The test was administered to 10,000 young adults (age 18 to 24) in nine countries. Americans came in dead last.

Americans have paid dearly for **ethnocentrism—an unwillingness to acknowledge the value of other cultures.** Many of our most serious national crises have resulted from cultural tunnel vision.

Because of its diversity, the United States has often been called "The Great Melting Pot." This industrial metaphor is unfortunate because it implies that human beings are like mineral ore—to be smelted and perhaps combined with newer, stronger metals, leaving a gray soup—uniform in quality, color, and texture—to be converted, in turn, into useful, inanimate objects. As Peter Marin says, "What we like to think of as the 'melting pot' often seems more like a superheated furnace that must be fed

Collaborate

Cultures and Subcultures

A. Take a moment to list three cultures of which you are a part (for example, male, Asian-American, Roman Catholic).

1. ______________________________
2. ______________________________
3. ______________________________

Now list three subcultures of which you are a part (for example, trail bike racer, soap opera addict, fantasy gamer).

1. ______________________________
2. ______________________________
3. ______________________________

Read these aloud in your group. Are your lists mostly similar or mostly different?

B. Share with the group any cultural patterns you've established with your closest friends (special greetings or handshakes, private language, in-jokes, things you always do together). How did these patterns originate? Are you still comfortable maintaining them?

C. Discuss how another culture or subculture intimidates or offends you. Give an example of something that bothers you. Why does it bother you?

D. Have you had extensive experience with another culture so that you now feel comfortable around people from that culture? Describe how this came about. Do you know any second languages? If so, how has this knowledge affected you?

On **Your** Own

Cultural Interview

Interview a person from a culture as different as possible from your own. The interview should take about half an hour. Plan your questions beforehand. Then summarize, in writing, answers to the following questions from this interview:

Briefly introduce your subject (name, cultural background, and so on).

Summarize the cultural patterns of that person's life that differ from your own.

Tell what you learned from interviewing this person.

If you'd like, offer to buy lunch for—and eat with—the person you interviewed.

continuously with imported values and lives, whose destruction creates the energy and heat of American life."[1]

More encouraging (and more accurate) metaphors emerged during Reverend Jesse Jackson's campaigns (in 1984 and 1988) for the Democratic nomination for President of the United States. In 1984 Jackson formed what he called a "Rainbow Coalition," a culturally diverse group of individuals dedicated to the protection of human rights and the eradication of poverty. For Jackson the rainbow's first significance was biblical: in the book of Genesis, it was a symbol of covenant after a disastrous flood. In secular lore, it represented economic hope to wanderers who sought the pot of gold at the rainbow's end. As a natural phenomenon it was a thing of beauty—composed of many colors blending together but still separate and unique.

Later, Jackson described the United States as a patchwork quilt such as his mother used to make from scraps of cloth and potato sacks. Each patch was, in itself, small and useless; stitched together, they formed a beautiful, durable, and useful fabric—a symbol of warmth, protection, and love. Jackson's message was clear: none of us—white or black, rich or poor, liberal or conservative—can make it on our own. Each patch is too small. But together, celebrating our differences as a source of strength, we will accomplish much.

HOSTILITY ON CAMPUS

Like any community, **a college campus is not immune to crime, violence, and racial hostility.** Often this takes the form of psychological violence—epithets shouted or written as graffiti, white supremacist symbols painted on doors. Hate crimes have risen steadily in recent years.

Usually it is more subtle: innuendo or special treatment by instructors, a tolerance of ethnic jokes, the absence of culturally specific music in student unions, or the absence of minority emphases in the curriculum or course materials.

[1] "Toward Something American," *Harper's*, July 1988, pp. 17–18.

Most often, cultural bias on campus is unconscious and unintentional—the result of isolation and ignorance. Some real-life examples:

- An African-American student at a midwestern university noticed that each time a race-related question came up in her psychology class, everyone turned to her for the answer. "I wear glasses too," she said. "Does that make me an optometrist?"
- An American student complimented a West Indian student on his excellent command of English. The West Indian was a little puzzled, since English was his native language, so he graciously returned the compliment.

People accomplish more when they work as a team.

Sometimes trying *not* to be prejudiced results in a new kind of stereotyping on campus. For example, the assumption that Asian-Americans are talented in math and science has induced many to pursue careers for which they have no interest or ability, while neglecting critical reading and writing skills. Some colleges offer intercultural communication courses and sponsor consciousness-raising workshops in which students are instructed in "Arab table manners" and "Japanese business practices," thus reinforcing the misperception that all Arabs are alike and that the Japanese are predictable people. Although offered with the best of intentions, these courses often result in even more subtle forms of cultural stereotyping.

GENDER DISCRIMINATION

The emergence on college campuses of women's studies programs, gay/lesbian/bi support groups, "Take Back the Night" rallies, and informational programs on acquaintance rape and sexual harassment attests to the continued virulence, even among educated people, of gender discrimination.

Institutionalized discrimination against women in American society is supported by the facts. In 1997, among adults working full-time, year-round, women earned 76 cents for every dollar earned by men.[2] Women workers with college degrees earned only slightly more than men who had never graduated from high school. And many women with executive talent have discovered the "glass ceiling" that keeps women in middle management from the upper levels of power in business and industry.

In the college classroom, women report more subtle forms of prejudice—including demeaning references such as "dumb blonde" and "she's here to get her M.R.S. degree"; the use of gender-specific pronouns to reinforce sex roles (doctors, politicians, and mechanics, for example, referred to as "he," whereas

[2] *Time* magazine, June 29, 1998.

nurses and secretaries are "she"); interrupting women more often than men; and using course materials that fail to reflect women's achievements.

Collaborate

You Be the Judge

Some colleges have adopted antiharassment policies that prohibit students from subjecting others to verbal abuse based on race, religion, gender, handicap, ethnicity, national origin, or sexual orientation.

In 1991 a student was expelled from Brown University for shouting abusive epithets directed at African-American, Jewish, and homosexual students. He was defended by the American Civil Liberties Union (ACLU), which argued the university had violated the student's constitutional right of free speech. The ACLU contended that, even though the student's remarks were offensive and repugnant, they were protected under the First Amendment.

What do you think? Divide class desks into two groups facing each other. Those who believe the student's rights were violated should sit on one side; those who feel the university acted appropriately should sit on the other. Debate the issue by having members of each group briefly explain why they chose the side of the room they did. After each person has had a chance to speak, anyone may offer a rebuttal of a view expressed by the other side.

Collaborate

Gender Issues

A. Take a look at the following statements culled from newspapers published within the last seven years. Discuss in your group how they may be instances of gender bias.

1. Female lobbyist "Just as Capable" (*MSU News*)
2. Nothing Man-Made Visible from Moon (*Detroit Free Press*)
3. "This [work of art], called Cysuno, is part of the $90,000 collection lent to the museum by Dr. Marshall Goldin of Glenview, Illinois, and his wife." (*Lansing State Journal*)
4. A New Start As Man and Wife (*Lansing State Journal*)
5. "Perky Kathleen Sullivan, who co-anchors "World News This Morning," and ABC news honcho Roone Arledge have been making the columns for months. The romance hasn't hurt Ms. Sullivan's career. In January, she'll begin anchoring 'World News Tonight-Saturday.'" (*Detroit News*)
6. "As befits the scion of a Hollywood family (father Tom was a football star and commentator, sister Kelly was once married to John DeLorean, and sister Kris was hitched to Ricky Nelson), Harmon looks to the late Gary Cooper for inspiration." (*Family Weekly*)

B. Spend about five minutes writing down, in question form, things you've always wondered about the other sex.

1. ______________________________

____

2. ______________________________

____

continued on next page

Collaborate *continued from previous page*

3. ______________________________

____

4. ______________________________

____

5. ______________________________

____

Then form two groups—men in one, women in the other—and pose your questions to the other group for their answers.

C. Spend five minutes brainstorming as many adjectives as you can that you feel describe the other group.

______________ ______________

______________ ______________

______________ ______________

______________ ______________

______________ ______________

______________ ______________

______________ ______________

______________ ______________

Give the other group a brief time to respond to each. Which adjectives were accurate? Which provoked a negative reaction?

D. Spend about ten minutes in your same-sex group brainstorming answers to these questions:
What's the best thing about being female (or male)? What's the most frustrating thing about it?

The best thing about being female (or male):

____

____

____

____

____

____

The most frustrating thing:

____

____

____

____

____

Get together with the other group and discuss your answers.

On Your Own

Gender Bias in the Language

In the right column, write the male equivalent for what appears in the left column.

Female	Male
Little old lady	________
Spinster	________
Old maid	________
Broad	________
The little woman	________
Bimbo	________

Can you think of other derogatory terms for women that have no male equivalents? Make a similar list for men. Which list is longer?

Cultural hostility may be directed against anyone.

Depending on the composition of a college's student population, cultural hostility may be directed against anyone: foreign students; Jews; Latinos; Native Americans; Asians and Asian-Americans; Pacific Islanders; Arabs; whites; students with disabilities; older students; students who are gay, lesbian, or bisexual; and members of the opposite sex. In all cases, prejudice is a manifestation of the desire to dominate another culture on the basis of perceived differences.

Discrimination in any form is incompatible with the idea of college, a place where we learn to evaluate arguments—and people—on the basis of their merits.

STAGES OF CULTURAL GROWTH

For persons of a dominant culture (for example, white males in the United States or wealthy people in a poor community), the change from an ethnocentric to a multicultural worldview can involve three stages:

1. ***Ethnocentrism.*** My culture is best; all others are inferior. I don't like people who are different from me—never have, never will. I was born and raised that way. If it was good enough for my parents and grandparents, it's good enough for me.

2. ***Understanding.*** As I have more contact with people of other cultures and learn more about them, I can see why they act the way they do. Their ways and customs are OK for them. In fact, I've

Tips

Sexual Harassment

It usually happens to women, but not always. On a college campus, it is usually student to student, but not always. When it does happen, everyone on campus—students, faculty, and staff—should know how to recognize it and what to do about it.

If someone who has power over you (an instructor or a boss) makes your sexual response a condition of your employment, makes sexual comments, or exerts sexual pressure that interferes with your educational environment, that's sexual harassment. A professor could hint that your sexual compliance and your final grade might somehow be linked. You could get negative performance evaluations on the job because you refused to go out with your supervisor. A fellow student could threaten to embarrass you somehow if you don't go along with his or her wishes. Or harassment could be more subtle: a pattern of insensitivity and intimidation or gender-biased treatment in a classroom or residence hall.

Sexual harassment is a serious matter. Not only does it violate college policy, it is a violation of state and federal law.

If it happens to you, you can—and should—do something about it. Make a written record of the offensive behavior, with dates and witnesses. Talk to students or coworkers; they may have experienced similar pressures and want to support you if you decide to take action.

1. Let the offender know how you feel. Describe the action you find objectionable and unwelcome and say how it makes you feel. It's possible the person was unaware of the action or its consequences, will apologize, and stop.
2. If you're afraid to confront the person, contact someone in a position of authority (your supervisor, the offender's supervisor, and administrator). You can also call the Personnel Office, Counseling Services, or the Dean of Students.
3. You may want to file a formal grievance. Check your student conduct code on when this is appropriate and how to proceed.

Be assured that your complaint will be taken seriously and treated in private. The law will protect you. Sexual harassment can be stopped.

already learned to like some of their food, clothing, music. I respect their right to be different. Live and let live.

3. ***Multiculturalism.*** My lifestyle is a composite of the best things I have seen in other cultures, and I've seen a lot. These things have enriched my life, even though I'm still me. I feel comfortable around all kinds of people. I'm open to new experiences, and I continue to grow in positive ways.

For persons in groups who have felt the sting of discrimination all their lives, the pattern of growth may be somewhat different:

1. ***Concession.*** I'm what the dominant culture says I am. I wish I could be more like them. But at least I'm not like those other minority groups.
2. ***Radicalization.*** They're just trying to put me down. I accept the way I am—in fact, I think I'm just great. Those other cultures are OK too, even though they're not part of mine. We've all got to stick together against the dominant culture. Eventually we'll pay them back for the way they've treated us.
3. ***Multiculturalism.*** My lifestyle is a composite of the best things I have seen in other cultures, and I've seen a lot. These things have enriched my life, even though I'm still me. I feel comfortable around all kinds

Assistive learning devices for students with disabilities are becoming more common.

of people. I'm open to new experience, and I continue to grow in positive ways.

The radicalization phase of development is usually characterized by hostility toward the dominant culture and close bonding with one's own culture.

Recently, some students with hearing impairment have entered the radicalization phase of cultural development. A few years ago, students at Gallaudet, a university for students who are hearing impaired, succeeded through sit-ins and demonstrations in blocking the appointment of a hearing president. Meanwhile, many hearing students, stirred by the 1986 motion picture *Children of a Lesser God*, spent hours learning sign language, only to discover when they applied to Gallaudet that the hearing-impaired students didn't want them there.

Students who are physically challenged are a rapidly growing culture on American campuses, representing nearly 8 percent of the total enrollment. Their demands that colleges become barrier-free and provide them with braille textbooks, print-enlarging machines, and assistive listening devices were answered by the passage on July 26, 1990, of the Americans with Disabilities Act (ADA)—legislation that persons with disabilities are calling their own Civil Rights Act. All public accommodations, including colleges, are now required by law to make a reasonable, good-faith effort to provide barrier-free access to all persons. If you are among the 43 million Americans affected by the ADA, you are responsible for making your learning and living needs known to those in a position to respond. And respond they will, or face litigation, whose costs will far exceed those of providing access.

Collaborate

Experiencing Prejudice

A. Everyone has been a minority at some time or another. Can you think of a time when you felt different? When you were excluded from a group? When you were called a hurtful name? Describe the experience to your group and tell how you felt about it at the time. How do you feel about it now?
B. Describe a moment in your life when you became aware of a prejudice you had against another culture. How do you feel about that culture today?

If you find it difficult to answer these questions orally, write your response first and read it aloud to the group.

On **Your** *Own*

Labeling in the Media

Bring to class a picture from a magazine, an advertisement, a headline, or a printed quote that shows labeling or stereotyping. Show it to the class and explain how the message it sends injures the dignity of the stereotyped group.

Tips

Put the Person First

Language can play a key role in creating and maintaining attitudes that are harmful to persons with disabilities. Certain words used to describe individuals with disabilities (cripple, moron, Mongoloid, junkie, victim, and so on) have extremely negative connotations. These terms are hurtful because they focus on the *person* as the disability rather than a person *with* a disability.

Here are some hurtful terms and their more appropriate substitutes:

Hurtful term	Preferred term
the disabled	person with a disability
Mongoloid	person with Down syndrome
the blind, deaf	person with a visual or hearing disability
wheelchair bound	person who uses a wheelchair
deaf and dumb, deaf-mute	person with a hearing and/or speech impairment

Rather than getting tied up in knots trying to remember the appropriate term, here is a simple rule to remember: *Put the person first.*

WHY CHANGE?

All humans have ethnocentric tendencies at one time or another. The culture in which we were "born and raised" can be a cocoon that offers comfort and security during a time when we need these things. But our cultural identity is always changing, and when a cocoon prevents us from becoming fully human and causes us to deny the humanity of others, it is time to slough it off and proceed to the next metamorphosis—to stretch our wings and explore the variety of the world.

Moving through the stages of cultural development toward a multicultural outlook can involve some painful struggle. Why make the effort?

There are many benefits to opening our eyes to the diversity around us, but the most obvious answer is that we have no choice. Our world is rapidly becoming a global community. **We must prepare ourselves for a future in which all cultures and nations will, of necessity, depend on each other for survival.**

On **Your** *Own*

How Do Others See Me?

Think of three words other people might use to characterize you.

1. ____________________
2. ____________________
3. ____________________

Are they accurate or flattering? Are they unfair or misleading? How do you feel about being labeled in this way? Where did people get this impression of you? What could you do to change other people's perceptions of you?

Collaborate

Stereotypes

For each of the items below, make a list of any associations that come to mind. (Your reporter can read each item aloud and write down what everyone says.) For example, if the item is "children," you might come up with innocent, naughty, playful, grubby, little, cute, and so on.

Straight-A student ______________________

Person who is blind ______________________

Janitor ______________________

Person born in England ______________________

Person with AIDS ______________________

Old woman ______________________

Person who is homeless ______________________

Professor ______________________

Person who is mentally ill ______________________

Police officer ______________________

College athlete ______________________

CEO ______________________

For each item, discuss the accuracy of your associations. Overall, what percentage are flattering, neutral, or demeaning? Are stereotypes useful? Dangerous? In what ways?

Where do we get our stereotypes? Brainstorm at least five sources (for example, cartoons).

Finally, discuss what you believe to be common stereotypes of students at your school.

Closer to home, the demographic composition of the American work force is rapidly changing. White males are already a minority among working Americans; their representation in the workforce is expected to decline to 39 percent by the year 2000. By the year 2000, one-third of all American workers will be minorities. A culturally diverse labor force will require managers who are sensitive to the uniqueness and differences of their employees.

By being open to other cultures, we soon discover **people are more alike than different.** We find our lives enriched by new clothing and hairstyles, foods, approaches to problems like fatigue and stress, spiritual insights, words and expressions, and new styles of music. Our society benefits from the knowledge and creative gifts of artists and scholars who have visited our country or become American citizens. And our own self-worth is measured by the respect with which we treat those who are different from us.

LABELING IS DISABLING

Perhaps you have a roommate of a different race or nationality, or an instructor with an accent. You may have participated in class discussions on sensitive issues and heard opinions expressed that would shock your parents

Collaborate

Team Names and Mascots

In recent years, some colleges have changed their team names and mascots to eliminate negative stereotypes. Eastern Michigan University, once the Hurons, became the Eagles. St. John's University, formerly the Redmen, is now the Red Storm.

Consider the following team nicknames and discuss them in your group:

- the Washington Redskins
- the Florida State Seminoles
- the Atlanta Braves
- the Cleveland Indians

1. Are these names offensive? What about Atlanta's "tomahawk chop," or Florida State's Seminole war chant? Do these names and traditions perpetuate negative stereotypes, or are they harmless? If you are Caucasian, would you be offended by team names like "the Washington Ofays" or the "Chicago Honkies"? If you are a woman (or a pacifist), how would you feel about being among the University of Massachusetts "Minutemen"? What about the Fighting Irish of Notre Dame, the San Diego Padres, or the Hope College Flying Dutchmen?
2. Think of other team names that refer to specific groups of people: can you imagine why any of these might be offensive?
3. Think of a racial or cultural epithet that makes you angry. How would you feel if your school fielded a team with that name? Do educational institutions have a special obligation to fight prejudicial stereotypes? If so, what can students do to help?
4. Debate this issue.

Last night I discovered a new form of oral contraceptive. I asked a girl to go to bed with me and she said no.

Woody Allen
Writer/filmmaker

or neighbors. And you are certainly familiar with American undergraduate jargon that transforms students into "nerds," "jocks," "geeks," and "dweebs."

Some students are even prejudiced against themselves ("I'm terrible with names." "I'm ugly." "I'm no good at math.").

Using labels is a lazy intellectual habit—a convenient way of simplifying a world characterized by complexity and variety. Labeling is demeaning—to ourselves as well as to others.

Embracing diversity means accepting and enjoying a world of dazzling and infinite variety. It means affirming the particularity and uniqueness of every individual.

SAFER SEX

Despite our many divisive misconceptions of others, sex unites—and perpetuates—the human race. However, in recent years the discussion of sexuality on college campuses has taken on a solemn tone. The alarming worldwide AIDS epidemic and spread of other less virulent sexually trans-

Tips

About HIV and AIDS

Human **I**mmunodeficiency **V**irus, or HIV, destroys important cells in the human immune system over time. This disease of the immune system is known as **a**cquired **i**mmuno**d**eficiency **s**yndrome, or AIDS. People who test positive for HIV have been exposed to the virus, but may not have developed AIDS.

1. The first case of AIDS (Acquired Immune Deficiency Syndrome) in the United States was reported in 1981. Within ten years, over 1,000,000 Americans were infected, and many millions more worldwide. The epidemic has taken an especially heavy toll in Africa: it is estimated that half the population of Uganda will die from AIDS by the year 2000.
2. Prior to 1985, when blood and sperm banks began screening for the virus, AIDS could be transmitted through blood transfusions and artificial insemination. Today, the virus is most frequently transmitted by sexual intercourse and infected hypodermic needles. Three-quarters of new HIV infections in 1994 occurred among addicts. About half these cases, according to the Centers for Disease Control in Atlanta, involved the exchange of sex for crack cocaine.
3. The percentage of women who have contracted HIV is rising rapidly. About 1 percent of Americans with AIDS are infants.
4. HIV itself does not kill. It attacks the body's immune system, allowing any number of "opportunistic" illnesses, such as pulmonary tuberculosis, pneumonia, and cervical cancer, to spread unchecked. Development of AIDS generally occurs about ten years after infection.
5. **You can't contract the virus that causes AIDS through casual, everyday contact (shared food and utensils, phones, towels, toilet seats, swimming pools). HIV is not communicated through the air, tears, sweat, or saliva. It's OK to hug and kiss a person who is infected with the virus.**
6. Common AIDS symptoms are persistent fever, extreme fatigue, unexplained weight loss, diarrhea, skin lesions, and swollen glands. These symptoms can indicate any number of simple infections, however, and don't mean you have AIDS. Some people infected with HIV develop no symptoms and remain in good health. To find out if you have the virus, get a blood test. HIV tests are free, confidential, and widely available. Testing positive doesn't mean you have AIDS.

mitted diseases (STDs) such as chlamydia and herpes have made college students properly cautious and discriminating (if not downright paranoid) about choosing a sexual partner. A passionate embrace may be arrested by frank and clinical questions: "Who have you been with? Did you use protection? How long have you been sexually active?" Celibacy has gained newfound respect as students become more knowledgeable about the failure rates of even the most reliable forms of birth control and health protection.

Carry me back to old virginity.
Graffito

Even though condoms and spermicides are free or cheaply available at most campus health services, only 40 percent of sexually active college students use them. A generation ago, the principal worry about sex among college students was pregnancy, which often led to "shotgun marriages" or an illegal and dangerous abortion. Unwanted pregnancy remains a concern: a recent survey at the University of Michigan revealed that about one-third of all campus pregnancy tests were positive, and about one-third of the pregnancies were unwanted and unplanned. A 1987 survey found the incidence of unintended pregnancy among the general population of 20–24 year olds to be 60 percent.

Today, you must protect yourselves and each other from unwanted pregnancy and from incurable and life-threatening disease. All college students

A Quiz

Here are the six leading causes of death for all Americans in the 24–44 age group. Can you rank them in order?

A. Cancer **1.** _____

B. Suicide **2.** _____

C. Unintentional injury **3.** _____

D. Homicide **4.** _____

E. AIDS **5.** _____

F. Heart disease **6.** _____

(Answers: 1 E; 2 C; 3 A; 4 F; 5 D; 6 B.)

Source: Federal Centers for Disease Control and Prevention in Atlanta, Jan. 1995.

have a responsibility to be informed of the dangers of promiscuity and to ensure that their sexual activity is as safe as it can be.

Of course, the only completely safe sex is no sex at all. No protection device on the market today is failsafe.

If sexual abstinence is unrealistic, you can **make sex safer by maintaining control over your behavior**. Students often talk about "losing" control when they have actually given it up. Consciously or unconsciously, they reassign responsibility for their actions to the "power of alcohol" or to the "stronger will" of their partner. Make—and own—your own decisions.

What part of "no" don't you understand?

Anti-rape slogan

ACQUAINTANCE RAPE

How serious is this crime? One study found that 7 percent of the women on 32 campuses had been sexually assaulted during the previous year. Other studies show figures as high as 40 percent. In all studies, a disproportionately high percentage of acquaintance-rape cases involve first-year students.

Getting an accurate picture of the problem is difficult because college women are often reluctant to report an assault. They may hope to avoid public exposure or getting another in trouble. They may feel partly responsible for having given mixed signals, or because one or both parties were intoxicated.

Tips

Strategies for Safer Sex

1. **Be especially cautious when using alcohol.** According to the American College Health Association, over half the visits to campus health centers are related to alcohol and other drugs.
2. **Communicate with your partner.** Having sex shouldn't be easier than talking about it. Be open with your concerns and desires and respect those of your partner. When you sleep with someone, you sleep with everyone that person has ever slept with. Ask about your partner's sexual history, HIV status, and possible intravenous drug use.
3. **Use a condom.** Whether you are male or female, carry a latex condom and use it in combination with contraceptive foams, jellies, or creams. Make sure they contain nonoxynol-9, which has been proven to kill HIV (the virus that causes AIDS) on contact. Put the condom on carefully before intercourse (pre-ejaculatory fluid can contain sperm and transmit disease) and remove it only after withdrawal. Never reuse a condom.
4. **If your school clinic does not offer contraceptives or condoms**, make an appointment with your physician to discuss the options available.

On **Your** Own

Reviewing My Personal Pledge

Take a moment to review your personal pledge (p. 51). How are you doing? Have you managed to keep your commitments so far? Were any overly ambitious or unrealistic?

If you find you have been less successful than you had hoped, don't be discouraged. Instead, think about your original goals and why you were prevented from accomplishing them. Then recommit yourself to a new set of goals for the rest of the term by completing the Revised Personal Pledge below.

Revised Personal Pledge

1. I will ______________________________
2. I will ______________________________
3. I will ______________________________

______________________ ______________________
Signature Date

> I do not wish them [women] to have power over men, but over themselves.
>
> Mary Wollstonecraft, *Author of* Frankenstein

College men are often confused by charges of rape after what they thought was a mutually consensual act. They argue the woman didn't protest and in fact seemed to encourage what was happening, or, if she did protest, they viewed it as encouragement. Some men are taught by their fathers and male peers that when a woman says *no* she actually means *yes*. In this view, women deliberately tease men by creating obstacles a man must overcome by force.

Such views no longer find a receptive audience. **Aggressive sexual behavior without a partner's consent is not condoned; instead, it is increasingly considered a criminal act.** Norms of acceptable sexual behavior are changing: sex without clear mutual consent is assault under the law.

Both men and women share responsibility for the problem of acquaintance rape and must work together to find a solution for it.

Men must understand that criminal assault, as legally defined, can occur even without direct physical contact—that it occurs whenever a woman's physical or psychological privacy is invaded against her will—and that it is a serious crime with serious consequences. "No" means no, and "Yes" means yes, and "Maybe" (or the absence of a refusal) does not imply consent.

Women must be clear and assertive in their signals—both in body language and in spoken language. They must learn to recognize danger signals and react quickly, before suffering ensues.

Both men and women need to be conscious of the effects of alcohol and take responsibility for their own behavior.

SUMMARY

College is a time to clarify and strengthen our values. When our value system is weak, we tend to behave passively or aggressively rather than assertively. The clarification of values and the development of strong relationships go hand in hand.

Encounters with cultural diversity in college can be a source of anxiety or a stimulus to learning and growth. Your challenge is to achieve an appreciation and respect for these differences while continuing to take pride in your own culture. There is also, still, much prejudice on American college campuses; nonetheless, American college students have taken leadership roles in rejecting prejudice and affirming the value of cultural diversity. Relationships that bridge the differences between us are well worth cultivating.

Finally, when relationships become intimate or sexual, our values are, once again, put to new tests.

Strategic *Plan*

Look over your Self-Assessment at the beginning of the chapter and identify an area in which you'd like to make a change. Then develop a Strategic Plan, using the format below.

I. Situation Analysis

A. One problem I'm having with values and relationships is ______________________

____

B. One change I think I could make is ______________________

____

C. The benefits of making the change are ______________________

____

D. The consequences of not changing are ______________________

____

E. Some obstacles I'll have to overcome are ______________________

____

F. Some resources I'll need are ______________________

____

II. Goals, objectives, deadlines, and indicators

A. My goal is to ______________________

____

Deadline: ______________________

Indicators of success: ______________________

____

continued on next page

Strategic *Plan*

continued from previous page

B. Here's what I'm going to do to achieve my goal, along with a reasonable deadline for each task:

OBJECTIVE	DEADLINE
1. ______________________	______________
2. ______________________	______________
3. ______________________	______________
4. ______________________	______________
5. ______________________	______________

III. Self-test

YES	NO	
☐	☐	**A.** Are my goals and objectives stated simply and clearly?
☐	☐	**B.** Does each one have a single focus?
☐	☐	**C.** Are they stated in a positive way?
☐	☐	**D.** Are they realistic?
☐	☐	**E.** Can I achieve them by the deadline?
☐	☐	**F.** Will I know if I've achieved them?

Journal **Ideas**

1. Do you feel your values are strong or weak, according to the criteria outlined in this chapter?
2. Do you feel your values have been derived primarily from others or from your own experience?
3. How would others describe your interpersonal manner? Do you have a lot of friends, or is finding friends a challenge for you? Discuss.
4. What is the extent of your experience interacting with people from other cultures? Have you met any international students? What observations have you made so far?
5. Do you feel comfortable with members of the other sex? Looking back over your life, where do you think these feelings (positive or negative) came from?
6. Describe an instance of labeling or stereotyping you have experienced or witnessed. Have others hung a label on you? Do you ever stereotype others? How?

Web **Search**

Search the last ten years of *USA Today* for news stories about sexual harassment, using *USA Today*'s own search tool (http://search.usatoday.com/). For much of this ten-year period, the legal definition of sexual harassment operated on the assumption that sexual harassment always involved members of the opposite sex. On what date did the Supreme Court rule that federal law also applies to same-sex harassment?

11

Staying Healthy, Stressing Less

Self-*Assessment*

Check the statements that apply to you.

- ☐ **1.** I take time to attend to my health.
- ☐ **2.** I seldom eat junk food.
- ☐ **3.** I sleep well at night.
- ☐ **4.** I feel well rested and alert and wake readily in the morning.
- ☐ **5.** I seldom feel stressed out.
- ☐ **6.** I exercise regularly.
- ☐ **7.** I don't smoke and I drink infrequently or not at all.
- ☐ **8.** I am rarely bored.
- ☐ **9.** I am rarely ill.
- ☐ **10.** I schedule time for rest and recreation.

If you checked fewer than half, this chapter will be especially valuable to you.

Write **Before** *You Read*

A. Spend about a minute surveying this chapter. Then write three questions you expect to find answers to in this chapter.

1. ______________________________

2. ______________________________

3. ______________________________

B. Spend another minute writing down any thoughts that come to mind about the topics below. Write freely and rapidly.

1. Eating and exercising: ______________________________

____

____

____

2. Sources of stress: ______________________________

____

____

____

____

3. Alcohol: ______________________________

____

____

____

____

PREVIEW

Your first year in college is a good time to make a candid assessment of your overall well-being and to formulate a lifelong plan for your own wellness and fitness. This chapter encourages you to examine your attitudes toward health, exercise, sleep, leisure, stress, and drugs, and think about how they may affect your relationships and your hopes and plans for the future. In addition, it invites you to consider making changes in your lifestyle that will yield a fuller, richer, more satisfying—and longer—life.

THE WELLNESS CONCEPT

Soaring healthcare costs, along with new insights into the relationship between physical and mental well-being, have revolutionized our attitudes about personal health.

Americans are living longer, and our quality of life is improving thanks both to medical breakthroughs and an increased awareness of healthful lifestyle choices. Whereas doctors and hospitals once provided health care on a reactive basis (responding to a need or crisis), health maintenance organizations (HMOs), business, and industry now promote a proactive approach through planned holistic programs of wellness and fitness.

Wellness is not just the opposite of sickness. It is a comprehensive, deliberate strategy for living a full and happy life. "An apple a day keeps the doctor away" is not just a bit of folk wisdom, but a way of life for millions of Americans who have stopped smoking, reduced their consumption of alcohol and cholesterol, and taken up vigorous exercise programs.

Be careful about reading health books. You may die of a misprint.

Mark Twain
Writer/humorist

FOOD FOR THOUGHT

By all appearances, college life is not conducive to eating well. If you commute or have a family, job, and community responsibilities, you may be relying on fast food, "grazing," and prepackaged meals full of fat, starch, and preservatives. If you live on campus and have an all-you-can-eat meal plan, you may actually be eating all you can eat at every meal or overdoing the starchy, greasy items that often dominate institutional offerings. You may also be feeding quarters into vending machines between classes and ordering the occasional 3 A.M. pizza.

Never eat more than you can lift.

Miss Piggy

Still, despite the jokes about cafeteria food, most college students eat reasonably well, especially those on meal plans, according to a recent study by Washington State food science professor Kathy Beerman. Residential students ate the most fish, vegetables, and fresh fruit (and the most cookies). Fraternity students were served a well-balanced diet but also consumed the most beer, sodium, and foods high in cholesterol. Commuters, who tend to eat on the run, relied most heavily on snacks and fast-food restaurants.

Because "you are what you eat," **do a body check**. How do you feel? How do you look? Are you overweight or underweight? Do you often feel dizzy, fatigued, run down? Are you prone to frequent headaches or indigestion? If so, your diet may be the culprit.

On **Your** Own

Do I Have an Eating Disorder?

If you're concerned that you might have an eating disorder (anorexia nervosa, bulimia, compulsive overeating), take the following quiz.

YES	NO		
☐	☐	**1.**	I begin to think about food within ten minutes of finishing a meal.
☐	☐	**2.**	I always count the calories in the food I eat.
☐	☐	**3.**	I weigh myself three or more times a day.
☐	☐	**4.**	I try out new diets, regardless of my weight.
☐	☐	**5.**	I often "feel fat," even when my weight is normal or after eating a light meal.
☐	☐	**6.**	I categorize foods as "good" or "bad".
☐	☐	**7.**	I judge myself as "good" or "bad" on the basis of how much or what foods I have eaten.
☐	☐	**8.**	I believe others judge me as a person based on how much or what foods I have eaten.
☐	☐	**9.**	Eating when other people are around makes me uncomfortable.
☐	☐	**10.**	I sometimes take laxatives or force myself to vomit after eating.

If you answered yes to five or more questions, you may have an eating disorder. Make an appointment with a campus counselor or your personal physician to learn more about eating disorders and what you can do about them.

On **Your** Own

A Tally

List everything you ate yesterday. What healthful foods were missing? What unhealthful foods were present? Were the total calories too much, too little, or about right?

Think about *why* you ate what and when you did. What positive dietary changes could you easily make?

If you truly want to feel better, look better, and think better, here are some suggestions:

- *Cut down on sugar.* There's not much good to be said about sugar. Its unpleasant side effects—weight gain and depression—last far longer than the momentary pleasure it brings. Go easy on salt too, especially if you or anyone in your family has a history of heart or blood pressure problems.
- *Avoid red meat.* It clogs the arteries with the wrong kind of cholesterol. Fish and poultry are good sources of protein and have less fat.
- *Maintain a balanced diet.* Every day of your life try to eat a piece of fruit, some green vegetables and some vegetable proteins (beans, seeds, nuts), some high-fiber bread or cereal, some cheese, milk, or

> I've been on a diet for two weeks and all I've lost is two weeks.
>
> Totie Fields
> *Comedian*

yogurt, and a tiny bit of fat or oil (preferably free of cholesterol or saturated fat).

- *Avoid food from vending machines.* Most of it is high in salt, sugar, fat, caffeine, preservatives, and/or additives.
- *Eat a substantial breakfast and avoid eating after supper.* The reason is simple: we burn a lot of calories during the day and very few while sleeping.
- *Be selective in the cafeteria.* Think before you put it on your tray. Choose the healthful foods and skip the sweets and starches. When you reach for that wedge of devil's food cake, imagine what it would be like if you slipped it into the hip pocket of your jeans, which is about where it'll end up.
- *Be careful at parties.* Alcohol is a major cause of weight gain among college students. At a party the salted snacks and beer aren't really free; you always pay for them later.
- *Manage the munchies.* It's OK to "graze" (eat when you feel hungry), as long as it adds up to a balanced diet over 24 hours.
- *Drink lots of water throughout the day.* It helps to flush your system.

GETTING ENOUGH SLEEP

Most people need seven to nine hours of sleep a night to function at their peak. Some get by on far less. We often find we need less sleep when we're

Fanatic About Food

One survey of residential first-year women revealed that five out of six were dieting at any given time. Another study found that 9 percent deliberately vomited at least once a month to lose weight. One-third of the women and one-fourth of the men in the study admitted they were "terrified" of gaining weight.

Separation anxiety is a major culprit, because many of us associate food with parental love. But there are other causes: boredom, loneliness, work-induced stress, the ever-present candy and pop machines with nearby ATMs for instant cash, starch-intensive all-you-can-eat cafeterias, a campus surrounded by bars and all-night pizza parlors, and nobody to tell you what you can or cannot do.

There's only one way to avoid gaining weight: consume fewer calories and get regular exercise. Exercise alone is an inefficient way to lose weight—you'd have to run fifteen miles just to burn up the calories from a small chocolate sundae. But moderate daily exercise does help increase your metabolism. And when you also take in fewer calories—particularly low-fat, high-grain calories—it is easy to maintain a healthy weight.

Self-administered cures for weight gain are often more disastrous than the cause. **Most students shed their initial weight gain within a year or two.** In fact, the carbohydrates and fats that account for most of the weight gain may play a useful role in reducing anxiety and depression. But cycles of binge eating and crash dieting can have catastrophic consequences, leading to serious eating disorders such as anorexia (self-starvation) and bulimia (bingeing and purging).

What's the solution? Once the clothes no longer fit, most students find their own solution simply by exercising self-control. But a study at the University of South Carolina stumbled onto an interesting fact: students who were involved in campus organizations experienced significantly less weight gain than those who were not. The conclusion: staying busy and having purposeful goals helps reduce overeating.

on vacation because we experience less stress. If you're able to deal successfully with stress by day, you'll be able to get along with less sleep at night.

Busy people often find it impossible to get the amount of sleep they need on a regular basis. If you find your sleep shortened or interrupted, **take brief (ten- to fifteen-minute) catnaps.** If you think you're likely to oversleep during this time, set an alarm. You don't have to fall asleep to get the full benefit of a nap. Just concentrate on letting your mind go completely blank. Cover your eyes, breathe slowly, and relax each muscle in your body. When you return to consciousness, you'll be able to work more efficiently.

If you have trouble falling asleep at night, it may be because your body is full of stimulants—caffeine, nicotine, and/or nature's own stress-induced drug epinephrine, commonly called adrenaline. There is no way to hasten the natural process of filtering adrenaline from the bloodstream; the best you can do is accept your wakeful state as unavoidable. Trying desperately to fall asleep will just add to your stress.

When you can't sleep, lie comfortably without tossing and turning, think pleasant and positive thoughts, and let nature take its course. Some people who treat insomniacs suggest running an imaginary film of your day. When you run into a conflict situation, stop the film, examine the conflict, and resolve it to your satisfaction before restarting the film. If you have a chronic problem with insomnia, instead of focusing on ways to fall asleep, **focus on avoiding stimulants and finding better ways of dealing with stress** during your waking hours.

As with diet and exercise, your body will let you know if you're not getting enough sleep. Your periods of concentration will grow shorter; you'll become forgetful, easily distracted, confused, and irritable. Obviously, these are not favorable conditions for learning.

Taking an exam after a sleepless night is a recipe for disaster. Cramming the night before an exam not only reduces sleep time but pumps the body full of adrenaline, which postpones or prevents sleep. Getting a good night's sleep after an efficient study session will help you remember what you learned and put you in a positive frame of mind for your exam the next day.

Exercise benefits both mind and body.

GETTING AND STAYING IN SHAPE

Mind and body work best when they work in harmony with each other; as the ancient Romans said, "*Mens sana in corpore sano,*" a sound mind in a sound body. If you stay in good physical condition,

Your fitness program should be enjoyable and challenging.

you'll sleep better, be mentally alert, have more energy, be less susceptible to stress, and have a more positive attitude.

All exercise programs emphasize five basic types of physical fitness:

1. ***Cardiovascular fitness.*** Your heart pumps oxygen through the lungs, into the vascular system, and to the brain. Cardiovascular fitness is acquired by aerobic activity (the kind that gets your heart pumping). Continued aerobic exercise produces endorphins, a group of natural chemicals in your body that cause feelings of elation and profound well-being—sometimes called "runner's high."

2. ***Muscle strength.*** Your muscles have enough mass to handle most physically demanding tasks without undue strain. Your lifestyle will dictate just how strong you need to be. But even if you don't need great physical strength, body building is a wonderful way to lower stress and build self-esteem.

3. ***Muscle endurance.*** Your muscles are capable of sustained, repeated activity. Muscle endurance is generally considered more important than muscle strength. Whereas strength is gained by lifting heavy weights, endurance results from repeated exercise with lighter weights, resulting in a wiry rather than bulky body

4. ***Body composition.*** The ideal is to decrease body fat and increase lean body mass. The former requires adjustments to your diet. The latter requires strenuous exercise.

5. ***Flexibility.*** Body flexibility is achieved by stretching rather than compacting the muscles—the ideal attained by dancers and gymnasts.

The physical education courses required for graduation were never intended to fulfill students' need for exercise in college. Their purpose is simply to introduce you to physical and mental fitness as a lifelong habit. They give you an opportunity to sample—from a wide range of physical activities—a few that you may want to adopt for life. These classes encourage you to think of your physical, emotional, and intellectual well-being as intimately connected.

Workouts and study sessions have a lot in common. Both require high motivation, strong self-discipline, clear goals, accountability, and measurable indicators of success. Both are sometimes fun, but when you're physically or mentally out of shape, they can be plain hard work.

When you're out of shape, working out is the last thing you want to do. If you've never studied much and haven't had a history of academic success, sitting down to study may have a similar lack of appeal. Believe it or not, people who have formed the habit of working out or studying on a regular

> 1. Avoid fried meats, which angry up the blood.
> 2. If your stomach disputes you, lie down and pacify it with cool thoughts.
> 3. Keep the juices flowing by jangling around gently as you move.
> 4. Go very lightly on the vices, such as carrying on in society. The social ramble ain't restful.
> 5. Avoid running at all times.
> 6. Don't look back. Something might be gaining on you.
>
> Satchel Paige
> *Baseball pitcher and Hall of Famer*

basis (often they're the same people) actually enjoy and look forward to both. They've had success and seen results from their hard work.

Essential in any fitness program (and in any study program) is to have clear goals. Use your first workout (like your first exam in a college class) for self-assessment, to find out where you are. If you decide to take up running, for example, time yourself over a measured distance. Just run naturally without straining or hurting yourself. Write the time, distance, and the date in a training notebook. If you want to lift weights, start with a very light weight. Do ten repetitions ("reps") of the exercise. Whatever you accomplish, write it down in your notebook.

Each time you work out, match or improve on your best prior effort. **Before each workout, set a goal:** today I'm going to run a mile without stopping or cover a mile in under eight minutes; today I'm going to do ten 90-pound reps on the bench press; today I'm going to do one set of twenty sit-ups. Every week or two, look back over your training notebook to **check your progress**. You'll feel a sense of accomplishment when you see how far you've come in a short time, and will want to capture this feeling over and over again.

One measure of the effectiveness of your study sessions is the grades you receive. In an exercise program you need similar "indicators of success." In addition to daily goals, **set mid- and long-range goals.** A mid-range goal for a swimmer, for example, might be to compete in an intramural swim meet some months away. A long-range goal might be to make the swim team or achieve a heart rate under 60. If you've taken up golf, a mid-range goal might be to score under 90 for eighteen holes; a long-range goal, to achieve a single-digit handicap.

As always, reward yourself when you achieve a milestone. The main reward, of course, is the level of fitness and skill you've achieved.

Before undertaking an exercise program, consider your fitness objectives, talents and interests, abilities, and overall health.

- What are your fitness objectives? Do you want to improve cardiovascular fitness? If so, good choices are walking, running, cycling, jumping rope, swimming, rowing, cross-country skiing, climbing stairs, court sports (badminton, tennis, squash, handball, racquetball, volleyball, wallyball, basketball), and aerobic dancing. Want to increase your strength? Try free weights or indoor machines (Nautilus, rowing, climbing) or, if you don't have access to machines, do push-ups, sit-ups, and pull-ups. Improve your hand-eye coordination? Try golf, tennis, bowling, or archery. To reduce body fat, combine an aerobic activity with a sensible diet. If you enjoy problem solving, try golf, rock climbing, or orienteering. Pick an activity known to give the results you want.
- What activities do you enjoy and find interesting? People who like aggressive competition should try court sports or martial arts. If you don't like competition but do like sociability, try aerobics or golf. If you want to exercise on your own, walk, run, swim, skate, cycle, or climb stairs. Above all, select an activity that sounds like fun to you. If your workout is drudgery, you won't stick with it for long.

> The only reason I would take up jogging is so that I could hear heavy breathing again.
>
> Erma Bombeck
> *Columnist*

- How do your talents and abilities match up with your fitness plan? If you have poor vision, for example, steer clear of activities that require fine hand-eye coordination. Pick an area in which you believe you have a pretty good chance of success.

Whatever activity you select, **consult a physician or sports medicine clinician before plunging ahead** on your own. A history of heart problems in your family, for example, need not prevent you from aerobic activity, but you will need to follow a cautious, prescribed program. If you have had a knee or elbow injury, you may want to do some preliminary rehabilitation of the muscles around the joint before placing strain on it. If overweight, you may want to combine a conservative long-range weight loss program with moderate exercise to avoid excessive strain on your heart and joints. If you're undertaking an intensive aerobic training program, combine it with weight training on alternate days to avoid injury.

A training partner can help you in several ways. First, it's safer to work out with a partner, especially in training with free weights: your partner serves as a "spotter," helping you out when you get "stuck" under a weight. Second, a partner can give you encouragement, pushing you to work a little harder. Third, you're less likely to skip a workout if your partner is waiting for you at the gym. And of course some sports like tennis require a partner. If possible, pick a partner somewhat more experienced than you are, someone who will push you to a higher level.

The most valuable physical activity is one that provides at least some aerobic benefits. Aerobic exercise keeps you breathing deeply for at least twenty minutes. This constant, vigorous activity makes your heart pump faster, oxygenating the blood. Over time, your heart rate gradually lowers. That means it's working more efficiently, beating less often but providing the same benefits. Aerobic activity strengthens the heart and cleanses the arteries, resulting in better health and longer life.

In any physically demanding task, let your body tell you how fast and how far to go. Forget the macho slogan "No pain, no gain." **When it starts to hurt, slow down.** Spend about ten minutes stretching muscles before and after each workout. Warm up before, cool down after.

> Each person has his own safe place—running, painting, swimming, fishing, weaving, gardening. The activity itself is less important than the act of drawing on your own resources.
>
> Barbara Gordon
> *TV producer*

A LIFE OF LEISURE

All too often, when college students do find free time, they "reward themselves" by eating, drinking, and socializing.

Parties are a fine way to release tension and make friends, but they aren't the only way. College is a good time to identify and develop interests, hobbies, and forms of recreation that will provide pleasure throughout your life.

The word *recreation* literally means to re-create. Ironically, people often choose leisure activities that re-create or reenact the conditions of their work lives. Business executives who spend their working hours strategizing and solving problems often relax by playing bridge or golf—problem-solving games with competitive partners. Mathematicians or computer scientists may adopt hobbies that emphasize form, structure, and logic—chess, classical music, mystery novels, stamp collecting. Artists may choose needlepoint or gourmet cooking.

A satisfying leisure activity tends to be similar to, yet different from, what you do for a living. Finding a hobby you enjoy requires some initial experimentation, a process of trial and error. A good hobby should be something that's always there, waiting for you like a good friend. Often the best hobbies don't require the presence of other people.

Some suggestions:

- *Playing an instrument.* You can do it alone or with others. After a few lessons (from a book or a teacher), you can make progress on your own, and there's plenty of sheet music available.
- *Handicrafts.* Visit a craft store or hobby shop and buy a kit. Making a birdhouse or doing needlework are therapeutic ways to get your mind off your work and end up with something useful to have, give, or show. You'll process stress and solve problems without realizing it.
- *Collecting.* Stamps, rare books, beer cans, butterflies, baseball cards—the possibilities are endless. The great pleasure is taxonomy—arranging, identifying, and classifying. If your life is chaotic, collecting is a way of creating a private, orderly world.
- *Volunteer work.* For people people, this is a way to use your talents to help others and experience personal satisfaction. Teach someone to read, take part in Special Olympics, be a surrogate parent to a child in a safe house. Animal lovers may wish to volunteer with the SPCA or animal rescue groups.

If you have many interests and are having a hard time choosing a major, consider designating one of your interests as a leisure activity or avocation. You don't have to choose between the cello and mathematics. You can do both—one for a living and the other for fun.

STRESSING LESS

A college campus is a pressure-cooker. Everyone—students, faculty, and staff—puts in long hours with high expectations and for little immediate reward. Many try to balance schoolwork with responsibilities to a family and a job. The result is a high level of stress.

Stress refers to the presence of the powerful drug adrenaline in our bodies. This adrenal secretion is the body's natural reaction to trauma. Its flow

Dolce Far Niente?

This Italian phrase means "It is sweet to do nothing." Doing nothing—just being a couch potato in front of the TV, for example, often seems a delightful alternative to people who are overworked.

But studies at the University of Chicago show that doing nothing is far from pleasurable. A person's self-esteem increases after a few hours of gardening; after a few hours of watching TV, it declines. People reported feeling irritable and depressed.

Human beings seem most happy when confronted by challenges that require their skills and develop their potential—jobs that seem like games. Children report their favorite forms of recreation are those that combine features of work and play: sports, music, art, computers, hobbies, and learning new subjects.

The conclusion of the study: People don't enjoy wasting time.

Collaborate

List Brainstorm

In a group of four to five, brainstorm three lists, first individually, then sharing your lists with the group:

1. List eight to ten specific opportunities to exercise on campus (for example, rollerblading or intramural team openings).
2. List five or six ways to eat well on campus (for example, where's the best salad bar? When and where can you shop for healthy snacks?).
3. List your "top ten" fun things to do that don't cost money (or that cost very little).

After you've read your lists aloud to the group, compile three composite lists of your group's best ideas to share with the class as a whole.

After all, tomorrow is another day.

Scarlett O'Hara, *heroine of Margaret Mitchell's novel* Gone with the Wind

into the bloodstream can be triggered by a physical shock, such as an auto accident. Or it can be "tricked" into action at the bidding of the brain when we feel threatened, as in the case of stage fright. In small amounts, adrenaline is a valuable stimulant, keeping us awake, alert, energetic.

In cases of severe trauma, it is secreted in much larger amounts, disabling the nervous system so the body feels no pain, as when an accident victim is said to be "in shock."

When stress is prolonged, we soon experience its destructive symptoms: irritability, self-pity, hypochondria, anxiety, depression, exhaustion, insomnia, loss of appetite, eating binges, apathy, dread, panic. These negative emotions, in turn, trigger any number of physical and mental illnesses: migraines, diarrhea, flu, ulcers, high blood pressure, sexual dysfunction, "nervous breakdowns," possibly even serious organic diseases like cancer and heart disease.

When persons suffering from stress treat themselves with amphetamines, alcohol, or barbiturates, the problems grow worse. **Stress can be lessened only by an effort of the will.**

Sixteen Stressbusters

One way of reducing stress is to anticipate and avoid stressful situations. When this is impossible, we can change how we respond to these situations. Here are sixteen stressbusting suggestions:

Stressbuster 1. Eliminate the word *problem* from your vocabulary and replace it with *challenge* or *opportunity*. When facing a difficult exam or a speech in front of class, think of it as a challenge to do your best and an opportunity to learn and grow. Say, "I'm looking forward to this. I've got a plan and I'm prepared. This is a chance for me to try some things I've never tried before. I'm going to feel great about myself because I'll know I tried my best."

Stressbuster 2. Get organized. Clear your desk. Make lists of everything you *have* to do. There will be things on your list you don't really have to do: buy flashlight batteries, write

Strenuous physical activity is the best antidote for stress

Aunt Jan, give Dave a manicure. Prioritize your list and do the important things first.

Stressbuster 3. Do it now. If you're faced with a difficult task, break it into a set of smaller tasks and do the first one immediately. Feeling guilty is a major cause of stress. Do what you must to feel positive about yourself.

Stressbuster 4. Say "No." Put yourself first sometimes. If you are working at full capacity and someone asks you to run for office, decorate the lounge, go to the mall or help with a paper, just say no. Do not feel guilty about it; you're entitled.

Stressbuster 5. Compromise. Give a little. Make a deal. In a disagreement, give up something to get something. If your term paper deadline is approaching and you haven't finished your research, write up what you've got, turn it in, and accept the consequences. If you're studying for an exam and time runs short, concentrate on remembering a few important points and let the rest go. Be human. Nobody loves a perfectionist. Give yourself a break.

Stressbuster 6. Don't take on other people's problems. If someone is angry with you, that's their problem. If someone comes to you with a problem, you can listen and sympathize without feeling obliged to solve it.

Stressbuster 7. Fake it. Pretending to be cool, calm, and collected often makes you cool, calm, and collected. Ask any public performer if this really works. Being cool is mind over matter. Use this technique in moderation and only in emergencies though; people who are too cool for too long end up never feeling anything. Similarly, smile and laugh once in a while, even if you must force it. There is some evidence that the "grin-and-bear-it" strategy works: smiles and laughter release endorphins that invigorate the spirit.

Stressbuster 8. Wait. A problem is not a problem until it's a problem. Ninety percent of all problems go away within 24 hours.

Stressbuster 9. Meditate. Clear your head with yoga, martial arts, or focused breathing. A good book will introduce you to many varied meditation techniques.

Stressbuster 10. Focus on physical fitness. People who are overweight, live on junk food, smoke, abuse alcohol, and don't exercise are far more susceptible to stress than those who take good care of their bodies.

Stressbuster 11. Build time into your schedule for relaxation. A schedule consisting of nothing but work, like a schedule consisting of nothing but play, inevitably produces stress. Create a balance. Set study goals in segments; when you com-

> Fortunately, analysis is not the only way to resolve inner conflicts. Life itself can be a very effective therapist.
>
> Karen Horney
> *Psychologist*

> The cure for anything is salt water—sweat, tears, or the sea.
>
> Isak Dinesen
> *Writer*

> Because the road is rough and long, shall we despise the skylark's song?
>
> Anne Brontë
> *Novelist/poet*

plete a segment, reward yourself by relaxing. Do something completely opposite from the stressful task: see a movie, bowl a few frames, go for a drive in the country. Get away from campus. Get a fresh outlook. Conversely, if you watch two hours of soaps in the afternoon, "pay the bill" with a two-hour study session.

Stressbuster 12. Visualize. Find a place where you can totally relax—an easy chair, a hot shower, a grassy meadow. Cover your eyes and visualize a tranquil scene. Move your eyes around as you see the birds, the mountains, the lake, the woods. Hear the waves lapping. Feel warm breezes on your skin. Inhale slowly and deeply, hold your breath for a count of three, and exhale slowly. Concentrate on the responses of your body. Focus on the arches of your feet, your ankles, calves, knees; work your way up, relaxing every muscle. If you feel tension anywhere, go back and release the tension in that muscle. When you feel totally refreshed and renewed, leap up and stride briskly and confidently back to your headquarters. (This exercise also works before an exam or a speech. You can do it in class and no one will be the wiser.) Relaxation/visualization audiotapes are widely available in bookstores and through mail order.

Stressbuster 13. Put your troubles in perspective. When you've identified the source of your stress (an upcoming exam, the behavior of a friend), frame the event in a larger context: your college career, your life, the entire student body, the population of the United States or the world, human history. Compare your challenge to the more difficult challenges others face: physical and mental abuse, the loneliness of prison and exile, hunger, disease. The point is not to minimize the seriousness of your challenge, but to gain a sense of its scope and intensity, to place it in a larger perspective.

Stressbuster 14. Get outside yourself. Notice others who seem stressed out. Give them a hug. Tell them you can relate, that sometimes you feel the same way. Listen without judging or giving advice. Take comfort in knowing that all humans, especially the most talented, suffer from stress. Be concerned with issues bigger than you and back your concern with action: chair a committee, raise funds, distribute handbills.

Put into words

Stressbuster 15. Talk it over. Share your problems with a friend or professional counselor who knows how to listen without making judgments. A major cause of stress is the unknown. When you verbalize your concerns, you begin to identify the causes of stress. Once out in the open, these are easier to deal with.

Stressbuster 16. Get help. If you're stuck in a dark place and just don't have the strength or clarity of mind to try the recommendations above, go to your resident adviser, a trusted mentor, or the counseling office. They'll help you sort things out.

> One reason I don't drink is that I want to know when I am having a good time.
>
> Lady Astor
> *Socialite*

ALCOHOL

Alcohol has its points. When consumed in moderation (a drink or two a day), it soothes the troubled spirit, relaxes, and according to one study, may reduce the risk of heart disease by flushing cholesterol out of the bloodstream.

Unfortunately, there's a downside too. Almost all the bad things that can happen to you in college are related to alcohol. National campus statistics show that alcohol is involved in about

- two-thirds of all violent behavior
- one-half of all physical injuries
- one-third of all emotional difficulties among students.

Alcohol is a factor in about one-third of all crimes, but it's a factor in 90% of college campus crimes. Most reported cases of sexual assault on campus involve consumption of alcohol—by both victim and perpetrator.

The best way to stay in control is not to drink.

In 1997 more than half of American college students drank to get drunk. Abusive or "binge" drinking (five or more drinks in a row for men, four for women) is on the rise, according to a comprehensive Harvard University study published in the *Journal of American College Health* (August 1998). Four out of 5 fraternity and sorority members were binge drinkers. Binge drinkers were 7 times more likely to have unprotected sex than non-binge drinkers, 10 times more likely to drive after drinking, and 11 times more likely to fail academically. College students consume over 430 million gallons of alcohol annually at a cost of about $4.2 billion a year—far more than they spend on textbooks.

The negative effects of excessive alcohol consumption can be deadly. Contrary to popular belief, **alcohol is a depressant, not a stimulant.** Although moderate alcohol consumption may briefly and initially stimulate sexual desire, it soon reduces sexual sensitivity; chronic use leads to impotence and sterility. Heavy drinking is sometimes called "death on the installment plan" because it is a major factor in respiratory diseases (such as bronchitis); stomach complaints (ulcers, gastritis); diseases of the nervous system (neuritis, epilepsy); muscle deterioration; intestinal problems; circulatory diseases (gout, cirrhosis of the liver, diabetes, heart disease); inflamma-

Tips

Intoxicated People

1. Alcohol makes people irrational. Don't argue or reason with intoxicated people and don't become angry or upset by what they say. Stay calm.
2. Caffeine, cold water, and physical exercise may wake people up but won't sober them up. The only cure is time—time for the liver to oxidize the alcohol in the bloodstream, which takes about one hour per drink.
3. Let the intoxicated person know you're concerned about his or her welfare. Offer reassurance, not judgment.
4. Encourage them to lie down and go to sleep. Get them to lie on their sides and put a pillow behind their backs to keep them from rolling over and choking if they vomit.
5. Call the police or your resident adviser if an intoxicated person becomes uncontrollable or if you sense a medical emergency.

> Partying is such sweet sorrow.
>
> Jean Kerr
> *Playwright*

tion of the pancreas; and (because it reduces the body's natural resistance) a host of infectious diseases. The suicide rate among alcoholics is 58 percent higher than among nonalcoholics. About one-third of all murders and traffic fatalities involve alcohol, with 60 percent of the latter involving teenagers.

If you choose to drink, **drink in moderation.** When you find yourself saying, "I really shouldn't," don't. Don't drink on an empty stomach. Before and during a party, eat protein-rich food (meat, cheese, milk), which slows down the rate at which alcohol enters the bloodstream, rather than starchy foods (crackers, chips). Limit yourself to one alcoholic drink an hour. (One drink means one glass of wine, one can of beer, or one shot of whiskey, all of which contain the same amount of alcohol.) Alternate your consumption between alcoholic and nonalcoholic beverages. Nurse your drink and respectfully decline "chugging" challenges or drinking games: they can kill you.

Make sure you are aware of local and state laws that govern drinking (using a fake ID, driving while intoxicated) and the consequences of violating them. Don't drive under the influence of alcohol, ever, and don't accept a ride from a driver who has been drinking.

If you're a party host, provide plenty of nonalcoholic beverages—sugar-free and caffeine-free soft drinks, juice, and flavored waters. **Don't pressure guests or your partner to drink** or make a keg or a bar the centerpiece of your party. Proceed on the assumption that anyone at the party might be an alcoholic who is struggling to stay sober and needs your support. And stay sober yourself. A good way to do that is to remember **you are legally responsible for the safety of your guests**, both at the party and on their way home.

Some colleges now offer "substance-free" housing for students who pledge not to use alcohol, tobacco, or other drugs in their room or hall. Some students choose this option because of pressure from parents. Others are recovering addicts or have family members who are addicted to drugs. Most choose it freely, in order to pursue a healthier lifestyle. More and more colleges are offering proactive drug and alcohol treatment programs for students, faculty, and staff. Rutgers University provides a residential drug rehabilitation center on campus to treat addicted students—students who attend daily counseling sessions and are allowed to leave only for classes. Almost every college in America has an active chapter of Alcoholics Anonymous.

> A custom loathsome to the eye, hateful to the nose, harmful to the brain, dangerous to the lungs, and in the black, stinking fumes thereof, nearest resembling the horrible stygian smoke of the pit that is bottomless.
>
> King James I
> *(c. 1604) on the evils of smoking*

SMOKING

Americans have been made acutely aware, over the last decade, of the health dangers of cigarette smoking. Millions of adults have stopped. Only about 20 percent of college students smoke at least occasionally, and just over 10 percent smoke regularly. Campus buildings have been declared smoke-free environments. In state-supported institutions, smoking in public buildings is often a violation of state law.

> I phoned my dad to tell him I had stopped smoking. He called me a quitter.
>
> Steven Pearl
> *Comedian*

Smoking harms the health of smokers and nonsmokers alike. You have a right to clean air. Assert your right by letting violators know you don't like their smoke. Express yourself kindly, but firmly.

If you're young and your smoking history is brief, quitting will be a lot easier now than later. If you're older and have been smoking for many years, it will be more difficult. In either case, **everyone is too young to smoke—and never too old to quit.** Now is the time.

> The best mind-altering drug is the truth.
>
> Lily Tomlin
> *Humorist*

OTHER DRUGS

The use of illicit drugs by college students has been declining steadily since 1985. In a 1990 survey, 33 percent of all college students admitted they had used drugs during the past year, down 4 percent from the year before. About 30 percent had used marijuana, compared to 50 percent ten years earlier. By 1994 the figure had dropped to 23.6 percent in the month that preceded the survey.

Although alcohol and nicotine are by far the most common addictive drugs on today's college campus, you may know someone who is using or abusing illegal or prescription drugs. Some symptoms of substance abuse are changes in behavior (skipping class, missing appointments); changes in personal appearance; mood swings and personality changes (hyper or withdrawn); social isolation; associating with drug users and suppliers; and defensive reactions to expressions of concern. If someone you know has a drug problem, contact your resident adviser, campus police, or counseling office. They will know how to help.

SUMMARY

Because most college students are exceptionally busy and at their physical peak anyway, they often neglect physical health at the expense of emotional well-being. College is a good time to adopt a wellness habit that will sustain you throughout your life: a healthy diet, regular cardiovascular exercise, satisfying leisure activities, effective strategies for coping with stress and an awareness of the dangers of alcohol, tobacco, and other drugs. Good health is fundamental. When you're not healthy, nothing else matters.

Strategic *Plan*

Look over your Self-Assessment at the beginning of the chapter and identify an area in which you'd like to make a change. Then develop a Strategic Plan, using the format below.

I. Situation Analysis

A. One problem I'm having with my overall wellness is ______________________________

____

B. One change I think I could make is ______________________________

____

C. The benefits of making the change are ______________________________

____

D. The consequences of not changing are ______________________________

____

E. Some obstacles I'll have to overcome are ______________________________

____

continued on next page

Strategic *Plan* *continued from previous page*

F. Some resources I'll need are ______________________

____

II. Goals, objectives, deadlines, and indicators

A. My goal is to ______________________

____

Deadline: ______________________

Indicators of success: ______________________

____

B. Here's what I'm going to do to achieve my goal, along with a reasonable deadline for each task:

	OBJECTIVE	DEADLINE
1.	______________________	____________
2.	______________________	____________

	OBJECTIVE	DEADLINE
3.	______________________	____________
4.	______________________	____________
5.	______________________	____________

III. Self-Test

YES	NO	
☐	☐	**A.** Are my goals and objectives stated simply and clearly?
☐	☐	**B.** Does each one have a single focus?
☐	☐	**C.** Are they stated in a positive way?
☐	☐	**D.** Are they realistic?
☐	☐	**E.** Can I achieve them by the deadline?
☐	☐	**F.** Will I know if I've achieved them?

Journal **Ideas**

1. Describe your overall state of wellness and fitness. What are you most proud of? What could stand improvement?
2. Describe your exercise program if you have one. What are the benefits and drawbacks? What kind of fitness would you like to attain?
3. How do you spend your free time? Do you have hobbies or outside interests? What do you think you might like to take up?
4. Describe your emotional health. Is stress a problem for you? Worry? Anger? Expressing your feelings?
5. Do you use alcohol or drugs when stressed? Do you have concerns about drugs and alcohol? Do any of your friends have a problem with drugs or alcohol? What could you do to address your own problem or to help a friend?

Web **Search**

1. Assume you are writing a paper about binge drinking on campus. Search InfoTrac College Edition© for three useful articles on this topic. Try each of the keywords below. In each space, write down the number of useful hits yielded by that search. Which keywords were the most useful in finding information on this topic?
   a. alcohol abuse on campus ______________________
   b. drinking ______________________
   c. college students and alcohol ______________________
   d. binge drinking + college ______________________
   e. binge drinking and college ______________________
2. Find a Web site called Welcome to Drinking: A Student's Guide (http://www.glness.com/ndhs/). Then take "The Knowledge Test" and "How to Determine if You're at Risk" and check your answers. How knowledgeable were you about drinking? Give the test to a friend or roommate. Then discuss your attitudes toward drinking in college. Do either of you show signs of being at risk? Of what?

12

Planning for Success

Self-Assessment

Check the statements that apply to you.

☐ **1.** I expect to complete a bachelor's degree in four years.

☐ **2.** I expect to transfer to another institution.

☐ **3.** I'm attending college part-time.

☐ **4.** I'm undecided about my major.

☐ **5.** I have studied my college catalog thoroughly.

☐ **6.** I'm finding that my courses are useful and relevant.

☐ **7.** I expect to find a job in my major field.

☐ **8.** I feel organized and satisfied with my degree pursuit.

☐ **9.** My favorite subjects and my career interests mesh well.

☐ **10.** I chose my major because it's what I wanted.

If you checked fewer than half, this chapter will be especially valuable to you.

Write **Before** *You Read*

A. Spend about a minute surveying this chapter. Then write three questions you expect to find answers to in this chapter.

1. ______________________________

2. ______________________________

3. ______________________________

B. Spend another minute writing down any thoughts that come to mind about the topics below. Write freely and rapidly.

1. Choosing a major: ______________________________

2. Choosing a career: ______________________________

3. Visualizing my future: ______________________________

PREVIEW

Careful planning is important if you expect to complete a bachelor's degree in four years. But how can you plan when you're undecided about your major and the job market is so unpredictable? First-year students should become thoroughly familiar with the college catalog, a source of vital information about majors, college policies, course content, and graduation requirements. Other sources are career counselors, major and minor requirement sheets (available in the reception areas of academic departments), faculty and staff mentors, more experienced students, and your academic adviser. Undecided students can use their time advantageously by acquiring the basic knowledge and skills needed to be competitive in a rapidly changing, technological workplace.

GRADUATING IN FOUR YEARS

It is still possible to complete a bachelor's degree in four years. However, your chances of doing so are steadily diminishing. Seventy percent of college students take more than four years to graduate; 53 percent take at least six years.

Some obstacles to the traditional four-year lockstep are:

1. ***Increased tuition and fees.*** Annual increases in tuition, fees, and room and board are forcing students to work more hours to stay in school. This often translates into fewer hours in class, full-time employment in the summer, or "stopping out" of college for a semester or more to earn money.

2. ***Transferring.*** As tuition and fees rise and our society grows more mobile, more students are transferring to colleges that are less expensive and closer to home. Because most colleges don't accept all transfer credit and all colleges have slightly different requirements for graduation, each time you transfer, you lose some ground.

Transfer Tips for Community College Students

- Arrange a preliminary campus visit by calling the Admissions or Articulation Office for an appointment. Most universities offer special "Transfer Days" featuring general information and a tour for groups.
- Apply for admission during your sophomore year—the earlier the better. Some colleges guarantee admission to students with an Associate of Arts degree, but you can apply before you have completed your degree. You must request an official transcript from your Records Office. (Remember that being admitted to a university does not guarantee admission to a particular college or academic program, which may require a separate application.)
- Keep written records of any contact you make with the transfer institution: date, time, and nature of any request, names of persons you speak to, and dated copies of all documents you send and receive.
- There is a separate application for financial aid; get it from the university's Financial Aid Office. Make sure you fill it out completely and submit it as early as possible.
- The university's Housing Office can help you locate housing on or off campus.
- Carefully read all information sent to you by the university, especially regulations and procedures for registration, financial aid, and housing.
- Remember to notify the university of any changes in your name, address, or phone number.
- When problems arise, attack the problem, not the person. Be patient, calm, and constructive.

3. ***Changing majors.*** Due to the uncertain economy and a rapidly changing employment picture, students switch majors now more than ever before. Unfortunately, some courses you've already taken may not apply to the graduation requirements of a new major.

4. ***Increased requirements for professional programs.*** In the past, an undergraduate education broke down this way:

General education requirements	40%
Major requirements	50%
Electives	10%

   Increasingly, accrediting agencies are expecting more hours of preprofessional training. Meanwhile, liberal arts colleges have resisted pressure to erode basic requirements and have even added new requirements, such as computer literacy, to the general education curriculum. This has crowded the curriculum, leaving less space for electives.

5. ***Withdrawing from/repeating courses.*** More students are withdrawing from or repeating courses to raise their GPAs and thereby improve their chances of getting into the best graduate or professional schools. (When you repeat a course, your cumulative GPA is refigured with the new grade factored in. Credit for the original course is deleted, but the course and grade remain on your transcript.)

6. ***Extra credentialing.*** To make themselves more attractive to employers, students are taking a more sophisticated approach to building impressive undergraduate resumés. This may translate into a second major or minor, study abroad, internships and co-op placements, or independent work on a research project or honors thesis. This all adds up to additional credit hours.

7. ***Returning students.*** In 1970 the average college student age was 22; today it is 26. Most returning adults are prevented from taking more than a course or two at a time by the competing demands of child care, full-time employment, and community involvement.

8. ***Tighter college budgets.*** Experiencing declining support from taxes, most public institutions have had to eliminate sections and classes with low enrollments, with the result that students must sometimes wait a semester or more to get the courses they need to graduate.

Ten Reasons to Attend a Summer Session

1. To take a course for personal enjoyment
2. To take a course that was unavailable in fall or spring
3. To graduate sooner
4. To stay in town and be near the person I love
5. To take a prerequisite for a course I need in the fall
6. To avoid having to take an overload next year
7. To really concentrate on one or two courses
8. To retake a course I did poorly in
9. To make up courses lost because of illness
10. To study abroad without losing ground academically

9. ***Stalling.*** Many students simply enjoy college life, are unsure what they want to do, or feel no particular urgency to graduate.

Each additional year you spend in college represents one year of earning power. Translated into the year before you retire, that one year could be worth many thousands of dollars. Taking a fifth year can be especially expensive if you're on a scholarship, because most scholarships are only good for four years.

If it is important to you to complete your degree as rapidly as possible, here are some suggestions:

1. ***Plan carefully.*** Read your college catalog and make sure you understand your degree requirements and their proper sequence. Make a schedule for your entire college career and stick to it. See an academic adviser early and often.

> Life is something that happens to you while you're making other plans.
>
> Margaret Millar
> *American novelist*

2. ***Take classes in the summer.*** This may cost you money because you'll be paying tuition and giving up earning power for the summer. But if you're trading your present earning power against an extra year at a much higher salary, taking out a loan with deferred repayment at low interest may be cost-effective. If you're enrolled in a four-year college, consider taking a required course or two at your local community college close to home. Tuition is lower, the hours are flexible, and the credit is almost certainly transferable. (There are limits, however, to the number of hours students may transfer from two-year colleges; check with your adviser or registrar.)

3. ***Apply for grants, scholarships, and tuition tax credit.*** Easing the cost of college will help you progress more rapidly toward your degree. Federal and state governments offer many grants and scholarships for students with financial need, demonstrated merit, or both. In 1997, President Clinton launched the Gear Up for College program to provide support to children from disadvantaged families. A number of states now offer tuition tax credit, and on August 5, 1997, the Tax Relief Act was signed into law. Taxpayers can claim a federal Hope tax credit of up to $1,500 per undergraduate student per year.

4. ***Test out of required courses.*** CLEP tests (College Level Examination Program) are available on most college campuses. They enable students to "test out" of a course by taking a test to demonstrate proficiency (equivalent to a grade of C or better) in most basic subjects. There is a fee for taking the test, but testing out saves both time and tuition.

5. ***Determine your career goals early.*** Many first-year students are just not ready to commit to a career. But it's never too early to think seriously about a career and to eliminate unrealistic options. Try at least to narrow your choices to three or four possible majors and take courses that are prerequisites for most of them.

6. ***Know your options before you withdraw from a course.*** If you're doing poorly in a course, meet with your instructor as early as possible to discuss your situation. In "skills courses" (composition, speech, music, art, and so on), instructors often look mainly for

improvement: Your final grade may represent the skill level you've achieved by the end of the course rather than an average of the grades you received. Some instructors will allow you to revise previous papers or do extra-credit work to improve your grade.

7. ***Register early.*** Plan your finances and your schedule well in advance of registration. Register for classes at the earliest possible time to avoid having to take classes you don't need or want. Find out which required courses are not regularly offered and take them at your first opportunity. Some courses are only offered every three or four semesters. Some may be taught by only one instructor, who may be on a leave of absence during the semester you planned to take it.

To make wise decisions about such matters, talk to an academic adviser.

ACADEMIC ADVISING

You're all set to graduate. You're getting married in May and moving to the West Coast after a honeymoon in the Bahamas. Your future spouse has been accepted to law school, and you've accepted a high-paying job beginning in June with a top accounting firm. You go to senior checkout to review your transcript, and the conversation goes something like this:

"You will need to take microeconomics."
"But I took that at community college. You gave me transfer credit."
"You got three hours of macro credit for that."
"But the course covered both macro and micro!"
"You can't get six hours of credit for a three-hour course. And anyway, didn't you get a copy of your tabulation of credit?"
"Yes, but I was advised to ignore that and proceed directly to Econ 301."
"Advised? By whom?"
"This econ professor."
"Which econ professor?"
"I didn't catch her name. I ran into her on the sidewalk."
"Well, I'm sorry, you were misadvised."
"You mean I won't graduate?"
"Not this semester."

Bad academic advising is available almost anywhere on a college campus. **Good academic advising is available only from a trained professional.** Asking a preoccupied professor on the sidewalk about a requirement or getting career counseling from your roommate is like asking your auto mechanic for medical advice.

Start with your catalog, the definitive source of information about college requirements. **Although catalogs are revised periodically, hang on to your first copy, because most colleges will hold you accountable for the requirements in effect at the time you enrolled. You, and you alone, are responsible for understanding and meeting those requirements.** "Nobody told me about that" is no excuse. If it's not in the catalog, don't worry about it. If it is, you're responsible for it.

Of course no one sits down and reads an inch-thick catalog from cover to cover. Academic advisers, however, usually know the catalog by heart. They can save you time by calling your attention to the sections that apply specifically to your situation.

On smaller campuses, academic advising is generally done by faculty who have had training in general advising. The advantage of this system is that your adviser can also provide detailed information about your major of interest.

The Academic Advising Office usually handles only "general advising"—that is, information about requirements outside your major. **Once you've declared a major, go to that academic department and ask to see the designated faculty adviser.** When you register, your schedule may need the signature of either a general adviser or a faculty adviser, unless you waive that right and take personal responsibility for your schedule.

Making the Most of an Academic Advising Session

1. ***Making an appointment.*** If you need general advising (to discuss general education requirements, possible majors, and careers), make an advising appointment shortly after the semester begins. Later, when the next semester's registration is under way, advisers are too busy to do much more than help you arrange a schedule. Academic advising offices may have walk-in hours, but they usually require appointments made well in advance during peak advising periods. Some offices stay open in the early evening to accommodate

Tips

What Documents Should You Save?

The safest answer: all. If that isn't realistic, get a sturdy box or small filing cabinet to store copies of the following documents throughout your college career:

1. **Your first college catalog.** Keep the one in effect when you first enrolled in college. Even if requirements change, only those in this catalog apply to you. Copies are available in the offices of Academic Advising, Admissions, or your campus bookstore. The college catalog contains an official academic calendar, policies, academic requirements, major and course descriptions, fee schedules, and other essential information.
2. **Scheduling plans.** Your plans should map out what you need to take each semester over your entire undergraduate career. Such plans are always tentative. You aren't bound by them, but they will help keep you on track.
3. **Academic progress reports.** These are unofficial transcripts. Examine them carefully when they first arrive. If there is a mistake, get it corrected immediately.
4. **Grade reports.** Treat these the same as progress reports.
5. **Tabulations of transfer credit.** If you transferred from another institution, these spell out exactly how the credit you earned there applies to your current institution.
6. **Financial aid statements and receipts.** Keep a record of all the expenses directly related to your education.

Keep for one year (or until the correct information appears on your unofficial transcript) any documents that might affect your academic status, such as course confirmations, drop/adds, grade changes, and official correspondence from faculty and staff.

students who work during the day. Call for an appointment two to three weeks before you plan to register.

2. ***Prepare.*** You'll get more out of this meeting if you do. (When you make your appointment, tell your adviser why the meeting is needed so the adviser can prepare, too.) Read the relevant sections of the catalog and advising tipsheets available in the Academic Advising Office or in your academic department. Write down questions as they occur to you. And remember, there is no such thing as a stupid question. If you knew everything, advisers would not have jobs.

3. ***Bring everything you may need to the meeting.*** Bring a course schedule, a catalog, and your own proposed schedule with alternate choices. Bring a list of questions to ask. Think about your personal preferences (avoid early morning classes, finish by noon on Friday, prevent work conflicts, include time for lunch). Think about your own strengths and weaknesses, and don't let yourself be placed in a class you're not ready for. Come with realistic expectations and a willingness to be flexible if what you want isn't available.

4. ***During the advising session, take careful notes.*** Jot down the name and phone number of your adviser (more questions may occur to you later). Many advising offices have "hotline" numbers to call or websites with answers to Frequently Asked Questions (FAQ's).

5. ***Check in with your adviser periodically.*** Requirements change. And if you find someone who has been unusually friendly and helpful, write a brief note of appreciation with a copy to the adviser's boss. It will be deeply appreciated and will help ensure good advising in the future.

Scheduling

The main agenda in most advising sessions is schedule planning. Look over the schedule book before your meeting. Notice that multiple sections of many courses are often available, especially in general education courses. Which should you choose? Here are some factors to consider as you decide:

1. ***Meeting days.*** Do you need to keep certain times free for job commitments? Do you plan to go home early on Friday?

2. ***Meeting times.*** Do you work best early in the morning, or does it take you a while to get going? Do you need to keep certain blocks of time free for lunch, work, meetings, labs? Do you want your classes back-to-back, or do you need time in between to study or relax?

3. ***Location.*** Can you find where the buildings are located? Will you have time to get from one class to another, especially after an activity class where you may have to shower and dress?

4. ***Instructor.*** Instructors listed in the schedule book are probably regular, full-time faculty members. If they are not listed, they are probably graduate assistants or part-time instructors. Ask for names of good instructors at every opportunity and try to get experienced

Collaborate

My Schedule

Get together in small groups. Take turns describing your current class schedule (courses you're taking, what the instructors are like, hours and days). Write your schedule below for reference.

Tell what you like and dislike about your schedule.

1. What are your favorite and least favorite courses?
2. How much time and thought did you invest in planning your schedule?
3. What factors will you pay closer attention to in the future?

Course	Times/Days	Instructor
________	________	________
________	________	________
________	________	________
________	________	________
________	________	________
________	________	________
________	________	________

faculty whenever possible. Advisers will tell you who the good instructors are if you ask, but it's considered unprofessional to criticize a bad one. Sometimes you can read between the lines. Some colleges publish student evaluations of courses and instructors (available in the library, bookstore, or residence halls). And, of course, students have their own network of information about whom to avoid, although this can be subjective: one person's meat is another's poison. Still, a great teacher can make a profound difference in your life. Whenever possible, make the instructor your first consideration in choosing your class sections.

5. ***Overall balance.*** Put together a schedule that balances courses with light or heavy workloads, heavy reading with computation or activity courses, dull requirements with exciting electives. Give yourself some breathing room between classes.

Keep in mind: you may not get your ideal schedule. Be flexible and list acceptable alternatives for each of your first-choice classes.

CHOOSING A MAJOR

If you are undecided on a major in your first semester in college, don't worry. You have plenty of time to make a smart selection. Selecting a major that will lead to gainful employment is often a worry for college students. The fact is, it's one of the least consequential choices you need to make. A long-term, follow-up study of Yale University graduates revealed some interesting facts: 25 years after graduation, only one of ten was working at a job even remotely related to his or her undergraduate major. Seventy-five percent were working in jobs that didn't exist when they attended college.

Employers don't hire majors; they hire people. And except for professions in which licensing is required (engineering, architecture, nursing, occupational therapy, education), after your first job employers will not likely ask or care about your college major. They will mainly be interested in how successful you were in your last job. As you select courses and eventually a major, choose what will prepare you for your *second* job.

Many students select a major by examining the current job market and choosing a "hot" field. But what's hot today may not be five years from now.

Since the average adult makes three to five career changes over the course of a lifetime, a better approach is to concentrate on acquiring the basic job skills discussed in Chapter 3.

- communication (both written and oral)
- creativity, critical thinking, and problem-solving
- organization
- leadership

These are the skills taught in general education courses—the solid foundation on which your major curriculum is built.

If you're undecided about your major, you're not alone: up to 70 percent of students change their intended major during the first year of college. And uncertainty doesn't come to an end once you've settled on a major, because technologies change, economies fluctuate, and life evolves.

> Always be smarter than the people who hire you.
>
> Lena Horne
> *American singer*

Academic advisers are trained to counsel undecided students. They can help you identify goals and explore possible majors. They will also steer you toward courses applicable to several majors so you won't waste time and tuition. And all undergraduates have a limited number of "free electives" (courses that count toward graduation but aren't specifically required). Use elective hours to take courses that interest you in a field you may not have considered. Concentrate on completing required courses during your first and second years and use those years to think about a major.

Use your first year of college to assess your abilities and interests. If you're getting C's in biology, think twice about continuing in pre-med. If you hate math, engineering may be a bad choice. If encountering pressure

See Your Adviser Whenever You . . .

- have questions about your academic status
- can't decide whether to repeat a course
- want to take a course pass/fail (credit/no credit)
- think about dropping a class
- do poorly in your classes
- feel unsure about your plans
- think of dropping out of school
- plan your schedule for next semester
- want to discuss life and employment goals
- want to know about career options in your major
- want to change your major
- need information about graduate or professional schools
- are unsure about requirements
- want to test out of a course
- need information about getting into a special program
- plan to transfer to another college
- want to switch colleges within the university
- want advanced placement in a class

Collaborate

Role Playing

Pair up with another student and take turns playing the role of adviser or career counselor. Interview your partner by asking the following questions and taking notes:

1. What did you like to do as a child? ______________________________

____

What was your favorite thing to do with your friends? ______________________________

____

What was your favorite thing to do alone? ______________________________

____

What do you think these activities taught you? ______________________________

____

2. What was your favorite subject in high school?

____

____

What extracurricular activities did you engage in?

____

____

Which were the most satisfying to you? ______________________________

____

Why? ______________________________

____

Were they activities you selected, or were you pressured into them? ______________________________

____

What talents or skills did you develop through these activities? ______________________________

____

3. What activities interest you most on this campus? ______________________________

____

What do you hope to get out of them? ______________________________

____

4. Describe your most significant accomplishments up to this point in your life. ______________________________

____

Why are they important to you? ______________________________

____

5. Do you have a "crazy dream"? Describe it, even if you think it's hopelessly unrealistic. ______________________________

____

continued on next page

Collaborate *continued from previous page*

______

______

______

Tell your partner what you heard, in summary form. Based on your partner's past interests and involvement, is he or she likely to:

1. Prefer working within an organization (____) or more independently (____)?

   Be a leader (____) or a follower (____)?
2. Be a specialist (____) or a generalist (____)?

   Know a lot about a little (____) or a little about a lot (____)?
3. Make a lot of money (____) or be content with a lower-paying job that offers personal satisfaction (____)?

   What do you think would be a satisfying major for your partner?

______

______

A gifted instructor can influence your choice of major or vocation.

from home to choose a major you're not comfortable with, ask yourself, "Whose life is it anyway?" You may find you are suddenly turned on by an inspiring instructor or to a field you had never considered before. If you work on a project into the early morning, endorphins blazing in your head, not wanting to sleep, eager to start again when the sun rises, then you've found your major and your career. Go with it, even if the employment prospects are slim; it's better to be happy than rich.

THINKING ABOUT A CAREER

One good way to explore possible careers is to identify and contact someone in the field that interests you. Arrange an appointment and ask questions. If possible, schedule a "day on the job" to "shadow" the person. To **find a mentor,** contact the career center or alumni office, an academic adviser, a faculty member or department head, a department secretary (often an undervalued source of helpful information), your resident adviser, an upper-class or older student, an athletic coach, a club sponsor, an administrator, or your work supervisor.

Keep away from people who try to belittle your ambition. Small people always do that, but the really great make you feel that you, too, can become great.

Mark Twain
American author/humorist

Sometimes I've believed as many as six impossible things before breakfast.

Lewis Carroll
Author, Alice in Wonderland

If you have a job without aggravations, you don't have a job.

Malcolm Forbes
Business tycoon

Colleges frequently have career centers that offer workshops on career planning, resumé preparation, job searches, and interviewing skills. Your center may subscribe to DISCOVER, a computer-based career-planning program that asks questions about you, then helps you develop a list of occupations to explore and majors that relate to those occupations. MAJOR-MINOR FINDER is a similar computer program that helps identify a field of study that matches your interests and preferred work environment. It also identifies jobs associated with these majors and the employment outlook. Your career center may also offer self-studies like the Myers-Briggs Type Indicator (MBTI), a 45-minute exercise that helps you understand your personality, or the Strong Interest Inventory (SII), which compares your interests and abilities with those of people currently employed in a wide range of occupations.

Co-ops and Internships

If your school offers cooperative education, take advantage of it. **A "co-op" is basically a paid apprenticeship** ($6 to $12 an hour) in a field that interests you. It's a good way to explore a career as early as your junior year while still earning academic credit. In fact, there's a 63 percent chance your co-op employer will offer you a permanent job when you graduate. Co-op positions are most plentiful (and offer the highest pay) in business and technical fields (engineering, computers, marketing, finance, accounting), but are available in other fields as well.

Internships are similar to co-ops. However, internships are more often available in the humanities and social sciences, and interns sometimes earn neither pay nor academic credit. An internship may last anywhere from a month to a year. In health, social work, and some educational fields, students acquire on-the-job skills in "clinicals," "practicums," or "field experiences." Like co-ops, **these arrangements provide hands-on training** in a real-time setting under the supervision of a professional in the field.

Because co-op positions and internships may not be available until your junior year, a good way to gain experience in the meantime is through **volunteering.** If you're thinking of journalism, join the staff of the campus newspaper. Students majoring in health fields can volunteer at local hospitals and clinics. Language students might offer their services as tutors for children learning English as a second language. Earth science majors can organize cleanup crews or join environmental awareness groups.

In short, **every hour of your day and all your experiences outside the classroom are opportunities to learn.** Make the most of each and every day.

There are several good computer programs that will help you identify a suitable career.

On **Your** Own

Choosing a Major

1. List three subjects you already know something about.

a. ______

b. ______

c. ______

2. What job or career-related experiences have you had? Community service? Counseling at summer camp? Athletics? A science fair project? Writing for your school paper? A family vacation in the Everglades? List three of them.

a. ______

b. ______

c. ______

What did you enjoy about these experiences? Problem solving? Working with young people? Learning about the environment? Making money? The self-discipline you acquired? Did you discover a talent you didn't know you had? Write your response.

3. List the names of three people who work in the fields that interest you.

a. ______

b. ______

c. ______

What are they like? What kind of background did they have that prepared them for this field? What do they do all day? How much money do they make? What are the opportunities for advancement in this career?

a. ______

______

______

b. ______

______

______

c. ______

______

______

On **Your** *Own*

Identifying Your Work Values

A good starting point for a career search is identifying your work values. This exercise will help you do just that. As you follow the steps, you will be asked to make some realistic decisions and trade-offs, which you will also need to do later in life. *This exercise must be done in pencil.*

Step 1 Review each of the work values listed below.
Step 2 If there are some values important to you but not listed, add them in the last three spaces (marked "Other").
Step 3 Eliminate the four values that matter least to you by crossing them out.
Step 4 For each work value, circle a number that expresses its importance to you for a satisfying career.
Step 5 Add up the numbers you circled and jot down the total. If the total is greater or less than 50, go back and change the numbers you selected until they add up to 50.
Step 6 In the right-hand column (marked "Rank"), rank order your values according to those that received the higher score. The value with the highest score, for example, should be ranked #1. If you assigned the same score to more than one value, decide which is more important to you and rank it higher.

Work values	**Low need/desire for**					**High need/desire for**					**Rank**
High income	1	2	3	4	5	6	7	8	9	10	_____
Prestige and recognition	1	2	3	4	5	6	7	8	9	10	_____
Independence	1	2	3	4	5	6	7	8	9	10	_____
Helping others	1	2	3	4	5	6	7	8	9	10	_____
Security	1	2	3	4	5	6	7	8	9	10	_____
Variety	1	2	3	4	5	6	7	8	9	10	_____
Leadership	1	2	3	4	5	6	7	8	9	10	_____
Expertise in a specialized field	1	2	3	4	5	6	7	8	9	10	_____
Challenge and adventure	1	2	3	4	5	6	7	8	9	10	_____
Creativity	1	2	3	4	5	6	7	8	9	10	_____
Good working conditions	1	2	3	4	5	6	7	8	9	10	_____
Other ______________	1	2	3	4	5	6	7	8	9	10	_____
Other ______________	1	2	3	4	5	6	7	8	9	10	_____
Other ______________	1	2	3	4	5	6	7	8	9	10	_____

When you have finished, discuss in your group which work values you ranked highest and lowest and why. What careers do your work values suggest you are best suited for? What careers are probably not suitable? Was it difficult for you to change your total to 50? Why do you think the exercise included this requirement? What did you learn from completing this task?

Tips

Will it Look Good on My Resumé?

In a tight job market, college students are more conscious than ever of the need to be competitive. The first year of college is not too early to think about the kinds of experiences that will make your resumé stand out. Some suggestions:

1. **Establish personal relationships with mentors.** Good recommendation letters lead to good jobs. A good recommendation should provide the personal insights that don't show up on a transcript, such as work habits (dependability, creativity, perseverance, interpersonal skills). Make an effort to establish personal relationships with instructors, employers, and staff members. Arrange office appointments. Volunteer for special activities. Try to get jobs in an academic setting (lab assistant, librarian's assistant) where you learn special skills and meet influential people.
2. **Seek out leadership roles in campus organizations.** Avoid relying on "vanity listings" to beef up your resumé. Making the National Dean's List or a Who's Who book only means you earned a certain GPA, which is already apparent to an employer by reading your transcript. Listing yourself as a member of Golden Key National Honorary Society (even though you never attended meetings) only means you could afford the initiation fee. These are vanity listings. Employers will want to know what you contributed to the organizations listed on your resumé and what knowledge and skills you acquired as a result of your involvement.
3. **Seek out opportunities for experiential learning.** Study abroad, internships and co-ops, fieldwork, clinical work, and volunteering are all ways of relating abstract learning to the real world of work. Here are some other strategies that will make your resumé distinctive:

- assisting a faculty member on a research project
- writing for the campus newspaper
- participating in student government
- conducting a canned food drive in your residence hall
- attending guest lectures and special events
- publicizing special events
- editing a literary journal
- assisting in a lab
- tutoring other students
- submitting a research article for publication
- attending or presenting your own work at a professional conference in your major field

If you have a word processor, start a file now called "resumé." Create categories (Education, Work Experience, Honors and Awards), then record your accomplishments as they occur. As your experience accumulates, you can eliminate less significant items in favor of more impressive achievements. If you don't have a word processor, a paper file will do as well. Jot down items on scraps of paper that you can retype more neatly later. Be sure to include dates, names, places, titles—any details you are likely to forget.

SUMMARY

Earning a bachelor's degree in four years takes self-discipline, careful planning, and the assistance of a trained academic adviser. Advisers can help you avoid mistakes that may have serious consequences. Careful scheduling is one key to success in college.

Some students, eager to start on their majors, neglect general education requirements that are the foundation for preprofessional courses and also teach skills that get jobs. There is plenty of time to decide on a major; first-year students should concentrate on developing essential skills. Meanwhile, seek out as many opportunities as possible—co-op, internships, and volunteerism—to explore careers and practice marketable skills.

On **Your** *Own*

Plotting Your Lifemap

The future is abstract and difficult to imagine. But focusing powerfully on a preferred future sometimes causes it to turn out almost the way you envisioned. One way to think concretely about your future is to construct a lifemap, lifeline, or chronology.

Start by writing the year of your birth in the lower left corner of a blank page. Then, add the year of your retirement near the upper right corner, listing several activities you plan to pursue. Beginning with your birth, "map" the significant events of your life, past to present, along a winding "road," or line, that stops—with today—in the middle of the page. Include events such as "family vacation to Canada," "learned to drive," "parents divorced," "moved to Ohio." You may wish to draw an icon to represent each event or spell it out, briefly. From the middle of the page, map events you expect will happen in the future ("graduated from college, "traveled to Australia," "got married") or that you hope will happen ("drafted by the Bulls," "made Broadway debut").

Hang on to your lifemap, update it annually, check it out now and then—especially as you make decisions about your future.

Collaborate

Lifemap Exhibit

Display all completed lifemaps on the classroom board or wall, at eye level. As you and your classmates tour this exhibit, you will become better acquainted with the range and shape of each person's life and his or her dreams for the future.

Strategic *Plan*

Look over your Self-Assessment at the beginning of the chapter and identify an area in which you'd like to make a change. Then develop a Strategic Plan, using the format below.

I. Situation analysis

A. One problem I'm having with planning my future is ______________________________

____

B. One change I think I could make is ______________________________

____

C. The benefits of making the change are ______________________________

____

D. The consequences of not changing are ______________________________

____

E. Some obstacles I'll have to overcome are ______________________________

____

continued on next page

Strategic *Plan* *continued from previous page*

F. Some resources I'll need are ______________________________

____

II. Goals, objectives, deadlines, and indicators

A. My goal is to ______________________________

____

Deadline: ______________________________

Indicators of success: ______________________________

____

B. Here's what I'm going to do to achieve my goal, along with a reasonable deadline for each task:

	OBJECTIVE	DEADLINE
1.	______________________________	______________
2.	______________________________	______________
3.	______________________________	______________
4.	______________________________	______________
5.	______________________________	______________

III. Self-Test

YES	NO	
☐	☐	**A.** Are my goals and objectives stated simply and clearly?
☐	☐	**B.** Does each one have a single focus?
☐	☐	**C.** Are they stated in a positive way?
☐	☐	**D.** Are they realistic?
☐	☐	**E.** Can I achieve them by the deadline?
☐	☐	**F.** Will I know if I've achieved them?

Journal **Ideas**

1. Do you plan to earn your bachelor's degree within four years? What must you do to accomplish this?
2. Do you feel you have a good understanding of the academic requirements at your college? What do you feel unsure or uneasy about, if anything? Make a list of questions and concerns.
3. If you have a general academic plan for your entire undergraduate career, describe it. What courses do you plan to take next semester? Next year?
4. If undecided, list three majors that interest you somewhat. What do you like about these subjects? What is the source of your uncertainty?
5. Describe your career plans, if any. What do you think will be most important to you in achieving these goals? Describe (a) your "dream" career and (b) a career you think is more likely.

Web **Search**

Make a list of useful Web sites for career information. Find sites that will help you do the following:

a. choose a career
b. perform well in a job interview
c. provide information about your chosen career
d. create an effective resumé
e. locate current job opportunities

Don't forget the Web sites on your own campus and the career center Web sites at other colleges and universities. Check to see if your college has a site that advertises current job openings on or off campus.

Appendix

ACTIVITY REPORT

A valuable part of your education is the chance to take part in extracurricular activities either on campus or in your campus community. As a course requirement or part of your grading contract, you may be asked to attend and report on one or more special events—a concert, lecture, sports event, play, or meeting of a student organization.

You'll get more out of this experience if you do a little research beforehand. For example, if you plan to attend some events during homecoming weekend, you could interview someone from the Alumni Office or look up old campus newspapers in the library to see what homecoming was like in years past. If you attend a play you might look up reviews of past productions, interview a member of the cast, or read the script. If attending a performance of *Messiah*, you might find out something about the composer, Handel, or the guest soloists.

Unless your instructor gives you another format, use the format on the following pages.

ACTIVITY REPORT

Name ____

Activity ______________________________ Date of activity __________

1. How did you find out about this event or activity?

2. Did you do any background research on the activity or the organization sponsoring the event? What did you learn?

3. Where did the event take place? Describe the environment (number of people attending, mood, atmosphere).

4. Other than the fact that it was required, what motivated you to choose this particular activity?

5. Describe the event itself. What happened? What were the high points and low points? How, if at all, did the audience affect you or the event?

6. What was your overall reaction? How did you (or others in the audience) benefit from attending the event?

Glossary

One way to take the mystery out of your college experience is to learn the campus code. Many terms describing how a college or university operates derive from Latin and Greek and are centuries old. Included here are some of the more interesting or unusual ones, as well as some newer useful terms that aren't explained elsewhere in the book. If you can't find the term you're looking for here, check the Index.

A

Accreditation. Colleges and professional programs get graded as you do. They have to meet certain quality standards to become "accredited," usually for five- or ten-year periods, by watchdog agencies. Avoid colleges and programs that lack proper accreditation.

Advanced placement. Achieving a minimum score on a "placement test" allows you to enroll in a more advanced course. Some students take "AP courses" in high school to prepare themselves for one or more AP tests.

Alma mater. Means "bounteous mother" in Latin. Once a way of addressing a goddess, today it's how college alumni refer to the college they attended. Alma maters are usually "sacred," "dear," or "old."

Alumnus, -a, -i, -ae. College graduates. An alumnus is a man; an alumna is a woman; alumni (-ae) is the plural. When in doubt, just say "alum." As soon as you become one, you will be asked to give generously to your sacred alma mater.

Assessment. A way of evaluating how much students learn. **Preassessment** tests what you know when you enter college or begin a course or program. **Postassessment** measures how much you have learned since then. The assessment movement is an effort to make schools more accountable for learning.

Audit. To enroll in a course for no credit, usually at a reduced tuition rate, on a space-available basis. Sometimes requires instructor permission.

B

Baccalaureate. Possibly derived from "laurel wreath." A four-year college degree. Sometimes refers to the ceremony (commencement) at which these degrees are bestowed.

Bachelor's degree. Possibly from medieval French chivalry, *bas chevalier*, a low-level knight just starting out. A four-year college degree. The B.S. (Bachelor of Science) has displaced the B.A. (Bachelor of Arts) as the degree of preference for most college students today because the B.A. generally takes longer and often requires a foreign language.

Board (Governing Board, Board of Regents, Trustees). Elected or appointed officials responsible for making major policy decisions. The college president reports to the board. Board members are accountable either to whoever appointed them (for example, the state governor or the ruling body of a church) or to the electorate.

C

Carrel. A study booth in the library. Often a special perk for graduate students.

Chancellor. In ancient times, a petty church or court officer (something like a notary). Today, the chief administrative officer, usually in a large university system. In some states the president is called chancellor and vice versa.

Coed. Short for coeducational. Once referred only to female college students, now more commonly a school or residence hall that accommodates both men and women. Coed residence halls are common, and some colleges are now experimenting with coed rooms.

Cognate. Required courses that are related to but outside your major.

Commencement. From the French *commencer*, "to begin." Graduation ceremony featuring a famous speaker who usually reminds graduates that a "commencement is a beginning, not an ending."

Common final. An identical final exam given to all sections of a class at the same time.

Community college. The term has replaced junior college, which implied inferiority. Some administrators don't like the word community either, because it implies, falsely, that only local students may attend. Community colleges are now referring to themselves as **"two-year colleges"** or "associate degree-granting institutions."

Comprehensive exam. An exam that covers all course material up to that point. To a graduate student, "comps" are a dreaded day-long test covering the entire spectrum of graduate coursework.

Convocation. Literally, a "calling together." Any all-campus gathering, usually at the beginning or end of the academic year.

Co-op. Earn while you learn. An actual paid job in your field of interest for which you earn not only money but academic credit as well. On-the-job experience makes you more marketable after graduation—a no-lose situation.

Credit hour. The basic unit in which academic credit is awarded, roughly equivalent to one hour (actually fifty minutes) of instruction per week. Sometimes distinguished from an **activity hour**: a lab, for example, may require four hours a week (four activity hours), but earn only two hours of credit.

Curriculum. In Latin, a "horse-racing track"; in English, a rat race. All the courses you must take, in proper sequence, to graduate from college.

Cyberspace. The entire realm of electronic communication.

D

Dean. In the Middle Ages, deans were high-ranking officers in a monastery. Today, a dean is usually the chief academic officer of a college (for example, Dean of Engineering), but there are nonacademic deans too (Dean of Admissions, Dean of Students, and so on).

Dean's list. Making the dean's list is an academic honor. If you're taking a full load and earn a certain GPA in a given semester—usually in the 3.25 to 3.50 range—you make the dean's list. The designation may appear on your transcript; you or your parents may get a congratulatory letter; a press release may be sent to your hometown paper.

Department head (or chair). Person in charge of an academic department, such as Astronomy or German, who reports to the Dean of the College. Heads are usually considered part of the college administration, whereas chairs are usually elected by their peers for a fixed term and are considered faculty members. Both teach, but have reduced loads.

Dissertation. A book-length manuscript that is supposed to extend the frontiers of knowledge. Required for the Ph.D. and some other doctoral degrees.

Dormitory. Originally "a place for sleeping," but housing experts prefer the term **residence hall**, which is probably more accurate.

Drop/add. To officially withdraw from/enroll in a course. After a certain date, you forfeit a percentage of your tuition if you drop a course. Usually you can't add a course after the first week of the semester/quarter. If you just stop going to class without filling out the proper paperwork, a failing grade will appear on your transcript. Be careful about dropping if your financial aid requires that you earn a minimum number of credits.

E

E-mail. Mail sent and received electronically.

Education. Interestingly enough, this term referred to the care and feeding of young barnyard animals until about the sixteenth century.

Elective. A course you choose to take, not a requirement, although you may need "elective hours" to graduate. Most students nowadays have very little room in their schedules for free electives and must ration them carefully. Restricted electives are courses from which you are obliged to select one or more to fulfill a major or minor.

Emeritus. An honorary rank bestowed on retired faculty. The word, according to a tired joke, comes from the Latin *e* ("out") and *meritus* ("deservedly so").

F

Faculty. Originally, a person with a special skill. In a college the term refers to teachers with formal, tenure-track appointments.

Fees. Fees may be assessed for any purpose other than the normal costs of instruction (tuition) and room and board. Special fees may be assessed to cover parking, student government, entertainment and athletic events, registration, graduation audit, campus maintenance, computer technology, and other costs. A **general fee** simply bundles many smaller fees together in a single payment.

Fraternity/sorority. The terms **fraternity brother** and **sorority sister** are redundant, since **frater** is Latin for "brother" and **soror** is Latin for "sister." What is more puzzling, it's called Greek life.

Freshman. The term is giving way to **freshperson**, which is less gender-specific but every bit as quaint, or **first-year student**, which is used in this book but probably has too many syllables for widespread adoption.

G

General education requirements. Courses in the liberal arts and sciences required of all students for graduation. One-third to one-fourth of your undergraduate career will be spent fulfilling general education requirements (also called core courses, distribution requirements, basic studies, general studies). Usually you can choose courses from a restricted list, arranged in groups by discipline. Because these are often prerequisites for advanced courses, take them first.

Graduate assistant. Sometimes called teaching assistant or teaching fellow. Some graduate students earn their tuition by teaching introductory courses or by assisting a faculty member on a research project (research assistants).

Grant. Money awarded for college without expectation of repayment. Grants are available from many agencies, both public and private.

H

Higher education. Any formal education beyond high school.

Honors degree. Sometimes used to refer to the "laude" designations, but may indicate the completion of honors program requirements. These usually include honors coursework and/or a senior honors thesis. May be general honors, honors in your major, or both.

I

Independent study. An individual course of study in a subject not covered by the normal curriculum. Usually requires at least junior standing, a willing and qualified faculty mentor, and a clear understanding of how the credit will apply to your degree.

Internet. A vast, global network connecting all persons who have capable computers.

Internship. Paid preprofessional employment for a quarter or semester. Sometimes it earns credit; sometimes it's required for a major; sometimes it leads to a job.

L

Lab. Short for laboratory. Lab instructors emphasize the first five letters of the word over the last seven. Provides hands-on experience, usually in the sciences; often requires a fee for materials and equipment.

Latin degree. Not really a degree but a transcript designation recognizing high academic achievement. *Cum laude* ("with praise") usually indicates a GPA in the 3.50 to 3.70 range; *magna cum laude* ("with great praise") in the 3.70 to 3.90 range; and *summa cum laude* ("with highest praise") in the 3.90 to 4.00 range.

Liberal arts. Required courses in the arts, math and science, and the social sciences, called "liberal" from the Latin *liber*, meaning "free." Liberal arts courses are supposed to free us from the chains of ignorance and prejudice. "The truth shall make you free," said Saint Paul.

Lower/upper division. Lower division usually refers to the first two years of college when students are taking general education courses at the 100 and 200 level. Upper-division students are undergraduates with at least junior standing who have declared a major and are taking mostly 300- and 400-level courses. Upper-division students generally qualify for independent study, co-op and internships, pass/fail, and other perquisites.

M

Major. Beyond general education requirements, your primary course of study, usually requiring at least 30 semester hours or 45 quarter hours in a single academic discipline. Double majors (a complete major in each of two disciplines) are difficult but by no means impossible. Individual interdisciplinary majors combine courses from more than one discipline and require prior approval by an academic adviser.

Matriculate. From the Latin word *matricula*, meaning "a membership list." Today, to matriculate means to be admitted and enrolled in a college.

Mentor. In Homer's *The Odyssey*, Mentor was Odysseus's trusted counselor. Today, a mentor is anyone who is (usually) older and wiser or more experienced than you and who is willing to help with advice and support. Mentors don't often advertise their services; you have to seek them out.

Minor. Beyond general education requirements, your secondary course of study, usually requiring at least 18 semester hours or 27 quarter hours in a single academic discipline. You may have more than one minor, or if you have a double major, none at all.

O

Oral exam. The instructor tests you orally, in person, one-on-one. Often scary for the student and time-consuming for the instructor (and therefore rare), but may be an expedient if you missed an exam due to illness.

P

Pass/Fail. Same as Credit/No Credit or Satisfactory/Unsatisfactory. You may choose to take a course pass/fail. Usually a C or better is required to pass. Some restrictions apply. A passing grade doesn't influence your GPA, but a failing one may.

Practicum. Like an internship, it provides real-time, hands-on experience in a professional setting (usually in health or education). Required for certification but often earns no credit or pay.

Preregistration. Formally indicating to the Registrar's Office your preferred course schedule for an upcoming term. This helps the administration adjust the supply of class sections to meet student demand.

Prerequisite. A course you are advised to take before being admitted to a more advanced course "Prereqs" are rarely enforced, but ignore them at your peril. Not the same as "perquisite," which is a fringe benefit.

Probation. Literally to "prove" you deserve to remain in college. If you are placed on probation (for academic or disciplinary reasons), you are given a limited time (usually a quarter or semester) in which to meet a set of conditions. If you fail to meet them, you may be dismissed or you may appeal to have your probation extended.

Proctor. A person other than the instructor who monitors a test. The word is an abbreviation of the Latin word *procurator* ("deputy, agent").

Professor. The term implies a person who "professes," or publicly declares a position, rather than a mere purveyor of facts. Some professors in England, like British judges in courts, still don priestly garb before entering the classroom.

Professorial rank. From the lowest to highest, they are assistant professor, associate professor, full professor. (Teaching assistant, lecturer, and instructor are all ranks but not professorial ones.) Not all professors have doctorates; some instructors do. Address as Professor So-and-so or ask what they like to be called.

Provost. Once the priestly personage second in command to an abbot. Today, similar to a chancellor, the chief academic officer, who is in charge in the president's absence. (Some say that if the president is the shepherd of his flock, the provost is the crook on his staff.)

R

Reference room. Room or section of the library where reference works (dictionaries, encyclopedias, bibliographies, manuals) are stored. Reference works can't be checked out; you must use them in the library.

Remedial (or refresher) courses. Today more commonly called "developmental" courses, these are designed to "remedy" inadequate academic preparation for college. Often required on the basis of low test scores in a discipline. Credit often doesn't count toward graduation requirement.

Reserve room. Room in the library where special materials are placed "on reserve" by instructors for class use. Some must be used in the room; others may be checked out for brief periods.

Residence hall adviser. Usually an upper-division student, an RA lives in a dorm and monitors, supervises, and mentors newcomers, often for a wage and/or tuition waiver.

Residency. State-supported colleges and universities charge lower tuition rates for residents of that state. Out-of-state students may qualify for residency after living in the state year-round for a specified period, obtaining a state driver's license, and meeting the requirements that vary from one state to another.

Sabbatical. Faculty may be awarded paid leaves for one or two semesters every seven years to pursue scholarly projects. At some colleges sabbatical leaves are automatic; at others, they are competitive and a great honor.

Scholarship. 1. What scholars do: inquire, investigate, disseminate findings. Scholars are "knowledge workers"; they trade in intellectual property.
2. Monies awarded—without expectation of repayment—for such work.

Seminar. A small class designed for upper-division and graduate students. Emphasizes independent research on a highly specialized topic and roundtable discussions chaired or led by a specialist in the subject.

Sophomore. Means "wise fool" in Greek. For centuries sophomores have given meaning to the saying, "A little knowledge is a dangerous thing."

Stacks. Shelves in the library holding books and periodicals. May be "open" (you can browse freely) or "closed" (a librarian gets the materials you request). If the stacks are open and you can't find a book, scan the area nearby: someone may have put it back in the wrong place.

Stopout. Unlike a dropout, a person who "stops out" withdraws from college intentionally and temporarily, for good reasons—to earn tuition money, get married, explore the world, do mission work—usually with the intention of returning.

T

Take-home exam. An essay examination to be completed outside of class within a stated time frame (usually 24 hours). Because you can consult any source, it's difficult to know when to quit reading and start writing. Not as easy as it sounds.

Tenure. A newly hired assistant professor usually has from three to six years in which to earn tenure. Contrary to popular belief, a tenured faculty member can be fired for incompetence, moral turpitude, or financial exigency, but not for doing controversial research or holding unpopular views. Tenure means academic freedom and job security. Galileo did not have it.

Terminal degree. The highest possible degree in an academic discipline. Usually the Ph.D. (Doctor of Philosophy) but may be Ed.D. (Doctor of Education), M.F.A. (Master of Fine Arts), and others.

Testing out. Getting a course requirement waived by taking a test and demonstrating your mastery of the course material. CLEP (College Level Examination Program) tests are nationally standardized tests usually administered four times a year by the Registrar's Office. A good way to save time and tuition.

Thesis. A lengthy research paper. A senior thesis (20 to 50 pages) may be required of honors students. A longer thesis (75 to 150 pages) is usually required of master's degree candidates. May also refer to the main idea or premise of a research paper.

Transcript. The formal record of earned academic credit and special honors (dean's list, *cum laude*, Phi Beta Kappa). Shows withdrawals, incompletes, repeated courses, pass/fail courses, and grades. A copy is kept in perpetuity in the Registrar's Office, which provides copies for a fee (paid by you) to employers and graduate schools. An "official transcript," as distinguished from a copy, bears the embossed college seal.

Transfer student. One who has transferred from one school (often a two-year college) to another (often a four-year college).

Transient. A transient student is just passing through, taking a course at one college (usually over the summer) in order to transfer the credit to another.

W

WWW (or World Wide Web). A popular "highway" for Internet explorers.

Index

A

B

C

D

Photography Credits

Page 1, Schuyler/Stock Boston; pages 3, 25, 29 (bottom), 91, 133, 135, 175, 177, 206, and 251, © copyright 1998 PhotoDisc, Inc.; pages 4, 52, 107, 113, 146, 148, 179, 185, 195, 274, and 232, David Gonzales; pages 11, 37, 50, 81, 119, 202, Hilary Smith; pages 20, 96, 117, 184, and 197, Isago Isao Tanaka; pages 27 and 29 (top), P. Channing/Pomona College; page 30, Brigid Nagle/Used by permission of Illini Media Company; pages 39 and 104, Sean Reed/Used by permission of Illini Media Company; page 47, Bruce Ayres/Tony Stone Images; pages 54, 149, 164, 204, Patrick Tower; page 58, Blake Ratner/Used by permission of Illini Media Company; page 67, Dana White/PhotoEdit; pages 100 and 187, Steve Handwecker/Used by permission of Illini Media Company; page 111, Chip Henderson/Tony Stone Worldwide; pages 140, Jim Kamp/Used by permission of Illini Media Company; page 155, Gary A. Conner/PhotoEdit; page 160, Used by permission of Illini Media Company; page 170, Kenneth Gabrielsen/Liaison International; page 193, Michael A. Dwyer/Stock Boston; pages 203, 211, and 250, Dick Schwarze/Used by permission of Illini Media Company; page 209, Joe Trojanowski/Used by permission of Illini Media Company; page 221, Bob Manoney/The Image Works; page 226, Used by permission of Bowdoin College; page 239, Kathy McLaughlin/The Image Works.